Before and Beyond Divergence

Before and Beyond Divergence

The Politics of Economic Change
in China and Europe

Jean-Laurent Rosenthal
R. Bin Wong

HARVARD UNIVERSITY PRESS
Cambridge, Massachusetts
London, England
2011

Library of Congress Cataloging-in-Publication Data

Rosenthal, Jean-Laurent.
  Before and beyond divergence : the politics of economic change in China and Europe / Jean-Laurent Rosenthal, R. Bin Wong.
     p.   cm.
  Includes bibliographical references and index.
  ISBN 978-0-674-05791-3 (alk. paper)
   1. China—Economic conditions.   2. China—Economic policy.
3. Europe—Economic conditions.   4. Europe—Economic policy.
5. Comparative economics.   I. Wong, Roy Bin.   II. Title.
  HC427.R66   2011
  330.94—dc22   2010033607

In memoriam
Kenneth L. Sokoloff (1952–2007)
Charles Tilly (1929–2008)

Contents

Preface

Why did China decline between 1400 and 1980, only to reestablish a major presence in the global economy? Why did Europe, a region torn by strife and suffering and economic collapse after the fall of the Roman Empire, become the birthplace of modern economic growth? These two questions are at the forefront of research in economic history. Answering them does not merely satisfy an academic curiosity; it also matters for understanding how the world is changing today.

Around the globe the unprecedented growth of economies during the nineteenth and twentieth centuries depended on innovations based on a model of technological change first developed in Europe. Those technologies were both capital and energy intensive. In the early twenty-first century we have become far more concerned about the natural world than we once were. Technological innovation today aims not only to foster growth but also to curb environmental degradation and ecological disasters. Nevertheless, we remain beholden to the approach to technological change that took root 300 years ago in Europe. We continue to expect the technologies begun by the Industrial Revolution to solve our problems.

At the same time, and in part because of the technological change that has occurred since 1700, we confront political challenges. Unlike the consensus over technology, there has been much less agreement in public discussions about the desired path of change in the spatial scale of polities. Nevertheless, in the past five decades the world has been moving away from European-sized polities (populations in the tens of millions of inhabitants and territories in the hundreds of thousands of square kilometers) and toward polities and economic spaces that are Chinese in scale (with population in the hundreds of millions of citizens and territories in the millions of square kilometers).

Whether it be in the sudden relevance of Brazil, India, China, and Russia to the world economy or in the attempts at forging free trade in Latin

America, East Asia, Europe, and North America, we are recognizing the importance of geographic scale for economic growth. At the same time, separatist movements from East Timor to Slovenia demonstrate that political scale does not simply reflect economic or technological imperatives. Moreover, the conflicts in Iraq and Afghanistan remind us that there are radical differences between internal peaceful political competition and civil and international strife. Hence as we debate economic globalization, we confront the importance of international relations. But ours is not some brave new world without precedent. The interactions between economic and political structures are long-standing and well-recognized phenomena in history. This book argues that there is much to be learned about how our world is changing by taking a longer view that examines hundreds of years of history.

Nowhere are the links between the distant past and the present more relevant than in the comparative economic history of China and Europe. Because the Industrial Revolution (the initial period of accelerated technological change) took place in Europe and in particular in Britain, scholars and pundits have fallen victim to the temptation of induction. Most of their reasoning begins with a known difference and constructs a plausible explanation of how that difference might have made China poor and Europe rich. As we shall see, this approach is shallow and often chronologically untenable. To begin with, China was once rich and is rapidly becoming one of the more prosperous economies in the world. We need an explanation of Europe's economic successes that also accounts for China's earlier achievements and more recent rise.

Our book offers a new explanation for the distinctive patterns of economic change in China and Europe. We argue that conventional arguments are either unfounded or can be reduced to the consequences of differences in political scale: although both China and Europe experienced long periods of unification and fragmentation, empire was the norm in China, while division prevailed more often in Europe. For much of its history, Europe was poor because it was at war. The rise of capital-intensive methods of production in Europe was the unintended consequence of persistent political strife. In contrast, China, which was often peaceful and unified, developed large-scale markets and took advantage of the division of labor. It was only after 1750 that the advantages of machine-based, capital-intensive methods of production became apparent. Before that time the recipes for growth of the Qing emperors were commonsense everywhere: promote the expansion of agriculture, keep taxes low, and do not interfere with internal commerce.

This book also proposes some methodological innovations. Because we are each specialists in one of these two regions of the world, we can make specific comparisons of similar processes. We pose, whenever possible, falsifiable propositions so that our explanations of particular phenomena can be challenged, qualified, or confirmed by future research. We begin with a review of some conventional arguments offered for both China's failures and Europe's successes. Some of these we reject because of their inability to explain known facts. Others we accept but place within a larger framework of explanation that allies price theory and political economy. We contend that this approach provides a more satisfying discussion of the issues and formulates better answers to the big questions than do the conventional narratives. Our collaboration suggests that the alliance of economic theory with expertise in the history of both China and Europe makes for better economic history.

We hope, first, that when readers finish this book, they will understand that political economy matters to economic history in basic ways. Second, we hope that we have demonstrated that the kind of history we explain matters for understanding present practices and future possibilities. Third, we hope that the political economy of earlier periods of Chinese and European economic history makes clear the distinction between the intentions of actors and the significance of their actions, including unintended outcomes. Appreciating this distinction can help us better plan our desired futures and be more modest about our expected successes.

Before and Beyond Divergence

Miracles, Myths, and Explanations in Economic History

In the past three decades scholars have reconsidered what set Europe off from the rest of the world as the site of state formation and economic changes that led to modern nation-states and industrialized economies. The themes, of course, are far older. They recur in the inquiries of great social thinkers from Montesquieu and Adam Smith to Karl Marx and Max Weber. Europe's, particularly England's, success moved scholars to assess other societies from a European benchmark. Quite diverse social science scholarship presumed that there was a unique and European-defined path to modernization and prosperity. But in the 1980s doubts about the intrinsic superiority of Western political and economic practices began to creep into public discussions as Japan's rise to prominence as the world's second-largest economy was followed by economic transformations in South Korea, Taiwan, Hong Kong, and Singapore. The political and economic evolution of East Asia raised serious questions about the Western origins of contemporary political and economic ideas and institutions.

Because of China's persistent high rates of economic growth, East Asia has once again become a region of fundamental importance to the contemporary world economy. Rapid growth for thirty years with a slowly changing legal system and little change more generally in political institutions also forces us to reconsider the extent to which we can account for the development of China with paradigms deduced from European history. If, in fact, European ideas and institutions are inadequate to explain China's successful growth, can we nevertheless put forward a method of comparison to evaluate the significance of similarities and differences between the two ends of Eurasia?

1

This book argues that this can and should be done. Rather than focus on the recent past, we consider the process of divergence that preceded the onset of modern economic growth in the eighteenth century. Our premise is that social scientists should integrate the legacies of history into falsifiable theories of historical change. Therefore, our enterprise is both more modest and more ambitious than most. It is more modest because we must focus on specific institutions and develop frameworks for making comparisons across societies and over time. It is more ambitious because at the end of the process we arrive at a sharper understanding of the links between politics and economics in China and Europe.

Ours is not the first attempt at such an analysis. In fact, comparative economic history lies at the core of efforts to understand why some places are prosperous and others are poor. Obviously, Europe and North America were the first places to experience modern economic growth, and they have also provided the heart of the evidence on which models of development have been based. The relative dearth of evidence on other parts of the globe has led comparative economic history to proceed in two steps. First, scholars find some trait that has been associated with success (e.g., representative government, the nuclear family, or Christianity); second, they seek to classify other societies on the basis of how close their institutions are to the favored one. Scholars have proffered many features to explain either Britain's or Europe's early success. These range from broadly cultural to more specifically social, political, and economic factors. Douglass C. North has led the way in stressing the importance of institutions to economic growth. Good institutions provide the rules and the sanctions to encourage productive behavior. People who enjoy secure property rights are more likely to engage in production and trade with others. Thus good government is crucial because only the state can provide laws and courts to make and enforce contracts. These maxims work well to give an account of how and why England succeeded economically in the seventeenth and eighteenth centuries in ways in which Spain or Portugal did not. Variations across Europe in early modern economic development line up quite well with the security of property rights and the effectiveness of law and courts in enforcing claims stated in contracts (North 1981). Because England was the first industrial nation, it makes apparent sense to consider the institutions found in England during the eighteenth and nineteenth centuries important factors in explaining the onset of modern economic growth. England's virtues extend well beyond improvements to production and exchange.

The logic of private property was intimately tied to ideas of "liberties," which elites vocally defended. In England propertied elites were locked into a struggle with the King that culminated in his defeat and the rise of Parliament. On the Continent elites also negotiated with their kings and invoked similar political ideas, even if the institutions that gave them voice were not as effective as those forged in England. The political and economic institutions developed in early modern Europe were thus intimately connected to economic outcomes after 1750.

The gains and pitfalls of this approach are clearly in evidence in North's recent work with John Wallis and Barry Weingast, *Violence and Social Orders* (2009). Although they stress the importance of politics for economic performance, they generalize the links between political and economic practices found in European and American history. They identify a grand historical arc leading to modern societies characterized by the replacement of polities with limited access by polities with open access. Limited-access orders (societies where privileged elites limit the use of violence) have elites who capture wealth and power. Open-access orders, in contrast, allow everyone to enjoy economic opportunities and political voice. In an open-access society political and economic competition prevails because the cost of forming either political or economic organizations is small and equal for everyone. At the heart of their analysis are institutions that North has previously referred to as the "rules of the game" (North 1990: 3–4). In this work the authors explain, "Institutions include formal rules, written laws, formal social conventions, informal norms of behavior, and shared beliefs about the world, as well as the means of enforcement" (North et al. 2009: 15). The trajectory of change from limited-access orders to open-access orders is complex and contingent because it involves dramatic changes to the political coalitions that ensure civil peace and to the structure of the economy. In particular, success depends on the emergence of increasing numbers of economic and political organizations that can realize peaceful economic and political competition. Empirically, European history exemplifies the process they are reconstructing, and within Europe, England figures most prominently and positively.

China, our focus for comparison with Europe, presents a case far less easy to fit into their framework. China's experiences of industrialization in the 1980s and early 1990s, for example, did not depend very much on the formal institutions of property rights, contracts, and third-party enforcement by the state, as North's approach would have predicted. Recently, Avner

Greif has rehabilitated informal institutions, showing that they play a critical role in sustaining trade, and arguing that the social structures behind these informal institutions can powerfully affect the path of economic change (Greif 2006). In this book we suggest ways in which quite different institutions can perform similar functions. In fact, many of the arguments deployed in the past fall by the wayside as soon as one realizes that neither China nor Europe is homogeneous. In fact, in most situations before industrialization, European and Chinese individuals confronted a similar menu of institutions. The distribution of the institutions that were used responded to simple economic logic. It was not until much later that the institutional menus began to diverge. In the case of contracts, many of the differences between Chinese and European institutions can be understood in terms of the degree and substance of formality versus informality. Chinese and Europeans deployed both formal and informal institutions; what differed was their relative importance. When economic conditions changed, both societies altered their relative reliance on formal institutions, sometimes increasing it and at other times reducing it. That both societies responded to circumstances encourages us to consider that some early modern Chinese and European economic practices were different simply because of circumstances. Moreover, in this comparison the degree of formality of transactions is not an indicator of efficiency.

Putting institutions into spatial as well as temporal contexts also matters to us. The national units that North, Wallis, and Weingast favor as their units of comparison are nation-states that compete with one another. Their focus is heavily on domestic politics, and war is little more than another form of public spending. This approach is inadequate for Europe because international relations cannot be separated from domestic politics. It is even more inadequate for China because after A.D. 1000 the Middle Kingdom was always larger territorially and demographically than many European polities put together. To this day much of what passes for international relations in Europe is domestic politics in China.

The need to specify geographic units of analysis as part of the research process (rather than simply relying on political boundaries at a point in time) is well understood in social science but is very often ignored for practical reasons. We cannot do so because differences in spatial scale and in the resulting intensity of armed conflict are central to our analysis of China and Europe. Although the division between domestic and international makes sense for many twentieth-century subjects, it is certainly extremely problematic when one is making comparisons between China and Europe in the past. We therefore reevaluate conventional political contrasts of European fragmentation to Chinese unity to identify the advantages of a large spatial unit to economic activity. In this comparative light Europe's competitive political system was extremely costly. The costs that accrued to Europe from fragmentation were quite visible because they involved violent political strife; the advantages were unintended and, indeed, unanticipated.

We do not propose an equally bold but alternative framework. Indeed, it is history and its uncomfortable facts that force us to depart in significant ways from the model proposed by North, Wallis, and Weingast. Rather, our claims are more limited because they are more precise. It may well be that in considering change in Africa, South America, or Southeast Asia, a researcher can take the structure of political institutions as given. If so, the lessons of neither Chinese nor European history would export well. Even that negative finding would be worth establishing. We suspect, however, that the study of long-run economic change is informed everywhere by encompassing "domestic" and "international" political competition.

Our finding that European national units are too limiting a spatial focus brings us to a second major inspiration. Kenneth Pomeranz has led the way in thinking carefully about the interaction between space and economic history. In *The Great Divergence* (2000) Pomeranz draws on frameworks that have long touted Europe's geographic advantages in terms both of intra-European trade and of access to New World resources (E. L. Jones 1981; Wrigley 1988; Allen 2009a). In contrast, China did not have these spatial advantages, and as others have emphasized, it also did not possess a political system that sought maritime expansion (Wallerstein 1974–1989 vol. 1). But his analysis also rests on a much deeper understanding of China and thus offers the richest comparison of China and Europe in the economic history literature.

Pomeranz's argument that in the areas of markets, consumption, and life expectancy China appears strikingly similar to Europe well into the eighteenth century extends a line of inquiry one of us began some years ago (Wong 1997: 9–52). Pomeranz's work has made very clear the challenge of explaining how economies similar in many ways during the eighteenth century ended up diverging dramatically in the nineteenth century. His explanation of economic divergence stresses two sets of reasons for the break between Europe and China, both of which are based on environmental differences. First, the location of coal in Europe closer to cities hungry for energy than was the case in China gave the English, in particular, a critical advantage over the Chinese when timber became scarce. This argument expands on prior work from Wrigley and has received substantial support from Allen (2009a chap. 4). Second, the close proximity of the New World allowed Europeans to avoid the difficulties attendant on increasingly scarce land. Pomeranz's study satisfies historians' desire for a narrative account of the past. At the same time, it engages economists with arguments they recognize (e.g., European economic successes depended on labor-saving possibilities from abundant land and energy). His explanation is temporally focused on critical changes that took place in the late eighteenth and early nineteenth centuries.

We share with Pomeranz a desire to anchor our explanation of economic divergence in time and place even as we search for more explanatory mechanisms that go beyond the circumstantial (location of coal or proximity of new and unexploited resources). But although we find European national units too limiting a spatial focus, we are not arguing for a world perspective on early modern economic history. We believe that the most persuasive explanation for Europe's late eighteenth- and early nineteenth-century transformations is best provided by comparing the politics of economic change within China and Europe in the centuries that preceded their visible economic divergence. When one extends the analysis back in time, political reasons for different conditions in China and Europe come into sharp relief. These differences initially favored China because the empire could and did grow through Smithian principles of specialization and exchange, but the same forces later favored Europe when political fragmentation increased the likelihood of capital using technological and organizational innovations. Our approach stresses comparisons between world regions and how differences between them created an increasing likelihood of dramatic economic change taking place in Europe rather than in China.

Like Pomeranz, we also avoid invoking cultural traits as putative reasons for different economic outcomes in China and Europe. Unlike him, we do observe important differences between China and Europe that have been considered by some to reflect cultural traits peculiar to one or the other world region. For instance, China's eighteenth-century construction of a vast granary system can be considered the emperor's Confucian and paternalistic commitment to the people's subsistence security. Although eighteenth-century China's language of paternalism was no doubt difficult to translate into European languages, linguistic challenges did not prevent eighteenth-century thinkers from identifying it as enlightened despotism (Montesquieu). European rulers also expressed paternalistic aspirations. What they lacked were the capacities to implement their political desires while at the same time pursuing war. European rulers faced political challenges radically different from those confronting an agrarian empire like China. What others have ended up thinking of as cultural differences are in fact better understood, we argue, as products of choices made in response to very different kinds of circumstances. These different circumstances are not simply natural and geographic, like Pomeranz's access to coal or proximity to the New World, but rather are produced socially and politically under diverse ecological and environmental conditions across both China and Europe.

We are interested in explaining economic change in China and Europe according to a common set of economic principles and in observing how the political contexts influence outcomes. We seek to use economic theory to explain variations within China and variations within Europe, as well as variations between them. Price theory figures prominently in our explanation of economic change. Long before the visible divergence of China and Europe after 1750, differences in relative factor prices in China and Europe set in motion incentives to save on labor and invest in capital that figure prominently in Pomeranz's account, as well as in other scholarship on European economic growth. To explain these differences in factor prices, we will stress conditions that are the outcomes, we will argue, of more basic differences in the spatial scale of polities in China and Europe. In this analysis we parallel Robert Allen's recent work on the progress of industrialization in England (2009a). Indeed, Allen puts special emphasis on relatively high wages and low fuel costs in explaining why the technologies we associate with industrialization were developed and deployed in England. But his analysis cannot explain why Europe (and not just England) developed a cadre of skilled workers and techniques that blossomed most fully in Britain. Nor can it explain why wages were high in Britain after 1650 relative to the Continent without recourse to politics. Moreover, an analysis of politics cannot be restricted to comparing England with France or China. It must start by examining differences between two units of similar scale that evolved separately: Europe and China.

Like Pomeranz, we seek to get at the roots of the divergence, but we believe that our approach integrates more social science and history. We do not, however, aim to offer a close historical account of the many particular changes made possible by the differences between China and Europe that Pomeranz emphasizes. What we lose by presenting a less full history, we gain in temporal reach, for it is our claim that in 2050, when China will look much more like Europe economically than it does today, the factors we stress—institutions and political scale—should continue to help guide our exploration of the way polities and economies evolve, whereas the importance of endowments has faded as transport costs have collapsed. After all, China's coastal provinces have been able to boom despite their distance from coal fields and the New World's natural bounties. The interactions between politics and economics remain fundamental to explaining economic changes in the future.

We believe that China and Europe were set on their separate paths long before 1750, when energy or distant land resources became more important. These factors no doubt contributed to the path of economic changes in Europe and may well have exacerbated the relative performance of economies like that of England in the nineteenth century, but they were neither sufficient nor necessary for China's and Europe's economies to diverge. Similarly, economic change in China and Europe was not driven mainly by differences in people's intentions, abilities, or personal circumstances (however much these factors can matter at the individual or local level). From the perspective of what individuals choose, we think that some of the most important factors influencing different likelihoods of economic change in the early modern era were unintended consequences of actions taken for reasons largely unrelated to improving the economy. Finally, we reject the idea that some narrow institutional differences between China and Europe were sufficient to change likelihoods of economic success because, as we show, different institutions can work as near substitutes in different circumstances. To observe that institutions are different does not necessarily mean that one set is always better than another. We will argue that political factors made it increasingly likely that parts of Europe, rather than any parts of China, would make the transition to modern economic growth by the late eighteenth century, irrespective of their relations to the New World or the location of their coal deposits.

As historians, we reject the myth of a contrast between European growth and Chinese stagnation in the centuries preceding the very visible nineteenth-century divergence. The evidence is clear: China did not stagnate economically until the nineteenth century, and even then not all parts

of the empire were unable to grow. Analytically, slower growth is fundamentally different from stagnation with all its ghosts of overpopulation
and Malthusian economics. Before 1700 similar dynamics of market-based
(Smithian) growth worked through different political and economic institutions in China and Europe. The key reasons for economic divergence
were political, and these increased the likelihood that modern economic
development would take place in Europe before China. European advantages were unintended consequences of political differences with China.

To make our case, we proceed first with some history in Chapter 1 to
highlight the striking differences in political scale in Europe and China.
However, the same history makes us well aware that China experienced
long periods of fragmentation, and that the entity known as the Roman
Empire endured for centuries, even if we exclude its Byzantine temporal
extension. Unlike most social science scholars, we do not take the differences in political scale as given. As a result our approach to, and resolution
of, the problem of the consequences of political scale breaks with conventional interpretations

To answer this problem, we develop a sequence of frameworks. Chapter 2
considers the old Malthusian workhorse of household structure and demography as a possible source of significant institutional differences that
could help us account for economic divergence. Kinship relations and
population dynamics are implausible sources for divergence. Chapter 3
looks at the institutions enabling economic transactions in China and
Europe between the mid-fourteenth and the mid-eighteenth centuries. We
find that although the two regions were clearly not alike, their dissimilari-
ties stem from political scale and seem unlikely to have caused economic
divergence. Chapter 4 takes us to the realm of manufacturing or craft production, where we find that the urban location of much manufacturing in
Europe and its more frequent rural location in China are significant, but
not exactly in the ways conventionally argued and for reasons that others
have not clearly explained. In Chapter 5 we consider how production and
trade are financed and in ways similar to those we use in Chapters 2 and
3 discover institutional differences, but not ones we consider causally crucial to have set China and Europe on separate paths. In Chapter 6 we move
to public finance, and here we find differences that cannot be accounted
for by conventional contrasts of Chinese and European states in the early
modern and modern eras. The differences we discover affect economic change
in ways contrary to what previous scholarship has suggested, although the

impact on overall likelihoods of economic growth is limited. The variation in public finance institutions, clearly tied to the agendas for rule in an empire versus those prevalent among a set of smaller competing polities, completes our analytical revolution. Europe succeeded despite rather than because of political competition.

In Chapter 7 we return to the history introduced in Chapter 1 and offer our interpretation of why the equilibrium size of polities was so different for so long in China and Europe. Having taken political scale as given and having shown its importance in Chapters 2 through 6, we consider in Chapter 7 some reasons for the differences of spatial scale of polities in China and Europe. We show that the politics of economic change in China and in Europe were quite different and, as early as A.D. 1000, enter into self-reinforcing patterns. The thirteenth reunification of China by Khubilai Khan completed the process of divergence.

We put forward general arguments and exemplify them with Chinese and European data. Not only are our economic arguments intended to account for variations within, as well as between, China and Europe, but they should also prove confirmable or falsifiable by data from other places outside both China and Europe. Similarly, our arguments about the significance of political scale are largely applied to explain one set of outcomes in China and Europe (economic divergence), but in the conclusion we also suggest that they remain relevant to more recent times. Our book is thus intended to be exemplary of an approach to explaining economic similarities and differences in the world of the past that also applies to predicting future changes. Our goal is to identify causal mechanisms that we know work across varied particular conditions, like those suggested by price theory, and to apply them to conditions that we think are best explained by considerations of politics. The exercise is not intrinsically historical or limited to explaining what we already know to have taken place. Indeed, effective explanations of what has happened in the past can help us anticipate future possibilities because many of the social processes at work today have historical roots and antecedents.

Our method of analysis identifies what we find to be persistent myths about China and Europe. It also allows us to reject accounts of what made Europe so special or its growth so miraculous. We pursue explanations of economic change that can account for observable behaviors in China and Europe, and we invite readers to assess the persuasiveness of our analysis and to extend our approach to other times and places. We will count ourselves fortunate if we engage readers seriously enough to evaluate our approach and compare its advantages and limitations with those of other studies of economic change. We will measure our success by subsequent efforts to amass more evidence and formulate research that confirms, qualifies, or undermines our explanations.

1

Space and Politics

A thousand years ago China was a vast empire. So it was a hundred years ago. A thousand years ago Europe was politically fragmented. It was still so a hundred years ago. These contrasts might suggest that massive differences in the scale of polities are constants in the histories of these regions. From this perspective it would be easy for us simply to take the divergent political structures as givens and put our energies into tracing their consequences for economic change. We could then appeal to either geographic determinants or cultural constants for the early and persistent Chinese success at creating a large integrated political space (and for Europeans, the failure to do the same). We have decided, however, to avoid this approach because we are aware that this basic political contrast between China and Europe was neither constant nor necessary. As Maps 1.1 and 1.2 make evident, a bit more than 2,000 years ago China and Europe were both large-scale empires. To be sure, China was larger (the scale of the maps are slightly different), but as empires Rome and the Han were huge. What is more striking is that five centuries later the polities of China and Europe were both fragmented. Then from 500 to 1000 there were several long episodes of fragmentation in China and repeated attempts to put the Roman Empire back together in Europe. Given this more complicated history, we seek in this chapter to explain how it came to be that by 1279 (the end of the Southern Song) the European political equilibrium involved spatial fragmentation, while the Chinese political equilibrium featured spatial integration. Understanding this basic contrast is critical to our subsequent analysis of the political economies of growth at both ends of Eurasia.

An analysis of the history of China and Europe between 1300 and 1850 is necessary to begin exploring the evolution of each region's political economy and how it mattered for economic growth. Let us briefly consider a well-known example of the economic consequences of political scale to which we will return in Chapter 3. Empires afford greater opportunities for large markets and the kind of growth processes highlighted by Adam Smith than politically fragmented regions, in which, at the very least, war and customs barriers will surely impede trade. The opportunities for Smithian growth in empires can, of course, be undermined when rulers substitute themselves for the market (in particular, by using taxes to secure grain for politically sensitive locations like Rome, Beijing, or Istanbul) or interfere with the labor market (as in Russia's serfdom or Spain's American *encomiendas*) or land (as with the Ottomans' *timar* system for funding the army). But such intrusions into the market are not the peculiar proclivity of empires; other polities did much the same. Instead, we must accept the importance of the interactions between political structures and historical circumstances in shaping economic institutions.

For our purpose of comparing China and Europe, we set aside debates about the definition of *empire*. We will call empires those polities in Europe or China where a central ruler exercised effective authority over a large fraction of a contiguous region. Clearly, this definition is not intended to be general or prescriptive. Any reader familiar with the Ottoman, Hapsburg, or colonial European empires knows that these realms were neither geographically compact nor blessed with great political capacities. Furthermore, unlike the Roman Empire, where, after Caracalla, all free men were citizens, or the Chinese empire, where the Han were by far the dominant ethnic group, most empires have been ruled by a minority population that severely restricted the political rights of other groups. We choose this definition of empire simply because it encapsulates the key contrasts between Europe and China analyzed in this book. Our empire, therefore, is neither an ideal type nor a general phenomenon; it is just a practical appellation for spatially large polities in contrast to far smaller ones.

For most of this book we will trace the direct and indirect impacts of differences in the spatial scale of polities on economic development. We will argue that differences in political scale are critical to understanding the economic divergence between China and Europe, but we will not base these conclusions on the specific details of imperial political structure.

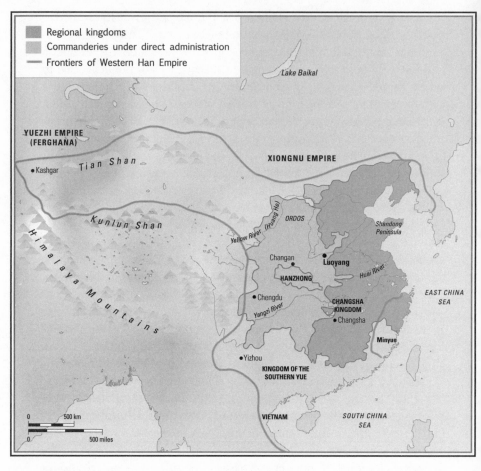

Map 1.1. The Han Empire, 207 B.C.–A.D. 220

Instead, we take the contrasting spatial scales of Chinese and European polities as key factors that both let and led rulers in these regions to develop different political priorities and policies. These policies, in turn, shaped the paths of economic change. Policies in other empires did not closely parallel those in China any more than policies in other fragmented states, such as those of Africa or Southeast Asia, reproduced the practices forged in Europe. Political histories embody much that is historically particular and spatially specific. For our purpose of comparing Chinese and

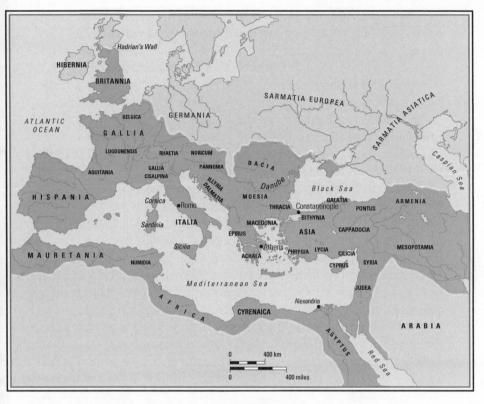

Map 1.2. The Roman Empire at its greatest extent, second century A.D.

European economies, we need attend only to the political histories of these two regions of the world.

In this chapter we seek to understand why, despite the existence of successful empires in both regions 2,000 years ago, the two political systems diverged to such an extent that 500 years ago fragmentation was as stable in Europe as consolidation was in China. In this largely narrative chapter we focus on early processes of empire formation. We also consider the structures of the empires and the challenges they faced. We then examine the processes that after A.D. 200 led to the permanent breakup of the Roman Empire and the repeated reconstruction of the Chinese empire. By the early centuries of the second millennium (the Yuan and Ming dynasties), a political economy had emerged in China that favored the maintenance of a large and integrated political space. Henceforth, dynastic transitions were painful but brief. In Europe a political economy had emerged that overcame the extreme political fragmentation and instability of the early Middle Ages but made the reunification of Europe extremely unlikely.

Rather than seeing the repeated successes of Chinese rulers at maintaining or reconstituting their empire as a direct and simple consequence of the spread of Han culture, we show how Chinese imperial rulers and their official elites learned from their mistakes in order to become more successful at promising and delivering internal order and welfare-enhancing projects. We also argue that in many ways Europe's political elites, from the rise of the Roman republic to the fall of Constantinople, were striving to establish the kind of prosperity that was achieved in China, but they failed. Continued political strife in Europe ensured that rulers who focused simply on public order, access to markets, and infrastructure development would not have survived. Instead, European rulers focused on gathering the resources they needed for war. In the process of raising taxes to pay for warfare, European rulers enshrined many specific concessions to local groups in a plethora of charters. These, in turn, proved to be an enduring brake on the spatial scale of political consolidation in Europe.

As noted earlier, one could attribute the existence of empire in China to a variety of extremely long-standing cultural attitudes or even to endowments. One could do the same for fragmentation in Europe. But such convenient explanations are belied by the fact that empires arise in a variety of settings across world history and well beyond China. Similarly, political fragmentation is not Europe's exclusive attribute. For economists, and many other social scientists as well, the evolution of the size of polities results from a competition between the heterogeneity of demand for public services and economies of scale in the delivery of these services. In our contemporary world scholars focus heavily on such domestic services as welfare, education, and infrastructure (Alesina and Spolaore 2003); in historical settings one must also include the military. The breakdown of the Roman Empire can thus be seen as the result of a collapse in the returns on maintaining a large-scale military, as well as an increase in the heterogeneity of demand for public services due to the influx of populations that had hitherto lived outside the empire. Similarly, the effectiveness of the Great Wall in containing nomadic raiders, as well as the overwhelming demographic size of Han populations in the empire, can be seen as making a large-scale polity easier to maintain in China. But this simple contrast, like many striking historical differences, requires closer analysis. The Great Wall had its parallels under the Roman Empire; such walls were just as much a European innovation as the military techniques that allowed Germanic tribes to defeat the Roman legions or the rise of siege artillery that eliminated petty lords in much of western Europe. A parallel contrast between China and Europe regarding the diversity of cultural identities in Europe and the dominance of Han identity in China requires us to consider more closely the hows and whys of social processes that led Chinese individuals to adhere to a common Han identity rather than privilege some more local identities.

From Early Empire to the Mongol Invasions: China's Memory

China's empire has very old roots, but sustaining and increasing the scale of China as a political entity required overcoming a number of challenges. Central to the establishment of the empire was the ability of the emperor to deploy overwhelming force over long periods of time because, as we all know, empires are generally created through military success. But sustaining the empire was a far more subtle endeavor. Consider the short-lived Qin dynasty. It achieved an imperial unification in 221 B.C., but Qin rulers fell only fourteen years after proclaiming their dynasty. As the standard accounts suggest, the Qin had a strategy of conquest but no imperial strategy of rule, and they fell to popular revolts prompted by their harsh demands for resources and labor from the common people (Bodde 1986).

Like the Qin, the next dynasty (Han) prevailed in warfare among rivals to assume imperial control, but unlike its predecessor, it developed policies of less harsh rule that allowed it to survive for some four centuries. The government opened new agricultural lands and maintained irrigation works that made these lands more productive. The typical rural settlement that the government sought to promote was an unfortified village with some 100 households, each owning its own small amount of land that allowed it to meet its material needs and pay taxes to the government. A society of prosperous small tenants was a persistent ideal of Chinese rulers (Nishijima 1986).

Benevolent rule was not a panacea, because not all Chinese were content to settle with the Han dynasty's rule. The emperors faced such serious challenges from elites that they lost power for fifteen years between A.D. 9

and A.D. 23 to a competitor whose failure to sustain his rule leaves him with the label "usurper" in history books. Although the Han ruling family regained power, the dynasty was unable to extend its authority to the local level. On the contrary, powerful landed elites controlled small areas and over time increased exactions from their peasants, thus sparking social conflicts that erupted into rebellion. Neither these magnates nor the Han dynasty could suppress the peasant uprisings. The social unrest proved fatal for the empire. Indeed, Cao Cao, the general who put down the rebels, took the opportunity to establish his own authority over a third of the empire. This potential founder of a new dynasty could go no further, however, in reconstituting the empire. After Cao Cao died in 220, his son did force the last Han-dynasty emperor to abdicate, but he could not extend his territorial control beyond the third of the empire he had inherited from his father. Three centuries of political division followed (Bielenstein 1986).

Once again the politics of violence are central to understanding this long period of fragmentation. Its causes include pressure from the Xiongnu, a steppe people who began to organize themselves as powerful foes long before the collapse of the Han dynasty. The Xiongnu had earlier responded to Han military efforts to push them further north and west with their own counteroffensive. Later, and to the Han dynasty's dismay, the balance of military strength shifted, and the steppe people gained more territory. Chinese leaders built walls in an effort to protect their initial territorial gains and then to protect themselves from nomadic advances, but nothing the dynasty did prevented the Xiongnu and other steppe peoples from becoming important military actors in the competition for control of northern China after the fall of the Han dynasty in 220 (Di Cosmo 2002).

For more than three centuries after 220, no set of leaders emerged either from within the Han's former territories or from the steppes who could build a successor empire. Political fragmentation in northern China proceeded to a very local level in some places, where militias were formed for self-defense and strongmen created their own small realms; other parts of the north were under the control of larger and stronger military rulers. In southern China military leaders ruled small kingdoms and faced two kinds of challenges. Domestically, they confronted powerful families who controlled large amounts of property; at the same time, they competed not only with one another but also with the much stronger northern regimes, which had richer resource bases and strong military traditions. While northern regimes had steppe warriors, southern regimes recruited tribal minorities, convicts, and vagrants (Graff 2002). Southern rulers also aspired to civilian political ideals that had been created under the Han dynasty; these principles helped rule an empire but offered little guidance to those seeking to build a new empire. By coincidence, this is precisely the period when the Roman Empire began to break apart. There, as in China, the same goals of achieving local security and reconstituting empire competed with each other.

Between the early third century and the late sixth century there was no unified empire on the Chinese mainland. In A.D. 400, had people been able to look across Eurasia, they would likely have doubted that an empire would form again either in Europe or in China. Although ethnic Han Chinese dominated demographically, in northern China they intermingled with a diverse array of steppe peoples, some of whom spoke ancient forms of Tibetan or Mongolian, while others spoke Turkic languages. These populations were organized into a series of culturally mixed small kingdoms. Their rulers were equally influenced by the steppe people's martial traditions and Confucian visions of imperial order. In particular, the military practices of steppe armies became the model for rulers of the northern portions of the former Han Empire. Yet whatever the differences that initially separated them, they were all exposed to Chinese political philosophy that affirmed the norm of empire and made recovery of empire the common goal. Although the rulers of the northern kingdoms were of diverse origins, they adopted the history of the Han Empire as a model for the world they had joined and wished to sustain (Tonami and Takeda 1997: 41–160).

To reform the empire required combining these imperial visions with sufficient military might, and it was by no means a foregone conclusion that any set of leaders would emerge who could conquer all their competitors. But such a leader did emerge in the north. Yang Jian built an army able to embark successfully on a march of conquest, first against other leaders in the north and then against southern regimes unable to mount successful defenses; his successes culminated in the formation of the Sui dynasty in 589. But just as in the case of the Qin, a strategy for conquest was not a strategy for rule. Sui leaders demanded too much of their subjects, who funded the building of the Grand Canal connecting the rice-rich south to the governing north and also paid for military adventures that took Sui armies unsuccessfully into the Korean Peninsula (Graff 2002: chap. 7).

The Sui rulers were replaced by a new set of leaders who established their Tang dynasty in 618 and proceeded to rule for nearly three centuries. The Tang focused on strategies for keeping the empire together. In doing so, they emulated and enlarged on the policies of the Han dynasty. For roughly half their period of rule, Tang emperors were successful in simultaneously expanding the empire's borders to the west and putting in place measures to stabilize the living conditions of their peasant subjects. At the same time, they extracted their revenues directly from the peasantry. The Tang worked to balance conformity with Confucian principles, and thus uniformity within the empire, with more practical considerations of the ethnic and cultural diversity of their subjects. The Tang capital of Changan became home to a diverse population of Han Chinese who intermarried with Di, Qiang, Tuoba, and other peoples, each of whom had distinctive languages, food, and clothing. Cultures and bloodlines mixed to create a range of lifestyles that together represented a cosmopolitan empire. In this setting lifestyles and cultural practices were chosen by individuals rather than imposed by genealogy. Imperial reconstruction was aided by the absence of any long period of anarchy like that which followed Europe's "barbarian" invasions. The arts, especially inspired by Buddhist influences from India and central Asia, flourished. Scholars sustained, without major interruptions, their classical traditions. Their Confucian ideas and institutions inspired the formation of a bureaucratic state with lasting political significance. Many of the principal organs of the Tang central government, such as the six boards, provided basic and important models for later Chinese dynasties (Adshead 2004).

The Tang dynasty shared the territorial ambitions of previous dynasties. Its rulers extended and opened the country's borders into central Asia. Like the Han dynasty, the Tang forged a presence to the west in several of the oasis communities along the Silk Road. These connections ensured that a diverse range of cultural influences originating in distant places would continue to enrich elements that later became considered typical of Chinese culture, including the poetry of Li Bo and the tricolored glazes of Tang porcelains. An open and expanding empire not only welcomed new cultural influences but also became ever more vulnerable to military threats, including those posed by some of the very troops who were expected to keep the empire safe from outsiders as the spatial scale of their responsibilities grew larger. Some of the military forces employed by the Tang state to maintain peace were recruited from central Asia and were descendants of the ethnically and culturally mixed groups that formed beyond the northern frontiers of the empire. Anxieties among some Tang court officials regarding the power of these military commanders led the general An Lushan to strike at the capital because he feared that the imperial court might attempt to limit or even undermine his power.

The Tang state was forced to seek strategic alliances with other steppe-region seminomadic military forces to defeat An Lushan's rebellion in 755. As a result, the Tang military had to withdraw from central Asia and accept a much-diminished empire. In the late ninth century domestic unrest among impoverished peasants and powerful local lords led to further troubles for the dynasty. Finally, in the early tenth century, the capital was captured by an enemy general. The fall of Changan marked the beginning of another period of political fragmentation in which rival forces established smaller kingdoms. For a period of nearly a millennium, from the Han to the Tang, Chinese dynasties found the balance between external expansion and internal cohesion difficult to maintain (Graff 2002: chaps. 10–11). As a result, the empire was repeatedly overrun and fragmented. Nevertheless, the empire was re-created later because subsequent rulers and their officials could draw on a growing repertoire of earlier ideas and institutions to which their own innovations offered their successors even more possibilities.

The Song dynasty, established by the general who came to power in the old Tang capital in 960, was no different. Its founder not only took over the remnants of his predecessors but also reconquered other small kingdoms that had emerged in what had previously been the Tang Empire. Nevertheless, the Song dynasty ruled a much smaller realm. It was in this smaller realm that a set of key administrative innovations occurred. These political processes may well have been spurred by the more rapid pace of social and economic change that was occurring at the same time (expansion of urban centers, small-scale tenant farmers producing for the market, improved transportation technologies, and new commercial institutions and merchant networks). Whatever their cause, Song political innovations should be seen as fundamentally new techniques of rule that reduced the transaction costs of internal administration. In particular, the dynasty created a civil service bureaucracy for which many officials were recruited on the basis of passing examinations; bureaucratic sophistication and specialization enlarged the government's capacities to mobilize resources and order local societies. However, domestic successes were undermined by a renewed vulnerability to states formed along the northern border by groups who combined military prowess with some of the bureaucratic institutions of rule developed within the empire. This military weakness ended up forcing Song rulers south, where they maintained a state that became one of several states on the Chinese mainland. Although the Song rulers' reach was not as extensive as that of some of the earlier empires, their retreat south was fortuitous because it also reinforced the dynasty's close connections to the emerging centers of economic and social change (Ihara and Umemura 1997).

Sitting in the Southern Song capital of Hangzhou in 1200, a well-informed observer of the dynasty's domestic conditions and foreign situation might well have been struck by the growing wealth of the country's cities and its increasingly precarious military situation along its northern borders, where a number of states, especially if they joined forces, could threaten the Song government. Without such a coalition or consensus among northern states, our observer, if he or she could think beyond the framework of Chinese dynastic history, might have imagined the possibilities of a multistate system emerging with militarily strong but commercially poor states in the north and a wealthy but militarily limited state in the south. In other words, the persistence of empire across the scale of space that had formed during the Han and Tang empires need not have been replicated thereafter. From the mid-eighth century, when An Lushan's rebellion ended effective central rule under the Tang, until the Mongol conquest of the Chinese mainland in the thirteenth century, there was no unified empire. Our imaginary observer, if he or she were particularly astute, might also note that even with a multistate system consisting of a few large realms (Rossabi 1983), the political equilibrium on the Chinese mainland need not have reached the level of spatial fragmentation found in Europe. After the Mongol conquest neither an imaginary observer nor subsequent historians were likely to recall the possibility that a multistate equilibrium could have become more permanent on the Chinese mainland.

Once again, the consolidation of the empire required a superior military force that could drive out its competitors, destroy them, or incorporate them. The Mongols did all three as part of an even larger enterprise that in the thirteenth century absorbed not only China but also much of central Asia reaching westward toward the Ottoman Empire. The Mongols' conquest of large parts of Asia created the world's largest empire. Their territories were so vast that it was impossible for a single leader to rule them effectively. In 1251 the empire was divided into four separate realms centered in southern Russia, Persia, the Mongol homeland, and China. The last of these was by far the wealthiest and most populous. From the vantage point of Chinese history, it is difficult to exaggerate the importance of the Mongol conquest; without the Mongols, northern and southern China (like the eastern and western Roman empires) might well have gone their separate ways. The Mongols simply destroyed all other would-be military competitors. When their far-flung empire fell apart, and the Mongols in China retreated to the pastures of Mongolia in the face of tremendous domestic unrest, a native Han Chinese dynasty could take over and establish its rule over the sedentary portion of their empire without facing serious territorial threats from strong "barbarian" forces in the north (Twitchett and Franke 1994 vol. 6, chaps. 4–9).

Clearly, the history of empire on the Chinese mainland over the first 1,500 years of imperial rule has a distinctive military rhythm. Empires formed and fell because of military offensives that often came from poorer external foes, but we can also see a pattern of internal processes that made the reorganization and persistence of the empire more likely. These involve the successful spread of Han culture among populations that were initially quite different in ethnicity, language, and social practices. These processes also involved the progressive creation of an effective structure of imperial administration. Thus some core elements of the mature Chinese empire have very old roots. But until the tenth century the empire withered away several times.

The persistence and growth of the Chinese empire and its equally recurring collapse lead to some reconsiderations of political economies of scale. Rulers were regularly tempted to expand their dominions in ways that were unsustainable. Furthermore, they were not always able to adjust their political organization to respond to new challenges (domestic unrest or foreign threats). Time and again we observe changes in internal governance or in the size of the realm that led to serious problems of governance and even the collapse of the dynasty. Over the long run, however, Chinese dynasties proved quite capable of learning elements of rule that made the empire more successful. The history of China before 1350 (from the Qin through the Mongols) can in fact be seen as a long apprenticeship in the strategies of internal rule.

Later dynasties, the Ming and even more the Qing, capitalized on their predecessors' experiences. Successful rule involved finding a balance with respect to the internal governance of the polity and its external relations. Domestically, emperors recognized the value of uniformity within the realm (which eased the flow of information) and a return to letting localities choose more specific institutions (which allowed innovation and specialization and reduced administrative expense). They also had to choose a level of requests for tax revenues from their subjects that was compatible with the services their officials provided. In each of these cases failure to maintain balance led to revolts and lower tax collection. Early on, rulers and their officials seem to have miscalculated repeatedly. In international relations imperial failures shine a bright light on the importance of balance. The Sui collapsed because their excessive appetite for territory brought about a reaction they could not control. Mongol rule of the Chinese mainland lasted less than a century; the Mongols viewed the people of the northern and southern halves of the empire differently and ruled them in institutionally different ways. What they had conquered they could neither transform nor rule for an extended period of time. Like their predecessors, they did promote conditions conducive to gains from trade and supported local governments that provided social goods inspired by Confucian ideas about good governance.

From Rome to Charles V: Europe Skirts Anarchy

From China's history one might well be tempted to build a theory of successful empire based on military innovation and an ideology of rule that equated a ruler's success with his benevolent treatment of his subjects. The history of Europe suggests that these are far from sufficient if empires are to endure over the long run. Indeed, the Roman Empire was built on a military technology that vanquished foe after foe for half a millennium. Its cultural practices spread throughout the Mediterranean world; and its rulers espoused views of administration that are not dramatically different from those inspired by Confucianism. But after A.D. 200 the empire entered into a slow, violent, and inexorable decline. As we discuss later, and others before us have noted (Scheidel 2009; Potter 2004: 530), the Roman Empire shared many similarities in its rise, expansion, and fall with the contemporaneous Qin-Han Empire. In a wider comparison of empires worldwide, the fall of the Roman Empire may or may not be exceptional. What strikes us is that every attempt to put the Roman Empire back together was an utter failure. If we have only the Qin-Han and Roman cases to consider, it is difficult to take one as the norm against which to judge the other unusual. To expand on our two cases, with attention to the kinds of concerns we raise in subsequent chapters, will remain a task for future work by other scholars. For our purpose, as we have already suggested, we wish simply to explain how and why the equilibrium spatial scale of Chinese and European polities ended up being so different.

Had a subject of the Song dynasty found himself visiting Europe in the tenth century, he would likely have been shocked by the parochial nature of polities and statecraft. Although some princes could claim to rule over an area as vast as a Chinese province, few could exercise the same authority as a Chinese ruler over more than a fraction of their territories. Their powers were hemmed in by what Stephan Epstein has aptly called "freedoms," a host of particularistic privileges that limited the prince's capacity to tax, to regulate the economy, and to provide public goods (Epstein 2000). The recipients of these freedoms, whether they were elites or commoners, peasants or urban dwellers, stood ready to revolt should the prince attempt to gain more power. Hence not only did monarchs face the natural consequences of fragmented polities, namely, the threat of conquest, but they also had to meet very serious internal limits on their authority. By Chinese standards, European monarchs were henpecked by their subjects. By almost any standard, the rise of nation-states in Europe is nothing short of a miracle.

Europe had not always been so fractious, and had Chinese travelers managed to make to it Rome around A.D. 100, they would have found a much more familiar polity. Like the Chinese empire, the Roman Empire was born from the fire of war: from Hannibal's invasion of Italy in 218 B.C. to Varus's defeat in A.D. 9, the Roman army was dealt only minor setbacks. Although Varus's loss of three legions in Germany was shameful, it had limited consequences for the empire, and the westward movement of tribes in northwestern Europe was contained for another 400 years. Expansion continued in the east until Trajan's army found itself on the banks of the Tigris. The year A.D. 116 marked the end of conquest, not because the army had found too strong a foe, but because Persia was simply too distant from Rome to keep.

Like China, Rome took its imperial responsibilities seriously. The first was keeping the peace. Although until A.D. 116 the empire grew, effectively pushing its foes farther from Rome, after that time an actual policy of containment prevailed (Goodman 1997: chap. 7). As in China, walls were built. By the standard of the Great Wall, Hadrian's stone barrier across Scotland was short. A much longer wooden palisade was built across Germany and parts of central Europe. Legions were stationed along the border, and by A.D. 150 one of the emperor's most important responsibilities was to secure the revenues to pay the troops; failure at that task easily marked him for death. The other key responsibility was the provision of public goods. Although historians have emphasized the emperor's lavish spending on "bread and circuses" in Rome and later in Constantinople, one should not forget that the cost of these activities is likely to have been quite small relative to the investments in useful infrastructure. Indeed, the political structure produced massive private and public expenses for infrastructure that included roads, as well as urban amenities like paved streets, arenas, theaters, temples, and waterworks. Such investments were particularly noticeable in the western half of the empire because these provinces had been relatively less urbanized before conquest (Goodman 1997: pt. 4). Although many of these costs were borne by elites rather than paid for with tax revenues, these "gifts" were a key element of elite political control (Veyne 1976).

Like the Han dynasty, Roman emperors promoted bureaucratic integration and a common set of cultural beliefs for elites. All around the Mediterranean and throughout western Europe, provinces saw cities mushroom with their triumphal arches, arenas, waterworks, and similar administrative structures. Not only were the men who lived in these cities considered citizens of their hometowns, but soon enough they were also citizens of Rome. In fact, by the time the western empire collapsed, all free men in the empire were citizens, as were many of the leaders of the "barbarian" invaders. One need only tour the remarkable archaeological remains that survive from England to North Africa and from Spain to Turkey to get a sense of the scale of expenditures that went into forging a common identity for the elites of the Roman Empire. At the time of Trajan and Hadrian, the empire was prosperous, powerful relative to its neighbors, and culturally successful because its diverse populations were adopting Roman ways. In short, one could easily surmise that the Roman Empire was following a course parallel to that of China around the shores of the Mediterranean. By the second century A.D. the elites of the empire were drawn from all over the Mediterranean basin, and the emperor could and did dispatch them to any of the provinces making up his domains (Potter 2004: chap. 2).

Success did not last very long. By the reign of Marcus Aurelius the empire was on the defensive. Over the next century the demands of military operations pushed emperors to divide the empire into western and eastern halves. Although Constantine reunited them to some degree in A.D. 324, he also moved the capital of the empire away from Rome, which over time promoted separation. By the time of his reign, war demanded that individuals with considerable authority be in command of large armies both in Asia and in Europe. Because the emperor could personally attend to only one of these two areas, he had to find someone else to lead wherever he was absent. A successful general in the other part of the empire was a natural rival. Less than a century later Rome was sacked (A.D. 410). There is no obvious date for the end of the Roman Empire; its western half ended in 480, but its eastern half endured for another millennium. Over that time the territories of the eastern empire were slowly but surely incorporated into the Ottoman Empire, but this new political entity proved unable to push into Europe north of the Danube or west of the Alps

The Roman Empire, like its Chinese counterpart, faced many interrelated problems. That it endured is a sign that it could overcome them, at least for a time. From a modern perspective two sets of difficulties stand out. The first was the political instability of a regime with no set system of succession; the second was the continued problems with the peoples beyond the borders of the empire. To begin with, a Roman emperor was foremost a military leader. This was particularly so because Caesar's and Augustus's claims to the throne came from their military prowess. Not surprisingly, the legions and the Praetorian Guard had much to do with the selection of emperors. Few emperors died peacefully. Most seem to have met their fate at the hands of angry soldiers or as a result of an internal challenge from a relative or a general; some later emperors died in battle. Succession contests were further heightened because there was no rule that required a single emperor, nor was there a rule that allowed the army as a whole to make a decision about who should be its supreme leader. Instead, as early as Galba (A.D. 69), troops in one region could proclaim an emperor and, if successful either in intimidating the sitting emperor or in battle, see their choice rise to the top of the hierarchy (Potter 2004: chap. 3). The convulsions that marked the deaths of Nero and Commodus, as well as the longer crisis of the third century, were all internal struggles over who should lead the empire. But despite this apparently fatal flaw the empire managed to survive many successions.

The second problem the empire faced came from military conflicts with neighboring peoples. These varied in intensity and structure. Along the eastern border the Romans faced organized polities. In the first two centuries after Augustus, Rome's eastern neighbors were of limited importance; it was Rome that chose where to mark the borders. The legions encountered only limited opposition. But by the reign of Caracalla, the Parthian kingdom could muster a powerful army. It bested the Romans in battle in A.D. 217; the rise of a new dynasty in Persia led to further battles, resulting in the capture of the emperor Valerian in A.D. 259 (Potter 2004: 254–256). Although the conflict in the East was expensive and protracted, like the conflicts over succession, it was a threat that could be contained. In fact, the East remained the more valuable and safer part of the empire even after Valerian's defeat.

It was another external threat—from the north—that eventually proved fatal. Seminomadic populations living on the northern edges of the empire, from the Black Sea to the North Sea, grew in military strength over the course of several centuries. Despite the defeat of Varus (A.D. 9), Rome was able to maintain the advantage over these peoples until a major invasion of Italy in 259; the final blow came a century later after the defeat of Valens at Adrianople in A.D. 378. But the empire did not collapse. Like their Chinese colleagues, Roman emperors tried to co-opt some of the nomadic populations. By A.D. 270 Aurelian and his successors regularly negotiated with Germanic tribes in an attempt to turn enough of them into allies as a means to pacify the frontier. That proved insufficient, and there were attempts to alter the empire's political structure both to meet different armies' needs for imperial leaders and to avoid the civil strife of contested leadership. Commanders were needed both in the West and in the East, and under Diocletian a remarkable political experiment was attempted: the tetrarchy. It involved two senior emperors and two junior emperors. The members of this ruling collegium could provide enough commanders for the troops. At the same time it offered the potential to co-opt new members in ways that should have discouraged revolts. By the reign of Constantine the experiment had failed, but it left open the idea that there would be eastern and western emperors.

Meanwhile, in the western reaches of the empire the Roman army enjoyed great advantages that allowed massive territorial expansion into regions that were sparsely populated by Mediterranean standards. As long as the Romans maintained their military advantage (which they did up to Marcus Aurelius), the western legions could police the frontier at low cost, and the ability of the emperor as a military leader was of little consequence. However, the relentless migrations of populations westward did not allow this equilibrium to persist. Indeed, these thinly populated territories could barely feed the legions stationed there, and these provinces could not provide enough soldiers to defend themselves. As a result, the emperor recruited auxiliaries from Germanic tribes and, if they served faithfully, settled them in the empire permanently. Because Rome's frontier blocked migration, the populations nearest the border were under pressure from populations migrating from farther to the east. Under these conditions instability was rife. The frontier populations, like those on the borders of the Chinese empire, were in close contact with Rome, at times serving as allies and at times launching raids into the empire. The Goths, who defeated Valens in 378, were refugees from Hun expansion. The Goths turned against Rome when local administrators failed to uphold their settlement treaty. From then to the sack of Rome, the western empire's decline was extremely rapid. Neither efforts coming from Constantinople nor those of Germanic tribal leaders could reunify the empire.

The collapse of the empire, seen in light of Chinese history, is not surprising. It was based on an idea of overwhelming military force that could not endure forever. What is more surprising, however, is the failure to reconstitute the empire. While a large and integrated polity survived in the East as the Byzantine and later as the Ottoman Empire, in the West the process of political fragmentation proceeded well into the Middle Ages. Even once the process of nation building characteristic of the early modern period was under way, it was territorially unambitious by Roman or Chinese standards. In fact, by the Middle Ages, within Europe, inheritance or marriage was a more likely way to create larger domains than conquest.

Why all this territorial fragmentation in Europe? It is clear that the Great Invasions—the massive population movements that occurred after 259—bear a great deal of responsibility. The invasions involved waves of populations whose demographic importance was locally quite large, and they had dramatic political implications (Bury 1928: 37). Whether the western half of the empire was always thinly settled or whether plagues or political disruptions drove population down is a matter of some debate. What is clear is that the Great Invasions were a process quite different from that of a military elite taking over an agrarian empire. The secular nature of the migration, as well as the serial nature of political change, ensured that dislocation was far more extensive than was the case with invasions of the Chinese mainland before the Mongols. It has often been argued for Europe that these ethnically divided populations had cultural practices and political structures incompatible with the Roman Empire (Bury 1928). The evidence on this point is far from compelling. Indeed, there is ever-increasing evidence that these populations were not fundamentally heterogeneous and that they were far more attuned to Roman culture than has been thought before. For instance, many "barbarian" leaders were also Roman citizens. What is also clear from the new scholarship is that notions of identity on both sides of the frontier were very fluid (Geary 2002). Having breached Roman defenses (or simply having taken over some piece of territory), invaders then faced the need to create the political conditions for lasting control. For example, the leader of a group like the Burgondes in fact faced multiple challenges. First, he had to hold together his "invading" army, for without troops his capacity to hold his territory would evaporate. Second, he had to find ways of ruling the local population that had been ceded to him. Most often this local population was larger than that of his "invading" group, but failure to establish his power would mean that his revenues would vanish. To achieve these two goals, invading leaders initially often chose to integrate themselves into what imperial authority existed. But the trend between A.D. 400 and A.D. 800 was unmistakable—the value of allegiance to some higher authority declined simply because no authority could guarantee protection. The Burgondes, for instance, were absorbed by the Franks. It became clear that to ward off the threat of a new invader or a neighbor, a ruler could rely only on the populations he controlled. The value of political and cultural practices that would have helped rebuild the empire collapsed, while the value of those that promoted local identity and local solidarity rose.

In western Europe the Roman Empire ended, but it endured in the eastern Mediterranean. Indeed, the polity centered on Constantinople (and later Istanbul) proved to be a durable empire. The direct successor of Rome managed to maintain a spatially large polity for several centuries, including some outposts as far away as Spain, Italy, and North Africa. For at least half a millennium after 378, the Byzantine Empire was the wealthiest and most powerful remnant of its Roman predecessor (Ostrogorsky 2002). It was also one of the locations where the knowledge and culture of the empire endured. Like its Song counterpart, however, it proved militarily incapable of reassembling the empire. In time, Constantine's heirs were replaced by Muslim rulers who took over all of the Roman Empire's eastern dominions and made its capital their own; but despite significant advances (at one time into Spain and part of France and more durably into the Balkans), neither Arab nor Turkish caliphs were able to put the Roman Humpty-Dumpty back together. Time and time again their advances were stopped either in the Iberian Peninsula or in the Balkans. Thus by A.D. 800 the former Roman Empire included a large polity in the East and many less stable ones in the West.

Medieval historians of western Europe have an uneasy relationship with the Byzantine Empire, and most prefer to leave it aside as a territory where feudalism did not take root. This is a convenient expedient because it allows us to think of the largest successor polity to the Roman Empire as non-European and thus beyond our concern (Patlagean 2007). From our point of view, ignoring the Byzantine Empire in European history has two consequences that we prefer to avoid. First, it makes the Roman Empire an epiphenomenon; political fragmentation, one might then argue, is the norm at the western end of the Eurasian landmass. The Iberian Peninsula, for instance, was fragmented before Rome took over from Carthage, and it remains fragmented to this day. European polities thus, for political or cultural reasons, can be assumed to be small. Including Byzantium makes this proposition untenable. Second, it reminds us that the political institutions of Rome did not vanish like some Atlantis but remained quite visible in the Byzantine state. Thus even in western Europe the idea of empire endured.

The Roman political institutions did not fade from memory because they evoked levels of security and prosperity that Europeans found wanting in their own times. Yet even the empires of Charlemagne (r. 800–814) and Charles V (r. 1500–1556) did not survive their deaths. Charlemagne succeeded in controlling a swath of territory from France to Germany and from the Netherlands to Italy, although he did not attempt to conquer either England or North Africa, and his Spanish campaign was a failure. Having achieved conquest, he thought to stabilize his polity by having himself crowned by the pope. He also began the process of creating more enduring means for stability, developing a centralized administration intent on providing some public services. But the empire did not outlast him. Upon his death his three sons divided his territories among themselves and soon were at war with one another. The upshot was that the eastern part of his domains down to Italy became known as the Holy Roman Empire, while the western part became France. By this time most political entities throughout Europe (kingdoms, principalities, duchies, bishoprics, and so forth) had no formal allegiance to the emperor.

By the end of the first millennium, one lesson that the rulers of the smaller polities did learn from Charlemagne's heirs was that they should not contribute to fragmentation. Hence the traditional practices of competitive succession or egalitarian claims were replaced by rules of primogeniture. Primogeniture ensured that one kingdom would not be divided into separate parts if a ruler had multiple male heirs, but it did not preclude a ruler of multiple kingdoms from dividing them among his children. Had rulers merged their territories into a single kingdom whenever they acquired new ones, Europe might have taken a very different political path.

Rulers, in fact, did the exact opposite of consolidating their disparate domains by formally recognizing a variety of localized practices in territories they acquired. These practices or customs covered subjects as varied as the nature of real property, relations between landlords and farmers (or lords and peasants), inheritance rules, units of weights and measures, mechanisms for deciding levels of taxation and the means to collect taxes, trade privileges, and more. In fact, late medieval and early modern societies were most often made up of many clusters of such rights for specific groups based on their social status, professional occupation, or place of residence. Until at least the seventeenth century, the trend was for the continued creation of such specific rights and hence for the continuing fragmentation of political space. We can use the ruler whose territorial sway could next rival that of Charlemagne as a case in point. Charles V of Spain was separately the ruler of more than two dozen territories; notably, he was king of Castile, king of Aragon, king of Naples, king of Sicily, archduke of Austria, duke of the Netherlands, and Holy Roman Emperor. Although the crowns of Castile and Aragon had been united under Ferdinand and Isabella, this did not imply that the territories were administered in a unified way, only that the heir to one throne would also inherit the other. Lordship of even the puny kingdom of Aragon involved the separate administration of many territories, of which the most important were Aragon proper, Valencia, the county of Barcelona, and separately the city of the same name.

Why did rulers in Europe accept such formal limits on their powers? To a large extent they were motivated by expediency. European rulers were well aware of the dire consequences of recognizing or granting economic and political rights to specific groups. Nevertheless, they ceded these rights both to reduce the likelihood of revolt and because it was often the only way to secure prompt tax revenue for the Crown. A local population might have conceded much greater authority to its ruler had he offered it the kind of economic and social environment that prevailed either in the heyday of Rome or around 1000 in China. But everyone was well aware that rulers could promise little more than Churchill's blood, toil, tears, and sweat. Indeed, the competition for territory remained keen for centuries, and rulers were eager to participate in this contest. Thus promises of using tax revenues for local prosperity would surely ring hollow. Instead, local populations wisely insisted on preserving their local privileges to limit their rulers' military ambitions. Certainly, a ruler who desired to extend his domain farther was unlikely to remove tolls or tariffs between two of his territories. Doing so would have reduced his revenues at the very time at which he needed them most. The political economies of empire and fragmented polities, as exemplified by China and Europe, will prove, as we demonstrate in subsequent chapters, to be significantly different.

Previous studies have argued that the size of polities in China and Europe shaped the path of economic change. For them, political competition among European states had positive economic consequences, and China's empire delivered stagnation. We will suggest that the costs of such competition were, in fact, heavy. Moreover, the advantages obtained from political competition and war making in Europe were indirect and unintended. Up to the eighteenth century, the direct and deliberate positive consequences of empire in China far exceeded the indirect and unintended benefits of political competition in other world regions. Many of the economic contrasts between China and Europe we develop in succeeding chapters depend on the different spatial scales of states in these two regions of the world. We will also discover that not all economic and institutional differences are equally important; some putatively economically significant differences between China and Europe historically did not in fact have clear consequences, while other assumed differences turn out to be not as stark as previously portrayed.

Our first chapter has addressed the historical reasons for the emergence of durable empire in China and the contrasting political equilibrium of small competitive states in Europe. Military factors and domestic political change clearly shaped the spatial scales of polities across China and Europe.

Up to the reign of Charles V of Spain, Europe had made little impact on the world, and China had had little interest in the western end of the Eurasian landmass. To the extent that Chinese and Europeans shared a common experience, it involved their difficulties in dealing with the steppe people. The thirteenth-century Mongols were the most formidable of these pan-Eurasia invaders. Their leader, Tamerlane (1336–1405), was the last great challenger to sedentary rulers in both the East and the West. Once it became clear that no military forces from the steppes would be able to take over both China and Europe, their political histories became largely unconnected for the next four centuries, and their economic histories were powered by often-similar but usually separate dynamics. In the next five chapters we explore the consequences of differences in political space for economic change in the era after Tamerlane. These differences help us provide an account of what the Chinese and European economies shared, how they diverged in the modern era, and why differences in the spatial scale of polities in China and Europe still matter to their economies today.

2

Population, Resources, and Economic Growth

The variation in family and household structure across Eurasia is astounding. Whether the age of marriage or the role of kin is involved, nothing seems alike in preindustrial China and Europe. Because demography matters for important economic phenomena, including the rate of savings, the structure of markets, and, ultimately, economic growth, scholars have leaned heavily on variation in household structure to explain the different pace of economic change in China and Europe (A. Smith [1776] 1976: 76–77; E. L. Jones 1981: 17–21). In doing this, they have relied on the notion that the European nuclear household (with one generation of adults) was demographically more prudent and more willing to participate in factor markets than the Asian extended household. Much of this logic was derived by considering mid-twentieth-century data where the connection between nuclear households, low fertility, high per capita income, and market interaction is particularly strong. More recently, rapid growth has taken place in many different societies, as has the fertility transition, weakening the traditional connections between culture, restrained demography, and economic growth. Hence we need to take a closer look at the historical evidence and the logic of the frameworks that invoke demography to explain economic change.

At heart, the arguments that seek to provide a demographic explanation for the fact that industrialization first began in Europe draw on a contrast between nuclear and extended households. The differences between household types can be purely demographic, or they can be related to the incentive to participate in markets. In our view these differences have been overstated. Chinese households, whether extended or not, like European

35

households, whether nuclear or not, practiced fertility restraint. Although extended-household societies may have been less involved with factor markets than nuclear-household societies, both extended and nuclear households were involved with factor markets to some extent. When technological progress provides incentives for a larger fraction of wage workers, we expect households in both types of societies to respond by entering the labor market at greater rates. Demography does not explain why China was poor.

To develop our argument, we rely partly on simple economic models. We forsake a purely quantitative approach because, as we will show, one cannot understand the evidence without a framework for understanding its institutional and social context. In this and the following chapters our models are spartan and thus leave out many elements of any particular situation. What these models lose in specificity regarding individual cases they gain in generality and transparency. They should be judged on a simple metric: do they allow us to highlight fundamental relationships and their implications, including some important ones the literature has so far ignored? If so, they are valuable tools. In framing our arguments we are particularly sensitive to the appropriateness of generalizations. Although nuclear households were dominant in Europe and extended households were the norm in China, in both regions there was a good deal of variation. To reduce Europe to nuclear households and China to extended ones is to maximize the differences between the two regions and thus bias the argument from the start in favor of the thesis that demography mattered for divergence.

We will argue that differences in the extent to which activities in early modern China and Europe were structured around families or markets created only differences in degree rather than in kind of economic change. Indeed, we think that lineage relationships offered Chinese households some economic advantages not available to European households, and that it is therefore difficult to establish persuasively that the institutional differences in household form actually favored certain European households over all Chinese ones in the era before urban industrialization. This assessment on its own still allows households' labor practices to limit the development of interregional and intersectoral labor markets. The evidence, however, suggests that households' or firms' choices did not determine where and when labor markets emerged and where and when workers moved into urban factories.

In this chapter we will begin our journey into a comparison of Chinese and European economic history. We will also begin to discard many of the routes chosen by other scholars because they either lead to dead ends or take us in circles.

Prudence and Poverty

The study of economic development in agrarian economies owes much to the early nineteenth-century theories elaborated by Malthus in his effort to explain the coevolution of population and well-being in England and elsewhere (Malthus [1806] 1992). Malthus recognized and brought to the fore of social science the long-run interplay between population and economy, but his work was hampered by a lack of solid evidence beyond England, a cultural predisposition to find the good in all things English, and a serious methodological mistake. Indeed, he projected the short-run correlation between social structure and economic outcomes (such as the English nuclear family and early industrialization) into a general truth (that nuclear families are everywhere essential for economic growth). The appeal of his conclusions did not lead to any significant questioning of the logic of his comparative model. In both logic and substance, he remains remarkably relevant to much work on comparative economic development.

Malthus's ideas have endured because they are both simple and general. As abstractions they are incontrovertible, but when they are deployed in comparisons across countries, his conclusions prove untenable. He posited four iron laws: (1) The resource base expands slowly, and thus in the long run there is a fixed negative relationship between population size and individual income. (2) In most societies nearly all women marry early and thus produce large numbers of children. The population is kept within the bounds dictated by natural resources by a "positive check": most people are poor, and mortality is consequently high. (3) A select few populations constrain their fertility rates below what is biologically possible, and they are better off. This "preventive check" requires that most women marry late and that some do not marry at all. (4) In such meritorious societies only individuals who can form a viable economic unit can marry. Thus marriage depends on parents or children accumulating the capital necessary to run a farm or a shop. In periods of high income, such capital accumulates faster, and thus individuals can marry younger, leading to higher fertility, while in bad times they are forced to wait and will thus either have fewer children or not marry at all.

These ideas are remarkably simple, and not surprisingly they are the basis of a large edifice of social science research (for an elegant synthesis, see Wrigley 1988). Scholars have extended Malthus's conclusions to posit that high-income economies are more likely to undergo industrialization for both supply and demand reasons. On the supply side, a high-income economy has the resources to invest in the (physical and human) capital needed for sustained growth, while at the same time, higher incomes are disproportionately spent on manufactures rather than food. We do not wish to quibble with the logic of these arguments; what is of concern to us here is their suitability for comparative economic history. In Europe, long after Malthus's death, British scholars have continued to extol the distinctive virtues of the British family relative to that of France, for lack of a better horse to flog. In their monumental study of the English population, Wrigley and Schofield (1981) tried to demonstrate that only the British practiced fertility control effectively. Later work has largely invalidated their claim that other European populations, in particular, the French, were less zealous in their preventive checks. Indeed, David Weir has shown that in the early eighteenth century French families were more sensitive to their environment than British ones; marriage rates and birth rates declined more, while death rates rose more in response to an increase in grain prices on the Continent than they did in England (Weir 1984). The truly distinctive characteristic of the British population experience is its uniquely (and clearly non-Malthusian) rapid increase from the mid-seventeenth century onward. Moreover, in the eighteenth century only one country started practicing fertility restraint of the kind that was supposed to accelerate industrialization: France. But its leisurely pace of demographic change did not turn the country into the workshop of the world. On the contrary, it seems to have slowed the pace of economic transformation.

Nevertheless, continuing work pioneered by Hajnal (1965), some social and economic historians are still interested in assessing economic performance on the basis of whether demographic structure is similar to or different from Malthus's prudent society, which they take to have been realized in early modern England (e.g., de Moor and van Zanden 2008). Most scholars, however, are now coming to recognize that secular economic progress was achieved in Europe in a wide variety of different demographic settings (Kertzer and Barbagli 2001–2002).

Although the range of European families is diverse, it remains relatively narrow, and one might therefore want to search more widely to seek confirmation of Malthus's ideas. Indeed, Malthus himself (and Adam Smith before him) speculated on demographic differences between Asia and Europe (Malthus [1806] (1992): 41, 183–184). After Malthus the speculation endured, carrying with it the unexamined inductive premise that Asia's development failure had demographic roots. One impetus for this comparison came from the extraordinarily high population density that European visitors encountered in certain parts of Asia. When Marco Polo returned from China with tales of riches and splendors, the dense populations he described were prosperous. Over time, however, this connection disappeared, and by the eighteenth century travelers were emphasizing the deep poverty of Asia's large populations. These conjoined density-poverty observations were not lost on social commentators. China's population size (the largest in the world for nearly all recorded history) was often invoked as a constraint on efforts to spur economic development (A. Smith [1776] 1976: 80–81). The serious Chinese famines of the 1870s, early 1920s, and late 1950s were taken as further evidence that the country labored under a severe Malthusian constraint: its population was too large for its economy to support. The Chinese government took this concern seriously enough to enact and enforce a policy of one child per household. Nevertheless, critics of China have continued to indict China's demography—nowadays for its tilted sex ratios. In the past, however, the theme was constant. For cultural reasons, Chinese families were unwilling to limit their fertility, whatever the social consequences.

Recent work in Chinese historical demography forces us to revise our thinking. To begin with, as Lavely and Wong (1998) point out, the growth rate of China's population was slower than Europe's over the long run (1400–1900). As detailed in Table 2.1, for the preindustrial period the two populations grew at the same rate (0.23% per annum), doubling between 1400 and 1700. Given that China was considered prosperous at the close of the Middle Ages, one can hardly blame demography for its poor performance. Similarly, slow population growth cannot explain either Europe's or any particular European country's prosperity. Indeed, those areas where economic growth was more rapid had the fastest population growth. For China, the literature has moved beyond casting doubt on the importance of the Malthusian positive check to documenting how some Chinese populations deployed their own preventive checks on fertility. In Europe the Malthusian preventive check involved women marrying late and or remaining unmarried. In contrast, Chinese women married earlier and more universally than their European counterparts. Although such marriage

Table 2.1. Population (in millions) and implied annual rates of growth for Europe and China, ca. 1400–1950

Year	Population (millions)		Growth rate (% per year)	
	Europe	China	Europe	China
1400	60	75		
			0.300	0.288
1500	81	100		
			0.211	0.406
1600	100	150		
			0.182	0.000
1700	120	150		
			0.406	0.760
1800	180	320		
			0.443	0.341
1900	280	450		
			0.961	1.035
2000	729	1,261		

Source: Lavely and Wong (1998: 719).

patterns prevented the operation of European preventive checks, the Chinese did control fertility, among other ways through postnatal selection of which children would be reared. Some Chinese populations, at least, had much greater spacing between siblings and ended childbearing at an earlier age than did Europeans (Lee and Campbell 1997; Lee and Feng 2001; Tsuya et al. 2010). In China, as in Europe, demographic growth rates were far below those biologically possible (Lavely and Wong 1998). Although the areas in which rigorous population reconstructions can be made have been limited to parts of northeastern China, this evidence requires us, at the very least, to invalidate the prejudiced view that all Chinese families sought or had high fertility.

Over the past millennium Jiangnan, the region near present-day Shanghai, has been the country's focal point for the most advanced forms of production, densest networks of markets and merchants, and most sophisticated types of consumption. If the Jiangnan population were regulated by the Malthusian positive check, we would expect it to grow rapidly, either after a positive economic innovation or after some political or demographic catastrophe had reduced the number of residents. But some scholars have suggested that population growth rates in this region were lower than those elsewhere. In particular, population change after the mid-nineteenth-century rebellions almost brought down the ruling dynasty was very slow (B. Li 2003; Bernhardt 1992). This observation might initially be thought to support the notion that the resource base of Jiangnan was near its carrying-capacity limits. But the region's high standard of living, both before and after the rebellions, implies that slow population growth was not likely the result of extreme poverty and the consequent Malthusian positive check. Instead, the population's slow expansion is consistent with the existence of preventive checks. Unfortunately, we have no direct evidence of fertility rates in this region. We cannot be sure how much of the moderate rate of population change was caused by family strategies and how much by emigration.

Famines play an important role in comparative economic history because qualitative evidence of their occurrence and of mortality crises is abundant, even in the many places where demographic rates cannot be measured far back in time. Famines in preindustrial societies are taken as a prime indicator of the operation of the Malthusian positive check (cf. Fogel 2004). Few would dispute that Jiangnan, China's wealthiest region, was productive enough to support its population well above subsistence, and that demographic constraints alone did not prevent capital accumulation. Other parts of nineteenth-century China did suffer serious natural disasters and famine, and many have assumed that crop failures and the lack of food led to hunger and death (B. Li 2003). It is no longer obvious that these tragic circumstances represent a Malthusian indicator of an agrarian economy overburdened by a large population. Instead, scholars have come to emphasize that in times of crisis, access to resources is economically, socially and, most important, politically determined. Famines typically occur in societies where the poor lack entitlements to food. People die even though there is food physically available, but those who need it the most fail to gain access (Sen 1981; Drèze and Sen 1989; Fogel 2004). In this light a Malthusian population explanation of the limited likelihood of economic development outside northwestern Europe appears less powerful than one that considers political institutions and crises. Indeed, politics, as well as other forces outside the demographic regime, can cause failures both in production and in distribution and in turn lead death rates to jump skyward, as China's catastrophic famine of 1959 to 1961 tragically demonstrated (D. T. Yang 2008).

Overall, the evidence increasingly suggests that China between 1600 and 1800 was not a society laboring under the positive check. Instead, much like Europeans, Chinese families controlled their demography. That their mechanisms for doing so were different from practices elsewhere does not mean that they were less effective. Moreover, other than in the traumatic political period between 1850 and 1978, mortality does not appear to have been very responsive to income. Although volcanic explosions like Tambora, foreign invasions, or large-scale civil wars could engender significant spikes in mortality, those events are irrelevant to understanding any particular demographic regime. In China, as elsewhere, famine and mortality crises were only rarely resource crises; far more often they were social crises. During the first century and a half of the Qing dynasty, in particular, there were very few episodes of severe food shortages, let alone major famines (Will and Wong 1991).

Our discussion of Europe's and China's demographic regimes has hinted at the fact that there were remarkable differences in these regimes within Europe and within China. For Europe, this has led scholars to emphasize the importance of the prudent nuclear family in both demography and economics. Because areas where the nuclear family dominated were at the center of the burst of economic change that preceded the Industrial Revolution, such arguments have had force both for comparisons within Europe and between Europe and the rest of the world. As we have seen, China has often been taken to be populated by imprudent extended households. But we know that extended households were never the only family structure in China, and they were more prevalent in the south and southeast than in the north and northwest. If nuclear households are considered prudent and extended households imprudent, glossing over the variation internal to China and to Europe builds in a bias that is favorable to Europe over China in ways that artificially inflate the relevance of demographic structure. If the logic of the prudent nuclear family leading to more prosperity were to hold, then those areas of China where families were smaller should have been more prosperous than those where families were more extended. There is, however, little evidence that northern China was substantially better off than southern China (Allen et al. 2007). Just as in pre-1600 Europe, within China the relationship between family structure and economic success is hard to discern.

Family structure and demography are important, even if they do not allow us to split the world into one zone of high fertility and mortality and another of low fertility and mortality. They are important because in the preindustrial era, when most enterprises were tiny, there were critical interactions between family structure and labor markets. As we explore these issues in the next section, we will once again find that generalizations about labor markets are based on a series of assumptions that bias findings in favor of Europe and against China. Equally important, if we abandon the idea that in most areas of Europe or Asia populations were at subsistence level, then it becomes worthwhile to chart the course of incomes and to understand how such resources were allocated to consumption, savings, and demography.

Real Wages

Measuring and comparing levels of incomes or well-being over long periods of time in any given place is difficult. Our task is made more complex because we seek to understand the changes in standards of living for the two ends of Eurasia. In doing so, we cannot settle for evidence from some time in the twentieth century and project such evidence back into earlier periods. Doing so would inevitably put China in a bad light, given the enormous differences in income levels that prevailed between China and Europe by 1900. A better solution is to rely on wage evidence from earlier centuries. To be sure, such data are imperfect for a variety of reasons, but there are excellent grounds to believe that the evolution of income roughly followed the evolution of wages. We know that when economies are growing rapidly, wages rise, and when economies run into trouble, wages fall. This, after all, is nothing more than the principle that in the long run wages are equal to the value of the marginal product of labor; when economies are growing, that marginal product is rising. Over a decade or so, some growing economies may experience little change in wages because technological change may substitute physical capital for either unskilled or skilled labor. In the long run, however, capital accumulation makes labor more valuable rather than less.

Even if we accept that wages in the long run are related to the performance of an economy, there remains a second conundrum. It is likely that the relationship between wages and growth in Europe was different from that in China because the relationship between households and labor markets was different. Rather than either assume the problem away, as recent work on relative wages has done, or assume that the problem makes the comparisons impossible, in this section we provide a framework for understanding how differences in labor markets might drive the wages we observe. This problem is not merely technical; it harks back to the long-held myth of self-sufficient, market-averse agricultural households. Suppose for now, as historians of both ends of Eurasia would often have it, that the myth is true (e.g., Reddy 1984; P. Huang 1985), and that many or most households do not participate in the labor market. By definition, autarkic households' incomes have nothing to do with wages, and wages can rise at the same time at which the incomes of autarkic households are falling or vice versa. Finding that wages were higher in, say, China than in Europe would tell us as little about the relative incomes of these two economies as comparing garment workers in the United States relative to civil servants in India. More generally, any comparison between Europe and China would be hostage to the fact that the fraction of households in the wage economy varied over space and time. Fortunately for us, self-sufficiency was at most an ideal, and one that may have been more imputed to agricultural households by later analysts than espoused or attained by the peasants themselves. The key is to recognize that most preindustrial households were both families and farms, units of consumption and savings as well as businesses.

Farm households found it expedient to participate in some factor markets, such as those for land or labor, for many reasons, but the root of such transactions lies in differences between the household's endowments of factors and its desired size as an enterprise. At any one time a farm household has some land, capital, labor, and skills. Here land and capital refer to the real assets a household owns or to which it has long-term rights. Labor refers to the work capacity of the household's members. Skills include talent and experience with farming or other endeavors. A household's endowments clearly reflect the history of its fortunes. Real assets will be large in a household that is productive and that saves rather than consumes, while its labor and skills depend on demographic strategies and age distribution. For very large numbers of households to have avoided factor markets would require far more predictability in demography and enterprise than is conceivable. Indeed, self-sufficiency requires that the family's ratio of land to labor remain roughly constant. Among other things, that would require that no family ended up with either more or fewer offspring than expected and that these children began contributing to household labor precisely at the time at which their parents were becoming older and less able to work. It also would require that ability be fully transmitted from parent to child over generations, so that better farmers (who could farm more land) never grew up in a land-poor household. Clearly, no one believes that such assumptions hold anywhere in the world.[1] The reader can rest assured that equally daunting assumptions must be made about savings behavior, the predictability of crops, and relative prices. Whenever these assumptions fail, there will be large differences in the marginal product of labor across farms. Peasants have long participated in factor markets to equalize these differences.

But we do not need to rely on mere theoretical arguments. Both in China and in Europe, land, even among farm households, was unevenly distributed so that almost no family obtained just the right amount of land to farm efficiently on its own. For Europe, evidence of such inequality abounds (see Baehrel 1961; Herlihy and Kaplish-Zuber 1985; and Soltow and van Zanden 1998; for an interaction with demography, see Emigh 2003). In China, as in Europe, most families had too little and some had too much land. The imbalance led them to hire in and hire out labor or to buy, sell, rent in, or rent out land. Of course, whether households entered the land or labor market depended on a variety of factors, and one might imagine that the burden of adjustment was laid squarely on the land market in many societies, effectively shutting down the labor market. But a very powerful force against this one-sided solution lies with variation in entrepreneurial talent: the ability of the household head to run the farm efficiently. A capable rich farmer would want to hire workers, while one who was less talented would be better off renting out at least part of his land. When a farmer was making these decisions, he could compare the cost of the labor he might hire with what he could earn from it, and if he was thinking of selling his services, he would also compare the return on more labor applied to his farm with what he could get as a wage earner. To be sure, the institutions behind these exchanges could be quite complex, and we will not debate the issue of when and where they would qualify as markets (Hoffman 1996: chap. 3). For our purpose, it suffices to recognize that few agrarian households could be self-sufficient, and thus that wages can tell us much about general economic conditions. From here we proceed in two steps: for the rest of this section we review the wage evidence, leaving its interpretation to the next one.

For Europe, economic historians have been able to measure wages in many locations and over long periods of time (the most famous early work is Beveridge 1965). They have been particularly fortunate that government agencies, municipalities, and charitable organizations, such as hospitals and monasteries, all kept detailed records of their expenditures and, in particular, of the wages they paid. What is even more remarkable is that a very large number of these account books survive and detail both wages and the prices of many of the commodities that one would want to include in a consumer price index. This effort has led to three relevant findings (Brown and Hopkins 1981; Allen 2001). First, over the half millennium that preceded 1800, wages fluctuated roughly inversely with the level of population. Although real wages were low before the Black Death (1347–1348), they rose steadily for the next half century and achieved a peak in the early fifteenth century that was not clearly surpassed until the eighteenth century. Second, at any one time the variation across places in the real wages of comparable occupations was as large as the variation of wages in a given place from 1600 to 1800 (Allen 2001). This kind of variation is surely not consistent with a Malthusian equilibrium everywhere. If the lowest wages are those of subsistence, then most places at most times were not at subsistence. Finally, the highest wages were found in the most densely populated areas (Ditmar 2009). Overall, European wages accord well with more narrative sources of economic success or failure.

Population densities were positively associated with levels of urbanization but were not closely tied to levels of agricultural productivity. Urban settlements certainly required agriculture to produce a surplus in order to be viable, but as George Grantham has noted, lower levels of agricultural productivity do not seem to have been a significant constraint on economic progress (Grantham 1993). Economic growth depended directly on the capacity of localities to structure their markets in ways that encouraged the division of labor and specialization. This reorganization was largely an urban phenomenon, which placed demographic demands on rural areas. Where and when cities boomed, agricultural productivity growth followed. (But as was the case in the Low Countries and the Veneto, imports of food were also often an integral part of the urban expansion.) The European demographic regime, on the other hand, was a more serious constraint. Fertility was simply not high enough to sustain large populations in what were biologically hostile environments. To put it simply, cities killed people at such a rate that the countryside had to produce a large surplus of births to sustain cities' demographic needs (Wrigley 1967). In turn, cities had to have high wages to induce the immigration necessary for their expansion. What is striking overall for the preindustrial period relative to the nineteenth century is the failure of advances in wages in one area (say, the Low Countries) to spread to the whole of the region. This localized success, far more than Malthusian subsistence, seems to characterize the preindustrial economy.

By the mid-seventeenth century, Robert Allen argues, a clear division had emerged. In northwestern Europe, particularly in Britain, wages were high and had a long-term tendency to rise. In contrast, as one moved south or east, workers earned less, and their pay tended to stagnate or fall (Allen 2009a). It was not until late in the nineteenth century that wages began to climb more generally. It is also likely that returns on land rose faster than wages (because land was a scarce and fixed factor and there was productivity growth in agriculture), and that although the price of capital had been falling since the Black Death, the capital stock had grown faster than the economy (Clark 2007; van Zanden 2007). Indeed, economic growth in Europe was at least partly a process of increased capital per worker. Hence the path of wages probably understates the aggregate level of increases in income. Nevertheless, because in most places the return on land and on capital accrued to a small number of people, wages remain the most representative form of income.

Until recently, income levels in eighteenth-century China were not a topic of concern because nearly everyone agreed that it was a subsistence economy. Debate centered on the degree to which the early twentieth-century Chinese economy was growing or not, with some scholars using wage data to buttress their arguments (Rawski 1989; Brandt 1989). For scholars who saw economic growth coming in the late nineteenth and early twentieth centuries, as well as those who remained skeptical, the eighteenth-century situation was assumed to be one of poverty. Either the eighteenth century provided a base from which growth subsequently emerged, or it was little different from the conditions in which the economy found itself in the early twentieth century (P. Huang 1985, 1990). Together, scholars all assumed or asserted that the Chinese were poor. The first revision of this view came from scholars who doubted that Qing China was such an economic failure, and the work of Kenneth Pomeranz (2000) provided tantalizing suggestions that in the Yangtze delta, at least, consumption might well have been quite high. In the last few years the debate has taken on new life as scholars slowly but surely bring wage evidence to bear on the matter (Yan 2008; Allen et al. 2007).

The effort to measure individual incomes in China before 1850 remains in its infancy, but already some important findings have emerged that are fully relevant to our endeavor. To begin with, from the eighteenth century to the twentieth century there have been considerable differences in real wages across China, and the range of variation seems to be on the same order of magnitude as in Europe (Allen et al. 2007; Yan 2008). Thus China was not simply an ocean of poverty; there were regions with relatively high incomes. It was also not simply a spatially static empire. As it expanded, the Han population migrated to what was a very large frontier (Pomeranz 2000: 84). But this migration presents a puzzle because individuals appear to have been leaving high-wage eastern and southern regions to settle in poorer western and northern ones. One can resolve this puzzle by once again breaking free from the idea of homogeneous self-sufficient households and considering that it is likely that wealth was unequally distributed within the richer regions. Successful lineages would have had little reason to migrate, but poorer people might well have been tempted to venture out toward the frontier. Indeed, poor people in prosperous areas could well have expected that combining the lower wages in poor areas with the income from opening land might be more desirable than simply the high wages in their home area. Such calculations were certainly important elements of the motivation for westward migration in the United States (Galenson and Pope 1989; Ferrie 1999). Chinese peasants could have made the same calculation of the income they might have gotten as tenants in the lower Yangtze versus the income possible as owners or occupiers on the frontier. Potential migrants could not make such decisions without some knowledge of factor prices—wages in the first scenario or the rental price of land in the second. Once again, households and markets are conjoined.

The evidence on wages also suggests that there was relatively little growth, if any, in Chinese real incomes between the mid-eighteenth and the mid-nineteenth centuries. If one takes into account demographic change, the findings can be reframed to note that despite an increase in population from some 200 million to well over 300 million, there does not seem to have been much, if any, decline in wages in many parts of the empire. The implications of this stasis are, on the one hand, that the divergence in economic performance between Europe and China is likely to have started before 1700 and was probably quantitatively significant before 1800; on the other hand, that those scholars who have argued for a

Malthusian involution in Qing China will find little comfort in the new evidence. That wages remained relatively stable despite a large population increase does not suggest that the marginal product of labor in agriculture declined at all.

Recently, attempts to compare levels of income in China and Europe or, to be more precise, between port cities at opposite ends of Eurasia have been stymied by a methodological conundrum. As Robert Allen has shown, this comparison suffers heavily from an index-number problem (2004). Rice was cheap relative to wheat in southern China, while the reverse was true in England. Wages were such that an English dockworker around 1700 was simply unable to afford a Chinese consumption basket in London. Similarly, a Chinese dockworker could not afford an English consumption basket in Canton. If one takes a composite index (making both buy a mixed basket), then wages in Canton and London were similar.

The index number provides arguments for scholars who favor a relatively high Chinese income in the heyday of the Qing dynasty. The larger issue, however, is how to interpret these findings. We begin with those lessons that do not depend on whether the labor markets in China and Europe had similar institutional structures. First, other data suggest that the wages of unskilled Chinese along the coast were higher than those in the poorest areas of Europe, but lower than those in the richest ones in the eighteenth century (Allen et al. 2007). Since the coastal areas were those with the highest income, one should conclude that the range of wages in regions of China and Europe overlapped at least through the early eighteenth century. Second, the lack of growth in Chinese wages between 1650 and 1850, when wages in western Europe began to surge upward, leads us to conclude that the country was falling behind. Third, no matter what trends or stasis obtained before the mid-nineteenth century, the subsequent 100 years witnessed profound political and social turmoil. Some economic gains were no doubt made in the twentieth century, especially in the region centered on Shanghai. Nevertheless, it is also likely that there were few sustained gains, so that in many provinces Chinese incomes in 1950 were similar to those of 1700. Political dislocations from 1850 with the Taiping Rebellion to Communist victory in 1949 force us to consider the possibility that in some places incomes might have been lower in 1950 than in 1700.

Clearly, then, the wage evidence strongly supports the thesis of a "great divergence," and on such data alone one would date it rather late, perhaps later than 1750. But as we will argue in the next section, such conclusions are unwarranted. Indeed, when wage data are placed in their institutional context, they become difficult to interpret and would place the divergence much later, perhaps as late as the 1820s. However, we believe that the structural and institutional divergence is actually far more ancient than 1820 and dates back at least to the early 1600s. Although the disconnect between wages and economic structure is partly explained by differences in how labor markets operated, most of the differences in wages come from the slow pace at which industrial technologies spread (Mokyr [1985] 1989: 5).

The Household and Labor Markets

Our interpretation of the available demographic and wage evidence also has a more proximate implication. It forces us to reexamine the conceptual frameworks that scholars use to interpret the economic histories of China and Europe. Indeed, the lessons we learn about the connections between fertility and mortality and, say, food prices depend on what kind of economy and society we are studying. Economic historians have, by and large, come to see most European economies and, in particular, households as embedded in markets. Hence prices tell us about relative demands and relative productivities. For China, most scholars would concede that the exchange of commodities was largely a market phenomenon, and one in which the state did not much hinder change or growth. Factor markets, however, find themselves squeezed between two institutions that are given far more importance—the state and the household.

Here we must focus on the interaction between markets and households, leaving aside politics, a factor that we will consider extensively in a subsequent chapter. The key question we want to tackle is whether China can blame its poor long-run performance on family structure. The traditional answer is yes, and the reason is that extended households substitute for markets, while nuclear households are embedded in them. As has been the case for fertility, scholars have assumed that (European) nuclear households were more favorable to markets. Indeed, a smaller household depends on markets precisely because of its varying labor supply over its life cycle. Moreover, the breakup of the household when progeny reach adulthood creates a demand for land and capital markets. Indeed, even in an initially egalitarian society some parents will find themselves short of children, while others are abundantly endowed. Hence there will have to be flows of land and capital from rich households to poor ones, or there will have to be flows of labor from poor households to rich ones (here *rich* means only that the household's land is large relative to its labor). In addition, the children must be set up with a livelihood before the death of their parents. Hence one generation must save (in land or finance) in expectation of the marriage of the next, and unless these plans are fully realized, there will be some borrowing of capital and land around the time of marriage.

Unlike Europe, where the nuclear household (one generation of adults) prevailed, China has been seen as the domain of the extended household and the kin group. In the classic Chinese extended household all the male descendants of a household head lived under one roof. Furthermore, the household head occasionally had more than one wife; finally, a potentially large number of permanently celibate males might also live with and under the authority of a kin head of household. Hence the household was large. Making the demographic unit even more complex were the important relationships among nonresiding kin groups and, even more broadly, lineages (groups of individuals who shared a distant patrilineal ancestor). What then of the relations between Chinese families and factor markets? To begin with, Chinese families may have faced less demographic uncertainty because the shock to individual couples was already partially averaged out in the extended household and even more so in the lineage group. Hence there was less demand for land and labor reallocation at every level of the sociodemographic structure. Furthermore, these large demographic structures reduced the demand for markets because they reallocated resources internally (Chaianov 1966). The connections between the despotic state and extended households as twin impediments to factor-market development can be drawn quite easily. For instance, an extended kin system may be efficacious when the law fails to secure the property rights of individuals against a despot's greed. Moreover, the authority of the lineage head may be more useful in securing such transactions than the justice meted out by corrupt public officials. Resources reallocated within the kin group are, in a sense, less visible than those reallocated through markets. In a more optimistic vein, the opportunities for long-distance trade in an integrated empire were more easily realized by extended households. They could secure their dealings by familial norms rather than having to rely on formal contracts left hanging on the whim of the judicial system, as nuclear households would have to do.

One can summarize the literature's argument in the following way: Extended households will have fewer interactions with the market than nuclear households. The larger the share of nuclear families in the population, the more market interactions there will be in the economy. More market interaction implies greater efficiency in the allocation of resources. Hence economies with more nuclear families will have higher incomes, higher wages, and higher growth. A positive correlation between the fraction of the population that is in nuclear households and wages is taken as proof of the argument. To a large extent the argument was developed inductively by scholars who believed that England was dominated by nuclear households and that it had been the cradle of the Industrial Revolution.

A more careful look at the argument will show, first, that societies with more nuclear households did indeed have larger labor markets. Second, the positive association between wages and the share of households that are nuclear obtains mechanically even if the market does not raise aggregate efficiency; thus a positive correlation between wages and nuclear households is not sufficient to make conclusions about efficiency. Third, the impact of household structure is largest when average firm size is smallest. In fact, once factories employ hundreds of workers, differences between extended-household and nuclear-household societies are negligible (because almost everyone is a wage worker).

Let us start with the first point. We develop the mathematical analysis in Box 2.1, but the mathematically disinclined reader can focus on the text. Firms (and farms) in preindustrial economies were small, so let us imagine that all the firms in the economy employ two individuals, an entrepreneur and a worker. Let us assume that each adult individual is equally likely to be good at management (then he is an entrepreneur) or not (then he is a worker). Now we can complete the model by laying out family structure. Suppose that a nuclear household has only one member who might become part of a firm (women are fully employed in domestic activities). In this setting half the households will have an entrepreneur, and they will hire workers from the other half of the households. Now examine a society with extended households that have two members who might become part of a firm. Some will have two entrepreneurs and will start two firms; others will have two workers who will both participate in the labor market, but some will have one worker and one entrepreneur, and they will not be in the labor market. In fact, the share of the worker-entrepreneur

Box 2.1. Family structure and labor markets

Assume that each firm or farm needs one entrepreneur and one worker. An individual can be either a worker (W) or an entrepreneur (E). A firm is profitable if and only if it is run by an entrepreneur and hires one worker. Capital markets are perfect, so we can ignore the other inputs into the firm. When families are nuclear, each family has one adult, and he or she must decide whether to be an entrepreneur or a worker. In a lineage system the leader decides whether to form firms (and which relatives to hire as entrepreneurs, including potentially himself), whom to hire as workers, and whom to send out to earn wages. Throughout we assume that the probability of being type E is one-half.

In nuclear households (one adult), E individuals become entrepreneurs, and they each hire one W adult. Half the population earns wages in someone else's firm.

Extended households are simply larger families. Consider a society where each household has two adults (the smallest possible case). The household can be of four types: (E, E), (E, W), (W, E), or (W, W). As in the case of nuclear households, it pays for each E adult to start a firm. Thus some households (E, E) have two firms, some will only have one (E, W, and W, E), and some (W, W) will have none. As in the nuclear-household case, half the population will be managers and half will be workers, but because (E, W) and (W, E) households satisfy their labor demand internally, their workers are not in the labor market and receive no wages. In fact, wage-earning workers (adults from (W, W) households) amount to only one-quarter of the population.

The extension of the model to households with more than two members and firms with more than two members is straightforward. For n adults, the number of different combinations of E and W is 2^n. Consider households that have m^e E adults and m^w W adults ($n = m^e + m^w$). Let $m = \min(m^e, m^w)$; then the share of households that have m^e E adults and m^w W adults is ($n!/2^n m!$).

It is easy to show the following: (1) If society 1 has households of size n_1 and society 2 has households of size n_2, then if $n_1 > n_2$, the share of the workers who are in the paid labor force is less in society 2. (2) The fraction of households who either hire or send out workers is larger in society 2 if $n_1 > 1$. (3) Let f be the number of workers needed in a firm. Although the qualitative difference between a society of size n_1 and a society of size n_2 holds for any f, differences among societies shrink.

population that is in the labor force in the extended-household society is half that of the nuclear-household society. An alternative takes the nuclear household as having two working members (husband and wife) and the extended household three or more, and again, a society with smaller households will have a larger share of its workers in the wage-labor force.

More realistic assumptions that consider gender roles carefully would dampen the difference, and making extended households larger would increase the differences between the two societies (in the extreme, where the economy is a single household, no one is in the labor market because everyone works for a relative). As we shall see, increasing firm size dampens these differences. In any case the basic intuition that larger families have less need for the market is extremely robust. It is important to emphasize that there is a radical difference between less and none. Even if we allow extended households to be very large—to have, say, ten members who can be workers or entrepreneurs and make firms very small, the labor force is still 10% of the worker-entrepreneur population. Labor markets remain active because a large fraction of households are either hiring at least one worker or have at least one member working in the labor market.[2] Thus factor markets are important everywhere at the margin and are available to respond to economic change. To rescue the idea that China's smaller factor markets were responsible for poor economic performance, one would have to believe that larger markets are massively more efficient. In fact, as we show later, China's smaller factor markets in the early Qing probably had no long-term impact because factor reallocation proceeded in other ways.

Beyond the simple scale of markets, we can make sense of the connections between sociodemographic factors and markets by considering the household as a firm. In that sense this section borrows heavily from the work of Gary Becker (Becker 1981), although our claims are less universal. To be sure, considering the household as a firm ignores many dimensions of its activities and its internal structure, but for the secular problem of interest here, treating families as firms proves both parsimonious and valuable. In particular, it allows us to ask: when will being a member of a large family, extended kin group, or lineage organization be economically valuable relative to being on one's own? Membership in an entity larger than the nuclear household is desirable because it gives access to resources without recourse to the market (and thus saves on the transaction costs of market interaction). On the other hand, the leaders of such entities make demands on individuals and must devote resources to ensuring that these demands are met. Thus membership in a larger demographic entity implies bearing the costs attendant on maintaining this organization. The question is not so much which household structure is best, but what combination of family structure and markets is best.

We can begin to answer this question by considering Coase's work on firms. In his celebrated article "The Nature of the Firm" (1937), Coase argued that markets stand between organizations. Obviously, a market stands between a producer and a consumer, but Coase saw the point as more general. A business will purchase some of its inputs and sell some of its outputs. Some inputs (say, the land on which a plant is located) may be owned, and some outputs (say, machinery made in the firm's own shop) may not be sold. That much is true of all enterprises. At the limit, however, one could imagine a firm that carries out only one step in a single production process and owns nothing: it buys all its inputs (including renting its equipment and plant) and sells all its output. Most often firms are somewhat vertically integrated (they carry out several steps in a production process), somewhat horizontally integrated (they make different kinds of products), or both. At another extreme we can imagine a full-command economy where a single firm organizes all production. When a firm extends its reach up or down one step in the production process, it is eliminating a market and replacing it with a structure of authority. For instance, if a miller buys a bakery to turn his flour into bread, he is no longer selling his flour. Hence the market for flour has disappeared, but the miller must now supervise the bakery. If he buys the bakery, he is effectively deciding that he prefers supervising the bakery to dealing with the market for flour. Coase argued that the extent of integration would reflect transaction costs, and that it was not possible to decide a priori whether firms should be integrated.

This logic has important implications for our households. An extended household is simply a more integrated family than a nuclear household. By analogy with Coase's firms, in some situations the extended household will function better than the nuclear household, but not in all. Unlike Coase's firms, individual families do not choose the extent of integration; rather, the prevalence of nuclear households is a historical pattern persistent both across space and over time. Because industrialization proceeded in Europe before the rest of the world, and in England before elsewhere in Europe, scholars have succumbed to the temptation of associating the nuclear family (and whatever other characteristic of England strikes their fancy, for that matter) with efficiency (see de Moor and van Zanden 2008). It now seems prudent to abandon that inductive reasoning. In fact, nothing obviously links industrialization with the nuclear household. Industrialization, after all, does not occur in small firms but in relatively large ones. When one has jettisoned a doubtful relationship between household size and economic change, the question whether the nuclear or the extended household is to be preferred is no longer easily answered.

One could extend this argument to demography. It would lead us to ask: are large or small family units going to do a better job at controlling the rate of population growth? In particular, following Malthus, we are concerned with the intensity of the operation of the positive check. Here we can see the full force of the firm metaphor. The small family will limit its fertility because, as Becker has suggested, parents care for the welfare of their children and thus have only as many children as they can afford. In particular, their calculation will involve their wealth and the prevailing wage rate (because someone who is not wealthy enough to set up a farm or an artisanal enterprise will have to work for wages). But to the extent that families want to have descendants and that mortality is both severe and random, they will tend on average to have more children than they would like. The small family is oblivious to the effect that individual fertility has on pay rates, the rental price of land, or capital because it takes all these prices as given. Consider now what a benevolent despot who seeks to maximize the individual income of the next generation might do. She or he will use the same reasoning as the altruistic parent, but at a social level. That will eliminate both the prudential motivation for high fertility and the externality caused by the aggregate effect of fertility on wages. One might well argue that extended households, being larger than nuclear families, will approximate the benevolent planner better. When one observes demographic behavior among large extended households in northern China, the exercise of Malthus's preventive check was quite intense, and the patterns of fertility unequivocally show that the head of the household chose its size deliberately (Lee et al. 1992; Lee and Campbell 1997). To take one example, the head of a large extended household or kin group would want to limit the fertility of the couples in the lower part of the hierarchy when wages were low. Indeed, he could then purchase any labor that he might need on the market without having to accept the cost of additional kin. Kin might seem cheap, but in an economy with abundant labor, they are in fact expensive. Familial responsibility implies that coresident kin (in particular, men) must receive a welfare no lower than what they could get on the market. Moreover, unlike outside workers, they cannot be fired in adverse economic circumstances. Thus unless the leader of a large kin group wanted to keep many retainers for military purposes, he had every reason to be responsive to the Coasian trade-off between making its own labor force and buying it.

It might seem that we have exaggerated the efficacy of larger households in dealing in the market or controlling fertility. Although the extended household offers a mechanism for regulating fertility, it requires a structure of authority. That authority is not necessarily benign, just as management in a firm cannot be assumed to be maximizing profits. One might consider two kinds of inefficiencies. The first is that the household head has a personal desire for a large household (because although that may make him poorer, it may also make him more powerful). The second is that the household head may repress everyone else's fertility while maximizing his own to the extent that the household is larger than the equivalent set of nuclear units. The evidence of Lee and Campbell does not suggest that either bias was large. It may be that in other political and cultural contexts, extended families have massive demographic impacts; that does not seem to have been the case in China.

The preceding argument suggests that differences in household structure and demography, while striking on their own, were not likely to have had much economic impact. Although extended households may interact less with markets, they do not suppress them, and although there may well be some transaction costs in dealing with family members, some that would be borne in market interaction are avoided. Although factor markets were likely to have been less active in China than in Europe, it would be preposterous to think that household heads would not have paid attention to wage rates or the rental price of land. In fact, our analysis suggests that even if we abstract from life-cycle issues, households in China and Europe would both be engaged in some markets at high frequencies. The model's starkness has further implications. Because whether one is in the market for workers depends solely on whether the household has an excess supply of entrepreneurs or workers, it follows that wages of workers in the labor market are an accurate measure of wages for all workers. Hence differences in wages would be a good statistic for the marginal product of labor in the whole economy. But that would make short shrift of the transaction costs that prevail in labor markets. We must elaborate the framework.

Households and Wages

In our model, individuals grow up as either entrepreneurs or workers, but now let workers be of two types: high or low ability. The better type could be more diligent, clever, or in other ways abler. We analyze the effect of this changed assumption on our model in Box 2.2 to show that wages are lower in extended-household economies than in nuclear-household economies even though aggregate output is identical. In this setting half the individuals are entrepreneurs, a quarter are high-ability workers, and a quarter are low-ability workers, and each household receives the luck of the draw. Assume that the marginal product of the better type is twice that of the less able type, so average ability is 1.5. Ability is not observable on someone's face or from a diploma, but it can be learned by employers over time. The family head knows the ability of the worker; an outside employer does not. Hence the initial wage in the labor market is simply the wage one would pay a worker with average ability. The question of interest to us is how do household structures affect average ability in the labor market and hence wages?

For societies with nuclear households, all workers are in the labor market, so average ability is 1.5. But as households get larger, only net surplus workers are sent to the market, and they will to the extent possible be the low-ability workers. The reason is that the paterfamilias who knows ability can promise his able worker more than the labor market can offer. As the analysis in Box 2.2 shows, this selection effect leads to market wages that fall as households get larger. The reason is that as households get larger, they send a smaller fraction of their workers into the labor market, and that makes it more and more likely that these will be low-ability types. Our model reproduces the findings of the literature that extended households interact less with the market than nuclear households and that wages are lower in extended-household economies than in nuclear-household economies without there being any productivity differences between the two economies. In other words, productivity differences are not necessary to produce the result that extended-household economies have lower market wages than nuclear-household economies. Thus differences in wages are probably the wrong diagnostic with which to date divergence.

It is also worthwhile to recall that we built our model to maximize the differences in labor-market participation between the two economies in order to reproduce the conventional wisdom that extended households

Box 2.2. Family structure, labor markets, and wages

The following model is an extension of the one in Box 2.1. An adult can be either an entrepreneur (E) or a worker with either high (W) or low (w) ability. As a result, individuals can be one of three types: E, W, or w. Half the population is E, one-quarter is W, and one-quarter is w.

One-adult (nuclear) households: including worker skills does not change the analysis; indeed, all workers work for wages. Note that the average skills of wage workers are the same as those of the population.

Two-adult households: wage workers are one-quarter of the population, and their average skills are the same as those of the population because they all come from households with two workers (WW, wW, Ww, ww)

Households with three or more adults: Consider first three-adult households. As in the previous analysis, half the population will be entrepreneurs and half workers, and half the workers will be employed in their family firms. Because the number of adults is odd, all households have an excess of either entrepreneurs or workers. For those that have an excess of workers, the question is whom they send out to earn wages.

Households that send workers into the labor market have either one entrepreneur or none. If they have none, they will send all their members into the labor market. Thus the average skills of the workers of these lineages will be the same as those of the general population. This is also true in lineages with one entrepreneur and two workers where the workers have the same skills. But now consider a household in which the two workers have different skills, for example, (E, W, w). It is reasonable to assume that household members have better knowledge of one another's ability than of the ability of an individual hired in the labor market. For simplicity, assume that the E member gets to decide which of his two relatives to hire and can pay whatever wage he wants, while the labor market cannot differentiate between high and low ability (W and w) of new workers, and thus their wages will reflect average ability. Clearly, then, the household can pay its high-ability worker more than the market, while the market will pay the low-ability worker more than the household would. Hence whenever households have choices, they systematically send out low-skill workers. Thus although average skills in the three-adult household society are identical to those of the two-adult household, average skills in the labor market are lower. Indeed, one can pursue this analysis and show that the selection effect increases as households get larger (for any household size n, the selection effect is smaller in economies with larger firms than where firms are smaller). If households are on average larger in China, we expect labor-market wages to be lower than in Europe independent of productivity.

are inimical to markets. It is time now to reconsider this premise. Pre-industrial firms were overwhelmingly small farm and craft enterprises; thus the assumption of firms with one entrepreneur and one worker is reasonable. But the process of industrialization is one in which larger and larger firms are created, thereby increasing the size of the paid labor force and reducing differences among societies with different types of households.

The argument that household structure and demographic regime were responsible for either the divergence in economic fortunes between China and Europe or England's early lead in industrialization is the result of convenient induction. Because the household-structure facts fit the case, other elements, such as the role of markets, were added without significant examination. More than anything else, there was something attractive about a framework in which economic development was produced by the meritorious and culturally induced behavior of northwestern European households. Culture in these theses set the stage in organizing households, and then economic logic took over. But as we have shown, there are serious flaws in the chain of logic that runs from culture to extended households to market participation and then to growth. Neither Chinese culture nor a stunted labor market prevented the creation of a large industrial labor force around Shanghai in the first third of the twentieth century or all around China in the last third. What is left is a purely cultural and historically circumscribed thesis: culture, one could argue, limited China's labor markets and growth in the preindustrial period. That is a far cry from the abstract generalizations of Malthus and many other scholars.

A less biased perspective might have led scholars to enlarge their temporal view back in time, and to ask why China was richer than Europe for such a long time if people were so imprudent and why Europe was poorer than China if its population was always so virtuous. Similarly, why have societies with extended households throughout Asia been able to have economies that perform so well today? Finally, recognizing that not all households in China were large or extended, one would have to wonder why heterogeneity in family structures persisted despite the supposed intrinsic superiority of the nuclear household. Any model that accounts for these facts will have to be more intricate so as to provide some advantages to extended households. Indeed, absent some countervailing advantages, extended households should break apart. In such a model the differences between China and Europe would be smaller, and one would then be more likely to wonder whether demography was that important after all.

Our argument does not require us to bear the burden of accounting for heterogeneity within China and Europe. Indeed, we are interested only in tracing the interaction of families and markets and in sustaining the observed greater reliance on factor markets in Europe. Since we do not seek to attribute either greater efficacy to one form of family structure or a permanent advantage to a society with greater markets, we need not worry about our simplifications. Indeed, consistent with the cultural and environmental variation that we know existed within the two regions, we would expect there to be variation in household structure and in the prevalence of markets.

We can distinguish different kinds of relationships if we accept that neither institutions nor culture determined a single outcome for China or Europe. If we also examine this diversity in a Coasian light, then we can expect to see the relationships between households and markets evolve over time as technology, relative prices, and transaction costs change. In fact, we may well be faced with a perfect wheel that turns from households to institutions and back to households, without any ability to assert some clear causal importance of household structures and demographic regimes for economic growth possibilities. Clearly, demography matters to labor markets, and clearly, labor-market institutions will affect the decisions of children whether to remain in a family enterprise, but it seems that there was considerable flexibility in these relationships both in China and in Europe.

What is clear is that neither region was locked into a particular mode. Although in China (and especially in southern China) the extended household was popular and in Europe (and especially in northwestern Europe) kin groups were small and rarely coresided, when opportunities changed, these social structures evolved. Consider some European examples. Le Roy Ladurie famously examined *frereches* (kin groups joined formally in a common enterprise), the prevalence of which increased during a particularly difficult time in Languedoc (1966: 160–168). But extended households were not found only in difficult times. Indeed, starting in the Middle Ages and through much of the preindustrial period, large families were key actors in Italian politics, where urban politics were family politics (Greif 2006). Even if households were nuclear in residence patterns, the larger kin group was of great political relevance. Extended kin groups were also an economically important unit; recall, for instance, that the Medici were bankers before they became princes. Their economic and political successes were kin-based stories rather than that of any single individual.

Nor do extended households simply mark a southern European predisposition for informal institutions over formal ones. David Sabean (1998) has documented the progressive rise of assortative marriage and an increase in marriage among close kin in eighteenth-century Germany as economic change made well-to-do heads of households more concerned with keeping their assets within the family. More generally, the persistently successful commercial banks of Europe, such as Barings, Mallet, or Rothschild, prospered and endured because they deployed the talent of more than a nuclear household. Thus coresidence is not a requirement for economic behavior to resemble that of an extended household. To be sure, in each generation some individuals would move and abandon the family's traditional business. The same was true in China because assets were often divided when the household head died (Lavely and Wong 1992). In other words, in Europe, even if the household was nuclear, the size of the economic unit could be a much larger kin-based group. This variation in kin-group sizes makes the wage information we have highly relevant. A young man who joined a trading firm rather than strike out on his own had to accept its discipline, but he would realize higher earnings by combining his labor with the experience of the other members of his kin group. His alternative was selling his skills in the labor market. If his parents were poor or inept, the labor market was likely to be the more attractive option. Conversely, a parent could decide whether to keep his sons in the family firm and face the risks that that entailed or to set them up in other professions and hire employees instead. Wages thus mattered in Europe because nothing required the firm to endure beyond its founder. As we shall see in Chapter 3, Europe's political fragmentation may have been partly responsible for maintaining the abundance of nuclear households working alone either in agriculture or in trade and crafts.

In Europe, Christianity eliminated Roman culture's focus on ancestors as an object of worship. The enduring importance of the cult of ancestors in China thus appears as a stark contrast. The contrast, however, is exaggerated because European elite families were clearly very concerned with their persistence and progress over multiple generations. More generally, to imagine households within China enduring for generations and to suppose that the culture of kin was static, one must ignore both considerable historical evidence about the culture of kin and the remarkable rate of internal migration (Lee and Wong 1991). Much of the flexibility lay in the fact that unlike in Europe, Chinese kin groups generally, and lineages specifically, were typically much larger than economic enterprises were. Hence what set of kin or what lineage resources were invested in what enterprise was a question just as relevant to the Chinese case as to the European one.

In Guangdong and Fujian provinces in southern and southeastern China, lineage leaders often owned land, the rental income from which went to maintain an ancestral hall and pay for expenses of lineage rituals (Faure 2007). Lineage leaders in Jiangnan sometimes set up charitable estates composed of agricultural properties that were rented out, the income from which went to support widows and at times other indigent members of the lineage (Rankin 1986: 87–88). But more important for our analysis were the instances in which kinship relations provided individuals with a network from which they could choose people to join them in economic activities. They could form firms based on the intimate knowledge and trust embedded in their kinship relations. These kinship networks could provide many people from whom business partners could be selected. The kin network could also then become the context within which problems in a business partnership could be raised and resolved. For Taiwan, which was both administratively and culturally part of Fujian in the eighteenth century, Johanna Meskill has reconstructed the multiple trusts and estates associated with a wealthy lineage, noting, "Joint holdings and individual holdings, while discrete were also interconnected. At times, estates or trusts collaborated with wealthy individuals in income-producing ventures; at other times, estates and trusts borrowed from one another or from individuals" (Meskill 1979: 245). The significance of kinship principles for the formation of firms in southeastern China is confirmed by the use of fictive kin relations in the formation of firms engaged in maritime trade (Ng 1983). As Teemu Ruskola has perceptively observed, where the Euro-American legal tradition takes the legal "person" as its key unit, the Chinese legal tradition used as its units those based on kinship relations (Ruskola 2000). We thus expect that kinship relations will prove an important resource for creating mechanisms required for economic growth.

Kinship relations played two related roles that facilitated economic growth in late imperial times. First, the kin group gave entrepreneurs a pool of likely partners. Second, kin relations provided a context for resolving economic disputes, a particularly important matter in the context of long-distance trade. We suggest that kinship practices in late imperial China offered opportunities to form firms and to adjudicate economic disputes without recourse to state-operated courts and laws. These kinship practices were further complemented by the activities of native-place and occupational associations. All these institutions were accepted by the state, which developed laws and courts to a lesser degree than in Europe. The difference between China and Europe is not, however, as stark as a focus on the household as firm might suggest, as we will see in Chapter 3.

When one is thinking about the deployment of lineage resources, one might well imagine that the price of land relative to labor is irrelevant. This is because the cultural predisposition of lineages to deploy their resources internally rather than through the market would imply that there is a relevant productivity of labor relative to land for each lineage rather than one in the aggregate for the economy. Evidence in favor of this would be the infrequent purchase or sale of land outside the lineage. Precisely because lineages were large, the sale of assets would be less frequent than in the case of nuclear households. That does not imply, however, that lineage heads did not have to evaluate the opportunity cost of keeping a piece of land in the lineage rather than using the same resource in some other way (increasing investments in other land, for example). If we consider labor, married males may have been rather unlikely to leave the kin group and its resources. The Chinese preference for male babies, however, led to practices of female infant neglect and infanticide that created unbalanced sex ratios and a stratum of men who could never marry (Lee and Campbell 1997; Tsuya et al. 2010). The larger kin group of extended family or lineage offered few advantages to such men. The growing amount of wage data over time implies that poor unmarried men were unable to benefit economically from extended kin relationships. Thus although it is entirely possible that, on average, individuals engaged in little wage work, there existed a very real group of Chinese men for whom the calculation was similar to that employed by Europeans.

This chapter has introduced our comparative approach. It has taken a set of apparently radical differences between Europe and China and has argued that these differences are not very important. To do so, we have combined evidence and economic theory. In this case, theory has been largely negative in that we argued against the notion that differences in wages between China and Europe were necessarily related to both household structure and the productivity of the economy. In developing the theory, we have been forced to confront a second key element: variation within Europe and China over time. We determined that this variation was problematic for any theory that bases Europe's advantage on the nuclear family. Rather than reject any theoretical argument, we decided to follow the implications of the simplest model one could build. This leads us to two important conclusions.

First, although differences in household structure may matter for the size of factor markets, they do not necessarily have any effect on how many households rely on these markets, nor do they necessarily imply that differences in markets have implications for long-run growth. In fact, just as we now reject the stereotype of an Asia ruled by a Malthusian positive check, we must also be careful to embed the information that we receive about prices and wages into the institutional context that produces them.

The second conclusion is that rather than considering the family group and its attendant economic unit as coincident and closed, we should consider that both are in steady interaction with markets. How much they interact with markets depends on transaction costs. We then examined the consequences of the fact that in many economic activities in Europe the family group was smaller than the economic unit engaged in production, while in China it was typically larger. Again relying on Coase's insight, we argue that it follows that the volume of trade in factor markets was likely to be larger in Europe than in China, but it does not follow that there would be efficiency consequences of this difference. Indeed, all heads of households had a profound interest in paying attention to factor prices in making decisions about how to deploy their resources. To suggest that the Chinese equilibrium is less efficient has about as much empirical content as to suggest that the modern integrated corporation is less efficient than tiny single-activity firms.

The next chapter moves from families and relative prices to consider differences in commercial institutions. Given the importance we have attributed to markets, it is pertinent to examine the contracting environment. This will offer us the first opportunity to consider the consequences of different spatial scales on the economy, and to evaluate an argument about China's relative failure that is nearly as prevalent as the demographic one: institutional lock-in. In doing so, we will discover again that persistent differences in institutions are necessary but not sufficient conditions for divergence.

3

Formal and Informal
Mechanisms for Market Development

The study of market institutions is a central endeavor of economics. Understanding how one party extends credit to another has sparked an abundant literature. One key lesson from this research is that not all exchanges can be supported by formal contracts. Some market transactions are too trivial to make a contract or a suit after nonperformance worthwhile. Others involve dimensions of performance that third parties cannot observe. In this case informal means and, in particular, reputation and repeated interaction serve to sustain markets and their implicit credit relationships. Because the size, frequency, and complexity of deals vary from one contract to another, both formal and informal contracting takes place, and some transactions are supported by informal means and others by formal ones. Many scholars have argued that in some places most, if not all, exchanges are informal, while in other societies contracts and courts play a central role. It is also commonly argued that differences in early history can have large and persistent effects on the types of transactions that ultimately prevail (e.g., Greif 2006; Hoff and Stiglitz 2004; Tabellini 2008). Scholars thus seek to classify societies as either group oriented (dependent on informal institutions) or individualist (dependent on formal institutions).

But the agreement to classify societies hides some serious tension about what institutions promote growth. Western Europe's success is often attributed to the capacity of commercial elites to wean themselves from reliance on networks, while Islamic and other Middle Eastern societies failed to do so (Greif 2006: 269–301; Kuran 2003, 2004). In contrast, students of Asia have often ascribed the success of these economies in more recent times to the wondrous flexibility and ubiquity of informal networks (Hamilton 2006). Formal institutions are claimed to be crucial in one set of cases and informal ones in a second set.

Most scholars would be willing to concede that individuals in China and Europe have been deeply involved in market transactions for centuries, but many students of comparative economics have seen Qing China as failing to develop the legal infrastructure to sustain formal contracting. In contrast, European states (in particular, the Dutch and the English) developed a law of property and contracts that facilitated commerce. China did not do so because the state failed to supply these institutions and the extended households and lineages had little demand for them. These conclusions, however, face problems similar to those uncovered in Chapter 2 regarding the argument that differences in household structure were responsible for differences in economic performance. Scholars who extol the value of networks tend to focus on long-distance trade, while those who favor formal enforcement tend to examine real estate transactions or local credit. As we shall see, the selection of evidence is largely responsible for the arguments that there were large structural differences in contract enforcement between Europe and China.

This chapter shows that the extent to which individuals in China and Europe used either formal or informal means of enforcing contracts depended on the nature of the transaction. The observed differences in the types of enforcement deployed in China and Europe were thus the product of differences in the economic environment, in particular, the scale of long-distance trade. The variation in institutions was largest when the two economies were most different in economic structure and spatial scale, but it shrank as the structures of the economies became more similar.

Our revision of the prevailing contrast between East and West is possible because of significant recent contributions by scholars of China and Europe. For Europe, Avner Greif's work on informal institutions has provided a new perspective on the sources of European growth (Greif 2006). It has spawned renewed interest in informal or private-order mechanisms as alternatives to state-based enforcement. Starting with Shiga Shuzo (2002) and Kishimoto Mio (2007) in Japan, scholars of China are discovering a rich formal contracting sphere. More recently, American scholars such as Madeleine Zelin (Zelin et al. 2004) and Melissa Macauley (1998) and Chinese scholars such as Liang Zhiping (1996) have shown that written contracts underlay the exchange of assets as diverse as land and equity in businesses and that magistrates intervened to resolve disputes. In both the European and Chinese cases, recent work reacts in part to a very large historiography whose primary effort has been to document the existence of a formal bias in Europe and an informal bias in China. We can now see that this dichotomy is far too simple to describe the interplay of formal and informal mechanisms in the history of both China and Europe (Wong 2001).

In order to reexamine Chinese and European contracting institutions, it is useful to take a moment to clarify what we mean by *formal* and *informal* enforcement mechanisms and to highlight the distinction between the two. Put simply, formal ways of enforcing agreements rely on government officials (e.g., judges) to decide disputed points and impose coercive or financial penalties when contracts are broken. Informal mechanisms, in contrast, require that private parties decide when contracts have been broken and what penalties to exact, whether that means shunning offending parties or other sanctions. It is common to suppose that choosing between these formal and informal mechanisms requires assessing the trade-off between the cost of enforcement and the losses associated with limiting the set of potential partners. Formal enforcement offers a broader set of potential partners, but it is costly, especially when transactions occur at a distance, because one has to be willing to go to court to settle disputes. Meanwhile, informal enforcement limits the set of potential partners to members of a group, but enforcement costs are potentially trivial as long as the duration of the transaction is limited.

This chapter proceeds in a manner slightly different from the one we followed in Chapter 2. We begin by examining the literature on long-distance trade and verifying that once we choose to compare similar activities, there are fewer differences between China and Europe than one might have supposed. Using this conclusion, we propose a framework for analyzing contract enforcement across types of transactions. This framework allows us to recast a much broader set of evidence and to argue that individuals relied on formal and informal enforcement both in China and in Europe. We then show that part of the differences between China and Europe came from differences in the scale of long-distance trade. The last section of the chapter argues that the extent of reliance on formal and informal enforcement varies over time. Although some societies might be locked into informal enforcement, this was certainly not the case for most European polities or for the Chinese empire.

Lessons from Long-Distance Trade

Consider long-distance trade, which for the preindustrial era we define as exchanges of goods where buyers lived 200 kilometers or more from sellers. Such commerce would have included trades between a foreign merchant and local consumers, those among merchants at trade fairs, or those in the early days of interregional exchanges. Initially, through the first millennium A.D. in northern Europe and many other parts of the world, these exchanges were infrequent and time consuming because they involved someone traveling several days, if not weeks, in each direction. Suppose, for instance, that a merchant arrived in a town after a long journey with a load of sugar. He faced two choices: he could sell his sugar for cash, or he could give credit to the buyer. As many have noted, a commercial system based on cash is going to be much smaller than one based on credit because it requires a coincidence of wants on all sides. In our case the sugar merchant must arrive when there is an accumulation of export goods of equivalent value that he is interested in purchasing. Extending credit would allow the merchant to unload his sugar and then seek out the return cargo that might offer him a better prospect for profit in nearby towns, but credit would be extended only if the lender (in some cases the traveling merchant and in others the local producer) could expect to be repaid. If the lender had to appear in court, distance made formal enforcement expensive and, if the distance was great enough, downright unprofitable. Even if one were able to hire a local agent, distance still raised the cost of relying on courts to the extent that few long-distance merchants were prepared to use them. Meanwhile, if the lender wanted to employ informal means to enforce repayment, the best he could do would be to refuse to have any further relationship with a recalcitrant borrower. As long as interactions were infrequent and small scale, such threats would have been as hollow as going to court. It is thus no surprise that the early commercial system was based on cash or barter. Hence we know that itinerant peddlers were typically paid immediately by their clients, merchants who met at European trade fairs early on could not carry balances from one fair to the next, and Europeans traveling to the coast of China brought silver to pay for their purchases. In general, when transactions were both distant and infrequent, buyers were not extended credit. This did not mean that credit was not desired; there simply were no mechanisms to support this kind of lending. As long as this state of affairs persisted, trade remained limited.

Societies, however, have devised a variety of methods to turn distant and infrequent transactions into either local or frequent ones. The most pervasive was to organize long-distance trade within networks. In that situation credit was extended within groups who shared ties of either family or geographic origin and who interacted frequently. This was true both in China and in Europe. These networks did not rely heavily on courts. Instead, their members respected their obligations because this was required for continued membership in their networks.

Dating back to the sixteenth century, Chinese merchant networks were large and widespread. The most famous consisted of merchants from Huizhou in Anhui Province who were important in the Jiangnan textile trade. These merchants bought cotton cloth produced by rural households at local markets. They then took the cloth to be dyed and finished in nearby market towns by businesses also run by other Huizhou merchants. Still other Huizhou merchants controlled the wharf from which many of the textiles were shipped to other parts of the empire. Huizhou merchants were engaged in a variety of trades and were located in many parts of the empire, but other merchant groups had more limited interregional routes. Merchants from the southeast coastal province of Fujian, for example, established businesses in the Jiangnan region either to export textiles and other products from Jiangnan back to Fujian or to import Fujian goods into Jiangnan. Regardless of the differences in spatial scale or range of goods traded, the same basic principles of trade among merchants sharing some combination of native-place and kinship ties applied (J. Fan 1998: 185–206).

The European research tends to highlight the diversity of informal institutions and to focus on a comparative analysis of their relative efficiency, but from our perspective, the striking fact is that informal institutions and merchant networks were at the core of most long-distance trade in preindustrial Europe. Whether one considers seventh-century Maghrebi traders in the eastern Mediterranean (Greif 1989) or the family trading firms established in the following centuries throughout Italy (De Roover 1953; Hunt 1994; Braudel 1966; Drelichman and Voth 2009; Muller 1997: pt. 3) and subsequently throughout Europe (Ehrenberg 1922; De Roover 1948; Neal and Quinn 2003; Trivellato 2009; Gelderblom forthcoming), one finds informal enforcement mechanisms. The same is true for the Protestant and Jewish commercial and banking houses of the early modern period (Lüthy 1959–1961; Trivellato 2009; Moulinas 1981). Finally, informal mechanisms were critical to the success of the family banks that linked cities in Europe in the eighteenth and nineteenth centuries, the most famous of which was the Rothschild banking family (Ferguson 1998).

The European literature has tended to make much of the importance of political boundaries. In the Middle Ages at least, European political fragmentation meant that long-distance trade was always, in effect, international trade. For many subjects the next polity was no more than a couple days' walk. Rulers and urban elites were suspected of discriminating against foreign merchants, but discerning where jurisdiction lay for a contract between two parties, both of whom were foreign to the place in which they made an agreement, was not always clear. For instance, jurisdiction for a debt contracted in Antwerp by a Parisian with a Lisbon merchant was very uncertain. Here China holds a lesson for Europe: political boundaries may be less important than sheer distance. Most Chinese merchants carried out the entirety of their business within the confines of their empire, and they could nominally have relied on imperial administrators to settle disputes. But they, like their European and overseas Chinese counterparts, preferred to remain in the informal realm. The reason is not that the empire failed to provide an appropriate institutional structure; rather, courts are just not very efficient at enforcing contracts over long distances.

Clearly, long-distance trade had an abiding affinity for informal networks, and financial capital (that most modern of enterprises) continued this tradition into the modern age. What is important for us is that this affinity seems to have little to do with any particular culture because we observe it nearly everywhere and, in particular, both in China and in Europe. This observation alone raises serious questions about the usefulness of recent analyses that emphasize differences across societies in the level of formality. If Europeans were so formal, why did they rely so extensively on networks and reputation in trade?

A Model of Competition between Enforcement Mechanisms

The next step in our analysis is to develop a framework for examining how contract enforcement is sensitive to the type of transaction at stake. We build on the simple but powerful insight from long-distance trade: individuals choose their enforcement mechanisms depending on what is available. Unlike the proponents of one mechanism or another, our approach presumes that there are advantages to both formal and informal mechanisms. To develop the model, we must return to why individuals want to engage in credit or to embed credit in other transactions.

Trade allows an individual to sell a good or service that he has in relative abundance for something he desires more. This process leads to an increase in aggregate welfare. At the same time, each party is well aware that his counterpart will seek to discharge his obligations at the least possible cost. Many individuals will be tempted to deliver goods of low quality, slouch in the delivery of services, delay payment, or, better yet, refuse it completely. In each such instance the value of the transaction to the individual's counterpart falls: exchange is beset by transaction losses. If these losses are not brought under control, trade may cease entirely. Henceforth, and for simplicity, when a party misbehaves, we will say that he cheats; if not, that he performs. Although issues of performance are far more extensive than just in credit transactions, these will serve as our guiding example. There, default, in particular, default that occurs as a result of actions or inactions of the borrower, is what the lender wishes to minimize. Once the loan has been made, the lender's profits fall directly as the default rate increases.

To reduce losses from default, individuals invest in information and expertise to determine the quality of the items being exchanged. Time transactions also require further institutions because although the buyer/borrower can observe what he receives today, the lender/seller does not know exactly what he will get in return. For such contracts, institutions that provide punishments for individuals who fail to perform are critical. Why should a lender bother to determine why a borrower fails to repay unless he has the means to punish the debtor who has engaged in fraud? Information and enforcement are thus complementary for time transactions because investment in information makes sense only if that information can be acted on. Effective action requires both institutions to detect miscreants and institutions to punish their misbehavior.

How do formal and informal institutions deter cheating? Informal institutions rely on reputation and other private sanctions. The parties to the exchange have incentives to perform because good past performance is a precondition to being able to engage in future transactions with members of a reputational coalition. The coalition contains all the individuals who restrict interaction (exchange) to members in good standing of the coalition.

The coalition can involve an ethnic minority, as in Greif (1989), or a lineage group or individuals of a given place of origin, as was common in China (Faure 2006). As game theorists have shown, cheating is most easily deterred when information flows are good, when alternative occupations are unrewarding, and when individuals are patient.

These conditions are highly intuitive. If information is poor, then one party cannot decide whether the other has cheated or not, and this dampens the effectiveness of exclusion. If individuals who misbehave can find other ways to secure income, then the threat of exclusion has little bite. This condition suggests that coalitions that govern exchange not just of one but of a large number of commodities and include many people are more powerful than those that involve just one type of transaction across a small group. Enlarging the coalition, however, increases information costs, and nearly all examples that we have of groups that engage in reputational behavior are subsets of the general population. Thus coalitions have costs because trade must be restricted, and hence a member may not obtain the best possible price for an item because the individual with the greatest willingness to pay may not belong to the same coalition. These costs will be highest when groups are small and goods are highly heterogeneous. Finally, if individuals are very impatient, they will want to enjoy the ill-gotten gains from cheating rather than wait for the more virtuous return of future transactions that follow good performance. Impatience is not simply a characteristic of the individual but is also a characteristic of transactions. If one engages in a particular kind of transaction (say, real estate purchases) sufficiently infrequently, the cost of exclusion from a future transaction will be outweighed by the immediate gain from cheating.

In the case of formal enforcement, the incentive not to cheat comes from avoiding a punishment that would be meted out coercively by an agent of the state. Again, would-be cheaters are deterred by the fear of prison, fines, or the damages the courts will force them to pay if they misbehave. There are costs and benefits to formal enforcement as well. Perhaps the biggest of these involve the setting up of courts and a legal system. There are also costs associated with the adjudication of specific disputes. These costs will depend on a variety of factors, notably, where the case will be tried. If the amount lost is sufficiently small, a cheater may not fear a suit simply because the costs of litigation outweigh whatever can be recovered. Moreover, pursuing redress in a court will depend on where a litigant has standing to sue someone who has cheated him. This could be where the contract was signed, where the cheater lives, or in some third location specified in the contract. The farther away the cheater and his assets are from the plaintiff, the more expensive the case is likely to be. The benefits of using a formal mechanism are that it does not depend on the identities of the parties to a transaction. This does not imply that transactions are anonymous: the parties to a given trade must still know a lot about each other, but their capacity to sanction a defaulter does not depend on the particulars of an ongoing relationship.

To build our simple model, we reduce the set of factors that affect the relative efficacy of formal and informal mechanisms to two: frequency and distance. As in Chapter 2, the interested reader can follow the mathematical analysis in Box 3.1. Given that the incentives to remain honest decline as transactions are geographically more spread out, while the incentive to cheat is immediate, the argument comes down to one simple rule: if the interval between transactions is too long, then these types of transactions cannot be sustained by an informal mechanism. Denote by T^* the largest time interval between transactions such that reputation sustains performance. When the expected interval between transactions rises beyond T^*, informal enforcement will fail. This stark result echoes much of the diaspora and social capital literature that argues that social networks play a critical role in supporting trade, and that they are also dependent on dense interactions. Similarly, the cost of punishing a defaulting borrower by taking him to court increases with distance even though what the lender can recover does not. Again, this leads to a simple argument: if the borrower lives too far from the lender, then formal contracts cannot sustain trade. Denote by D^* the largest distance between two parties such that it is worthwhile to sue in court if someone cheats. We further assume that D and T are not systematically related—that is, there are infrequent transactions among neighbors, such as real estate sales, as well as frequent transactions among neighbors (as in the market for occasional labor).

If we suppose for now that individuals decide to use only one type of mechanism to enforce one type of transaction (e.g., the market for livestock) and that they can select whatever mechanism they want for any particular type of transaction, which will they chose? Given the foregoing formulation of issues, there are four possible cases, as shown by the four regions in Table 3.1.

Box 3.1. Formal and informal contract enforcement

Consider a loan of value L. When the loan comes due, if the borrower defaults, he earns π and the lender earns 0. If the borrower is honest and repays, he earns a return of $h = \pi - (1+r)L$, and the lender gets $(1+r)L$. In the absence of any enforcement mechanism the borrower never repays $(h < \pi)$, and consequently the lender makes no loans.

Formal enforcement of a loan of value L. Here the borrower who defaults can be taken to court. If he is sued, he will lose, have to repay the debt with interest, and bear the court costs. Hence the borrower always repays if he thinks that he will be sued after default. Will the lender sue? If he does not sue, he gets nothing back. If he prosecutes, he wins $(1+r)L$ (gets his money back and some interest forgone). He also bears the costs of litigation (payments to the courts and to legal experts and time spent, including travel to the residence of the borrower/buyer). Those costs increase with the distance between his residence and that of the borrower, and we will denote them by $C(D)$. He will sue if $(1+r)L > C(D)$. Given a loan of value L, the lender always sues borrowers who live less than D^* away from him. It is easy to show that if courts become more efficient at enforcing judgments, then the maximum distance at which judgments get enforced (D^*) increases.

Informal enforcement of a loan of value L. When the loan comes due and the borrower defaults, he is always found out and is, consequently, excluded by his network from a range of transactions forever, so his best future alternative will earn him b per period, and $b < h$. If he repays, he is not excluded. Technically we are looking at a stationary repeated equilibrium (where no one ever cheats). The conditions under which network members exclude cheaters have been explored at length (see Greif 2006). For now, assume that the buyer interacts with the network once a period (the period can be very short). Let d be the discount rate; the discounted present value of receiving h forever is H. Similarly, the discounted present value of receiving b forever is B. The borrower contemplates the difference between $h + dH$ (being honest today and forever) and $\pi + dB$ (cheating and being branded a bad partner ever after). Then the net returns on being honest if interaction occurs once per period are $R(1) = h - \pi + d(H - B)$. If the interval between interactions is T periods, $R(T) = h - \pi + d^{T+1}(H - B)$. $R(T)$ is declining in T, and there is a unique T^* such that $R(T^* + 1) < 0 < R(T^*)$. It is easy to show that if the network is more valuable, then T^* increases.

Table 3.1. Contractual arrangements in trade

Interval between interactions	Distance between parties	
	$D < D^*$	$D > D^*$
$T > T^*$	Formal feasible	Formal not feasible
	Informal not feasible	Informal not feasible
	Prediction: formal	Prediction: cash-only transactions
$T < T^*$	Formal feasible	Formal not feasible
	Informal feasible	Informal feasible
	Prediction: ?	Prediction: informal

1. *Distant and rare transactions* (the upper-right-hand quadrant in Table 3.1): Because $D > D^*$ and $T > T^*$ neither mechanism will work, and trade in such conditions will be in cash.
2. *Distant but frequent transactions* (the lower-right-hand quadrant in Table 3.1): Because $D > D^*$, formal enforcement is not feasible, but because $T < T^*$, informal enforcement is feasible.
3. *Local but rare transactions* (the upper-left-hand quadrant in Table 3.1): Because $T > T^*$, informal enforcement is not feasible, but because $D < D^*$, formal enforcement is feasible.
4. *Local and frequent transactions* (the lower-left-hand quadrant in Table 3.1): Because $D < D^*$ and $T < T^*$, both formal and informal enforcement are feasible; hence our theory does not decide the issue. For the moment we will leave this case aside.

This framework has some immediate implications for thinking about the historical record:

- Societies that are wealthy should have both formal and informal institutions. Indeed, prosperous societies will enforce contracts for infrequently traded assets, such as land, and they will engage in long-distance trade. Because both China and Europe have been economically prosperous at various points in their histories, we would expect both formal and informal institutions to flourish in both places.
- Comparable transactions should be enforced with similar mechanisms, both in China and in Europe. It is unlikely that one will find

one society where the market for land rests on reputation while commercial finance relies on state enforcement and another where the reverse is true.

- If, as is commonly assumed, Chinese informal networks work better than European ones but European courts work better than Chinese ones, then some transactions enforced informally in China will be enforced formally in Europe, but that range will be small. The dominant effects will be that the geographic reach of courts in Europe will be larger than in China (so more low-frequency transactions might occur with credit in Europe than in China). At the same time, European networks will fail to sustain some distant transactions because the frequency of such interactions will be too low (see Table 3.2).
- Finally, if one economy has more long-distance trade and consequently evolves more efficient informal mechanisms, then it may well appear at a particular time that this economy is more informal relative to another that has less long-distance trade and uses formal mechanisms more. The relative prevalence of different mechanisms in any given society should evolve along with changes in economic structure. Thus finding informal enforcement in China and formal enforcement in Europe is not sufficient to tell us how the regions

Table 3.2. Contractual arrangements in trade with differences between societies

Interval between interactions	Distance between parties		
	$D < D_c$	$D_c < D < D_e$	$D > D_e$
$T > T_c$	Europe: formal China: formal	Europe: formal China: cash	Europe: cash China: cash
$T_e > T > T_c$	Europe: formal China: either	Europe: formal China: informal	Europe: cash Europe: informal
$T < T_e$	Europe: either China: either	Europe: formal China: either	Europe: informal China: informal

Note: In the darkest gray areas (■) Chinese and European transactions should be enforced in similar ways. In the lighter gray areas there are differences and one society has an advantage, either because both types of enforcement are available rather than only one (■), or because one type of enforcement is available rather than none (■). Only in the unshaded center box can one find the traditional opposition between informal China and formal Europe.

evolved. To maintain that the two regions had important differences in the evolution of their economies, one would need to find that similar activities relied on different mechanisms in the two regions.

The foregoing conclusions depend on the critical assumption that rulers supply an adequate level of formal enforcement and do not intervene to make courts inefficient or to disrupt trade networks. Although cultural and social differences are unlikely to alter the preceding arguments, political constraints can be important. This consideration clearly requires great care at two levels. First, we must ascertain that China's informality was not simply the result of imperial neglect or oppression (as has been suggested by E. L. Jones 1988: 135–136). Second, the foregoing argument probably cannot be exported to any and all settings or to all populations. The mere fact that there is a functional logic to develop formal mechanisms does not mean that rulers have the requisite capacity or proclivities to act accordingly. For example, as we saw in Chapter 1, during the eleventh and twelfth centuries European rulers more often than not failed to provide formal institutions (Bisson 2009).

Our interest here involves China and Europe after 1400. We must now ask, what were the political constraints on institutional choices? Political constraints take a variety of forms. Most importantly, the Chinese empire's very size encouraged the formation of networks of long-distance traders whose volume of activity was, for centuries, far larger than what occurred in war-torn and fragmented Europe. Looking not at the fifteenth but at the eighteenth century, one might believe that the empire failed to put in place a court system capable of providing formal enforcement to all comers. Conversely, European countries' tiny medieval size may have created segmented markets whose transactions were comparatively easy for courts to enforce. Moreover, war may well have made it difficult to sustain reputational networks on a large scale. Thus Europe may have been politically pushed into a more formal equilibrium than was efficient. The rest of this chapter is devoted to presenting evidence that both formal and informal mechanisms mattered in China and Europe; that their distribution in the economy can be explained by a common logic; and finally, that political factors were important in shaping the boundaries between formal and informal enforcement. Moreover, it is likely that the distribution of labor between formal and informal institutions that prevailed in one place at one time (say, medieval Europe) would not have been as practical in other places and at other times (say, Qing China or nineteenth-century Europe).

China and Europe: Similarities and Differences

Our earlier discussion of long-distance trade emphasized that both in Europe and China such commerce was carried out either in cash, in the case of distant and infrequent transactions (the upper-right-hand cell in Table 3.1), or with credit through informal networks, in the case of distant but frequent interactions (the lower-right-hand corner). Beyond a certain distance, which we put at 200 kilometers simply for illustrative purposes, courts could not effectively enforce contracts. It is not that courts did not perceive international trade as an attractive venue for the sale of legal services. On the contrary, they made every effort to attract business. By 1600 Low Country courts, for instance, promised to judge disputes among foreigners according to the law of the place where the contract had been signed (Gelderblom forthcoming: chaps. 7–8). But this provision benefited two merchants from Venice who happened to be in Amsterdam, not a merchant in Venice who wanted to recover from a Dutch counterparty. Indeed, in disputes between a local and a foreign merchant, one would expect courts to lean in favor of their own.

What then of interregional trade? In the case of very long-distance trade, the need to settle accounts voyage by voyage explains the fact that every ship that left Europe was laden with silver to settle its accounts on foreign shores. It would have been no different were the ships Chinese ones going to Europe with goods. In either case cash relationships were required irrespective of the location at which two parties of such different identities transacted their business. Nevertheless, the evidence of institutional change is clear. On the European side, both the Dutch and the English East India trade evolved from clubs of investors who funded a given ship's voyage to joint-stock companies that regularly sent out ships and established permanent bases in the East (Gelderblom and Jonker 2004; Harris 2005). During the eighteenth century, as transactions became more frequent between the same parties, credit arrangements became more common. As in the other forms of long-distance trade, interregional trade moved into the lower-right-hand box of our table. Various forms of credit were extended in Canton between Chinese and foreign merchants, as well as among foreign merchants. Brokers and agents in Canton and Macao rented space on ships, purchased goods, and arranged for their sale (Van Dyke 2005: 150–159). The China trade does tell us that we should develop flexible notions of distance and frequency that accommodate changing institutional forms that were far from fixed over time and space. Among new commercial ventures, those that were profitable tended to become more frequent simply because it paid for merchants to invest more in such voyages. As these markets expanded in scale, they allowed the establishment of informal mechanisms for time contracts where none had been feasible before.

We turn now to the third category of exchanges, identified in the upper-left-hand corner of Table 3.1. These are infrequent transactions for which formal enforcement is possible. Contracts that involve real estate are the prime example of this situation.

In Europe, as is well known, enforcement of local long-term contracts was a key element of local justice. This was true in the Roman law prevalent in the south, as well as in the common or customary law of the northern areas of the region. It was true in the countryside, where at first local lords and later royal officials provided judicial services. It was also true in urban areas, where political authorities often delegated the tasks of resolving disputes to merchant groups (guilds). Nevertheless, the enforcement of the decisions of guild officials relied on public officials (Epstein 1998; Ogilvie 2003). Over time, practices across the many discrete local jurisdictions were harmonized through the processes of centralizing state formation, but the principle of a judicial system that was close at hand persisted. Moreover, the bulk of the activities of local courts involved the adjudication of economic disputes (Duby 1974, 1979). It is not possible to estimate the value to the private economy of formal contract enforcement, but it is clear that recourse to the courts was widespread from an early date in the medieval economy, in particular, when disputes concerned land, long-term credit, or labor arrangements. In fact, when European economic historians want to trace the rise of formal institutions, they often turn to contracts about land and describe the evolution of tenure from a feudal system, in which individual claims were known only locally and were largely enforced by a local lord's thugs, to one in which a national justice system enforced titles to real assets (North and Thomas 1971; B. Campbell 2006). In many places titles and rental contracts were secured by registration in public information systems (Hoffman et al. 2000; Gelderblom forthcoming: chap. 8). Moreover, parallel registration systems allowed lenders to learn what liens had been placed on a particular piece of property. Thus formality and publicity were central to European conceptions of the organization of the land market and its attendant credit market. They are also central to the standard narrative of Europe's success.

Although most students of Chinese history already know that land was sold and rented in much of early modern Europe, many students of European history may not realize that agricultural land in late imperial China was also typically held as private property. There were regions where the imperial government interfered with the market for land in order to better control its supply of troops for duty on the frontier (Lee and Campbell 1997), but such cases seem more an exception than the rule. In the past two decades historians have unearthed a vast documentation trove of private contracts. These contracts show that in general, title to land was a matter of written record and that transfers of land involved written documents (G. Yang 1988). In fact, by far the most common forms of contracts that survive from imperial China concern land transactions. Although writing down transactions is a first step in creating some formality in the market, one might well do so even if the ultimate enforcement mechanism involves reputation. Indeed, a written agreement detailing the transaction and witnessed by multiple parties might reduce the likelihood of disputes compared with purely oral or private arrangements. But the documents often are also stamped by the local magistrate, suggesting that individuals were doing more than simply writing things down.

The crux of the matter involves the enforcement of these contracts. The earliest abundant local archival materials in China are from the eighteenth century, and they include legal cases heard by county magistrates. These show that one of the four most frequent categories of disputes brought before these magistrates concerned land transactions (the others involved debts, marriage disputes, and inheritance). These were typically between neighbors or kin. In some instances these disputes could continue for generations. Both the duration of some disputes and the more general indications of how long a given piece of land had been in the possession of a household and its ancestors suggest that public authorities were centrally involved in securing land assets. Further, they show that private property rights in land were well established in many parts of late imperial China.

The enforcement of local property rights by formal mechanisms and the enforcement of contracts in long-distance trade by informal mechanisms are common to both China and Europe. It is important for us to stress this baseline of similarities because scholars have been all too eager to point out the differences. In transactions where one kind of mechanism is clearly better than the other (distant but frequent and close but infrequent), China and Europe look alike. What about transactions where one could rely on either formal or informal mechanisms to sustain trade?

High-Frequency Local Transactions

Transactions that can be sustained by either formal or informal types of enforcement are high-frequency local transactions that occupy the lower-left-hand cell of Table 3.1. These include transactions between local producers and resident merchants, between resident merchants and local consumers, and between local creditors and local borrowers when credit is short term. Our simple model is agnostic about what type of mechanisms will be chosen. The conventional approach is to phrase the question as if the two mechanisms were mutually exclusive. Scholars have provided both logical and cultural grounds for this either/or approach. On the logical side, some have argued that when a contract is broken, the injured party will try to get redress at the lowest possible cost. Hence, the logic goes, if in China reputation is cheaper than courts, then individuals will cease to use courts. The cultural argument has been taken by others as equally powerful in supporting a strict separation between formal and informal mechanisms: in some societies where reputation is important, someone who tries to have recourse to courts will be tarred, while in places where courts are broadly available, reputation is of little value. Certainly these approaches are appealing because they provide the fuel for theories of divergence between a dynamic Europe creating anonymous formal markets and a static China mired in its informality. In fact, some have gone so far as to suggest that the introduction of Western institutions for economic transactions in the late nineteenth and early twentieth centuries was necessary for modern economic growth in China. Seen this way, the historical divergence between the Chinese and European economies was the result of a cultural-institutional lock-in (Ma 2006; M. Li 2003).

But although these arguments are seductive, they do not stand up to the evidence. Simply put, rather than being mutually exclusive, reputation and formal enforcement were deployed in conjunction. For Europe, where the research on local markets has been abundant, the evidence is compelling. It shows that although the role of reputation was more important in some transactions than in others (say, commercial credit rather than mortgages), it was never irrelevant. Similarly, although individuals were more likely to engage in litigation over land than over a basket of fruit or some small debt, willingness to sue over minor matters was remarkably high (e.g., for Burgundy, see Brennan 1997; Hayhoe 2008). That is why we have records of millions of court cases and registered contracts. One could conceive of these issues in many ways; the simplest is detailed in Box 3.2. Each actual transaction is either an informal or a formal transaction depending on the relative value of interacting within a network or with strangers. Within a network enforcement is informal and free, but

---

Box 3.2. Contract enforcement when both formal and informal enforcement are feasible

To resolve the issue of what occurs for frequent and local transactions, we must introduce some heterogeneity in the borrowers' characteristics. Moreover, unlike prior models, we want both types of arrangements to persist over time. In our initial model there was no default in equilibrium (it was a dominant strategy for the borrower to repay), and hence both mechanisms were equivalent (the seller never goes to court and never has to actually exclude anyone from trade). The argument presented here is illustrative of the kind of conditions under which both types of arrangements can persist in a locality.

Lenders are concerned about two issues: the interest rate and the likelihood of nonperformance. Each lender is a member of a reputational coalition or network and can make loans either to his fellows or to someone outside the coalition. If he transacts in the general population, he can expect the borrower to pay r_F. But in this case the seller faces some adverse selection (there are some borrowers who do not repay), and he has to go to court. He then earns $(1 + r_F)L - pc$, where p is the probability of nonpayment and c is the cost of formally enforcing the contract. If he makes a loan to a member of his network, information is good there, and contracts are always performed because the value of being honest is larger than the value of default for the borrower. However, using the coalition has a cost: the coalition is small (a subset of the general population), and thus the best interest rate offered within the coalition is $r_I \leq r_F$. It follows that all transactions where $(1 + r_F) - pc \leq (1 + r_I)$ occur inside the coalition, while the others use formal enforcement. It also follows that larger transactions are more likely to be formal. Beyond loans, this analysis suggests that goods where the range of willingness to pay is small are likely to be transacted informally, while those in which individual tastes really matter are transacted among strangers and are enforced by courts.

counterparties are few in number. Outside the network there are more counterparties; thus one can expect a better match, but enforcement is costly. Because conditions vary by type of transaction, by types of individuals, and by the circumstances when the transaction is contemplated, individuals interact regularly with both types of partners and rely on both types of enforcement. Although from the outset a transaction is either informal or formal, transactions that look identical can be enforced in different ways, depending on the identities of the buyer and the seller.

This kind of logic applied in the past. Since the medieval period a central feature of European society has been a judiciary that early on made its services available to nearly everyone (although slaves did not have the right to sue, manorial courts settled disputes involving serfs). Initially these very local courts were under the authority of local lords who either dispensed justice themselves or appointed whomever they pleased. In western Europe, at least, the combination of the decline of serfdom and the growth of the power of regional lords, cities, or even kings led to a professionalization of the judicial system and its progressive centralization. In economic matters centralization was limited in many places because rulers found it expedient to give people of commerce (merchants and manufacturers) a fair amount of autonomy in resolving their conflicts. But the royal justice system was always available to enforce commercial courts' verdicts.

Despite the deployment of a ubiquitous judicial infrastructure more than 500 years before the Industrial Revolution, merchants and private persons were all wary of ending up in court. It was universally agreed that procedures were long, expensive, and rarely rewarding. Instead, the general advice was to develop networks of relationships within which one could interact with trustworthy people. The mass of qualitative information that extols these strategies would not be understandable had informal mechanisms been unavailable to enforce time contracts. Thus Europeans relied on both formal and informal sanctions without hesitation.

For China, in contrast, we have so little evidence of formal mechanisms and such considerable material on informal ones that we have come to expect that a cultural preference for informal mechanisms can explain the persistence of informal mechanisms amid a general reluctance to use formal mechanisms such as courts. From our point of view, however, the case that has been made for China's informality is weak. It rests on two kinds of evidence, neither of which is conclusive. First, the fact that informal

institutions have been important to the Chinese economy from long before the Qing dynasty to the present has led scholars to assume that formal institutions did not matter. Although it is useful to recognize this long-
standing reliance on informal institutions, it is only necessary but not
sufficient to support the standard argument. The second kind of evidence
comes from the first half of the twentieth century. It should surprise no
one that in an era of weak government, official capacity to provide formal
enforcement of property rights declined. To be more specific, can we really trust the detailed survey evidence collected during this time, a period
that includes the Japanese occupation, to reveal the fundamentals of Chinese village society? To answer "yes" assumes such institutional rigidities
that one wonders how such a society could have survived for millennia. A
less distorted picture emerges if we return to the eighteenth century. In
this earlier period the state's involvement in local society was both extensive and valuable. We know, for example, that the imperial administration
kept detailed records of grain harvests and prices. It also deployed a variety of institutions to limit the impact of ecological variation (granaries and
water control). And, as we shall see later, it had the capacity to provide a
legal infrastructure for commerce and industry.

Some careful research has cast doubt on the idea that local dealings
were transacted only on an informal basis. Among English-language
scholars, Kenneth Pomeranz (1997) has shown the durability of a pickle-
making firm in northern China that did not rely on kinship ties or other
informal mechanisms for financing and management, but instead sold
shares and selected its management according to performance-based criteria. In a larger and more recent work Madeleine Zelin (2005) has reconstructed the operations of both large and small salt-producing firms in one
part of Sichuan Province. She shows that firms were able to obtain initial
financing for their operations by selling shares, that small and potentially
bankrupt firms could gain much-needed capital by offering additional
shares, and that large firms were capable of vertically integrating production and distribution operations—all of this with little or no reliance on
the kinship and native-place ties that we conventionally assume to be the
basis of Chinese entrepreneurial activities

Because their convictions about cultural differences have been so strong,
scholars have easily adopted stark conclusions about the institutional bases
of economic change, given the contrasting visibility of informal institutions in China and formal institutions in Europe. In their view, China and

Europe embarked on two alternative path-dependent patterns of change, and consequently their economies reached different institutional equilibria, with the European becoming more efficient than the Chinese. In this way of thinking, the absence of a judicial system in late imperial China on the scale of Europe's would mean that the Chinese never ended up expecting to use courts for most economic matters. Conversely, the European penchant for setting up courts to hear commercial disputes, beginning in the late medieval period, would prepare for the eventual emergence of the contracts and courts at the center of much of the new institutional economics story of European economic growth. Such a contrast can even be seen to affirm the idea expressed long ago by Adam Smith in his observations on China. Smith argued that economies grow to the point that their institutions permit and that these points will be different (A. Smith [1776] 1976: 106). It further echoes the belief of Karl Marx that Asian modes of production were incapable of growth and could be brought into the present only by the forceful transformation imposed by European powers.

Although we take issue with the arguments about institutional lock-in or path dependence, there were, of course, differences between China and Europe in the salience of formal and informal institutions. Our analysis of the use of formal and informal institutions depending on the kinds of economic transactions in fact implies that there should be substantial differences between Europe and China, but our framework explains these differences without recourse to an assumption about institutional lock-in; relative costs are enough. This approach is more attractive than one that assumes lock-in because, as we discuss later, the evidence supports the thesis that institutional change occurred in both regions.

The next section examines the persistence and even expansion of informal institutions for economic transactions in China. We argue that "informality" in China did not result from any cultural preferences that prevented the emergence of formal institutions. Rather, informal institutions were heavily used in the empire because China's spatial scale made long-distance trade both feasible and profitable. Formal institutions, like courts, were not very useful for commerce over hundreds of miles. In contrast, Europeans came to formalize their contracts as a consequence of political authority exercised on very limited spatial scales. Such strategies worked only because most exchange occurred on a local scale. Europe's political fragmentation and violent conflicts surely reduced the volume of long-distance trade. Thus historical narratives concentrate on how merchants overcame these barriers. It is less straightforward, however, to conclude that the same factors had any implication for how contracts were enforced in such long-distance interactions. Indeed, in China, such trade developed within the empire and was unfettered by transit taxes, but as we have seen, relationships were overwhelmingly informal.

The combination of European evidence of informal mechanisms complementing formal ones and Chinese evidence showing alternatives to the conventional informal mechanisms playing important roles shows us that the cases in the lower-left-hand corner of Table 3.1 are truly mixed, not simply between Chinese and European cases, but among cases in each region as well. Thus the contrast in the use of formal versus informal institutions is neither absolute nor fixed. Evidence of formal contracting in Chinese firms is quite limited at the moment. Nevertheless, existing evidence suggests that when Chinese entrepreneurs were presented with opportunities for which formal institutions were clearly desirable, they were able to develop such mechanisms, and they did so well before the examples of Western formal practices became known in China in the closing decades of the nineteenth century. The native development of enterprise forms warns us against the easy assumption that the Chinese learned about the superior virtues of formal institutions only from Europeans and after the latter had arrived on the scene. This assumption is twice flawed. First, the Chinese development of formal institutions before exposure to Western formal institutions means that they could adopt and adapt foreign models on the basis, in part, of their own previous practices. They could equally decide to forgo such adoption when they felt that their own mix of formal and informal institutions worked at least as well as, if not better than, the alternatives offered by Western institutions. Second, as we have already seen in this chapter, formal institutions are not unconditionally superior to informal ones, as the story line of the spread of European formal institutions typically implies. Indeed, informal institutions may well be clearly superior under certain circumstances. We now explain why this was the case for late imperial China.

Trade Institutions and the Long Shadow of Empire

This chapter has so far argued that formal and informal institutions were used both in China and in Europe. This stands in stark contrast to earlier scholarship that invokes cultural preferences as autonomous forces to explain the institutional choices made in China and in Europe (Landes 1998). One reason for exploring alternative hypotheses is that such explanations are difficult to evaluate: there are certainly cultural differences, as well as differences in commercial institutions, between China and Europe, but it is not clear how one can go from correlation (culture and institutions exist together in each place) to causation (specific cultural traits determine institutional forms) when we have only two cases to compare. Here we develop a thesis and offer a word of caution. The thesis is that divergent political processes over the long run led to different roles for formal and informal institutions in China and in Europe. The caution is that these contrasting historical processes did not lead to particular kinds of institutional lock-in. Rather, the relative roles of formal and informal institutions evolved over time and continue to do so to this day. It is this evolution over time that offers possibilities for confirming or disproving our argument.

Indeed, in our framework the relative importance of formal and informal institutions will depend on the distribution of transactions across our four quadrants. Political, technological, and environmental changes that lead to more long-distance trade will increase the role of informal institutions in the economy. Conversely, events that lead to an increased use of fixed capital assets will push the economy back toward formal institutions. To be sure, the distribution of transactions according to their frequency and the distance between parties cannot be evaluated with even a semblance of accuracy for any premodern economy (let alone over a millennium, as we would desire). Nevertheless, we can be confident from evidence for the tenth through the fourteenth centuries that the fraction of transactions occurring over long distances was larger in China than in Europe. We can also begin to chart the changing role of different institutions.

At the end of the first millennium A.D., China's lead in long-distance trade was a direct consequence of its more settled politics. China was more often than not an empire, while Europe was persistently fragmented. During the decline of the Roman Empire, some of the most important trade routes for bulk commodities were simply abandoned, and they took centuries to reestablish. Europe's commercial revolution was to some extent a recovery of trade patterns dating back to the Roman era. In China, political unification preceded commercial expansion. Chinese rulers did not view trade over distances of hundreds of kilometers as international trade but rather as domestic trade within their empire. Emperors had little reason to interfere with such commercial activities. That internal peace was the norm for many centuries over much of the empire was a key element that facilitated the flow of trade across the empire. Moreover, the fiscal need to intervene in trade within the empire was generally reduced after the mid-fourteenth century when the state returned to an earlier reliance on agricultural taxes as the main source of revenues and made only episodic use of commercial taxes before the mid-nineteenth century. For these political reasons, there was little state interference in the development of trade. Indeed, the central government generally worked successfully to keep lower levels of government from imposing their own levies or obstructing commodity flows in other ways (Wong 1999: 222–225).

As Chinese and Japanese scholars have documented, high volumes of trade in basic commodities (cotton, rice, sugar) covered vast distances in China by 1500 and especially in the eighteenth century (Xu and Wu 2000). Some of the organizational structures, including distinct wholesale, retail, and transport merchant functions, began to emerge in the Song dynasty (Shiba 1970). During the Ming dynasty major networks of merchants, each linked by multiple strands of native place and kinship, expanded the scale and scope of trade. The most famous were the Shanxi merchants and the Huizhou merchants. The former made their initial fortunes by taking grain to the northwest frontier to feed troops in return for licenses to sell government-regulated salt, while the latter also made fortunes controlling salt distribution in other parts of the interior of the empire. Both groups also engaged in other trade, such as timber and craft goods (Fuji 1953–1954; Fu 1956; Terada 1972). Additional groups of merchants developed trade with Southeast Asia from ports in southeastern and southern China. Some of their operations began in the eleventh and twelfth centuries, and their expansion continued up to the early seventeenth century.

China's early forays into long-distance trade, we argue, privileged the elaboration of a commercial regime based on networks and informal mechanisms. Even the best local courts in the world would have proved unable to adjudicate disputes between merchants who resided hundreds of kilometers apart. Hence networks developed early and intensely. Furthermore, these networks succeeded precisely because they became efficient at acquiring information about the activities of their members and about market conditions. In some cases, as noted earlier, these merchants went directly into local markets to purchase commodities. In others there was an interface between merchants transporting goods over long distances and local producers or consumers; these brokers *(yahang)* were the agents who either bought the merchants' goods or purchased goods from local producers for subsequent sale to long-distance traders. Merchant manuals counseled traders to be very careful about choosing a broker and suggested means to gauge the trustworthiness of a broker, as well as the demeanor desired to demonstrate one's own credibility (Lufrano 1997). For their part, officials worried about the asymmetry of knowledge regarding local market conditions that might allow brokers to take advantage of long-distance traders. Official involvement could go so far as to set rules to establish permissible behavior (Ch'iu 2008). These government efforts to influence the norms governing transactions complemented more informal strategies to enhance trust in transactions that lacked the advantages of large merchant networks. County magistrates also adjudicated disputes between brokers and traveling merchants as one of several kinds of commercial disputes that were heard during the eighteenth and nineteenth centuries (J. Fan 2007). Chinese merchants had recourse to formal dispute resolution, but the costs in time and money were considerable. As a result, informal methods prevailed as complements to formal ones. Given the size of the empire and the many other duties that local magistrates had, monitoring local markets was given over to local elites and merchants for the most part (Mann 1987). In sum, merchant networks using informal mechanisms to make long-distance trade possible proved to be the most salient and significant institutional context for commercial expansion. Trade beyond these networks under the sometimes-watchful and anxious eye of officials also took place, but formal mechanisms were not the major instruments for commercial exchange.

Much the same logic explains why European long-distance trade depended largely on informal networks. The absence of empire in Europe did not prevent long-distance trade. In fact, long-distance trade plays an important role in the narrative of the rebirth of the European economy after the Great Invasions, and in the narrative of all subsequent growth spurts culminating in the Industrial Revolution. The rebirth of the European economy was made possible by the demands of local elites for distant goods, including spices, fine cloth, and other manufactured products. Much of this commerce went through informal networks, such as those in the Mediterranean. At first these networks were centered in the East, but by the eleventh century they had come under the control of Italian cities like Genoa or Venice. The further growth of northern Italian cities was premised in part on the sale of manufactured goods all over the region. In the Spanish Netherlands, the growth of Antwerp centered around a Europe-wide textile market, while the rise of Amsterdam was based on its capacity to control trade in the Baltic, then in the Mediterranean, and subsequently beyond Europe. With the shifts in centers of trade and the growth of trade relations, more formal institutions came to be employed for economic transactions—in particular, in credit with the formation of exchange banks (the Wisselbank, the Bank of England)—but informal links continued to be the mainstay of international trade and finance (Neal and Quinn 2003). This remained true all the way to 1912, when J. P. Morgan made his celebrated remark that the most important trait of a capitalist was his reputation (Carosso 1967). As the Bernard Madoff scandal reminds us, informal relationships remain very important in today's financial world.

Despite all that informal networks could accomplish, however, it was still true that political fragmentation in Europe interfered with long-distance trade throughout the Middle Ages. Scholars of Byzantium, Genoa, or Venice have focused on the achievements of their cities, but what they have missed is that one key element in the competition between commercial centers was the use of violence, which seriously distorted trade. Had these cities been located in a real empire, they would have been forced to compete on purely economic grounds. Even after Europe's military capacities had propelled it to become the world leader in commercial exchanges, trade was hindered by politics. Even leaving out dramatic changes to European trade networks associated with war (e.g., Genoa's decline in the eastern Mediterranean after its loss in the war of Chioggia or Antwerp's decline during the Dutch revolt), any graph of the volume of trade shows dramatic declines during periods of war (Daudin 2005: 207–216; de Vries and van der Woude 1997: chap. 9).

Beyond war, trade also suffered from the policies of European states. All governments (absolutist and representative) tried to limit the extent of long-distance trade. The British Navigation Acts were not very different from Spanish commercial policies. The motives behind trade policies were varied, including the protection of local industries and stemming bullion outflows when a country's commodity trade ran up deficits. The reason for state interference in trade was, of course, the need for revenue for war.

Taxing long-distance trade was easy: in each territory most long-distance trade was international trade and went through a few ports. But European rulers did not stop there. Instead, they also taxed trade between their different domains. Trade between European polities, many of which correspond to regions within national states today, was thus limited by tariffs and prohibitions in the Middle Ages (Dincecco 2008). Under the Spanish Crown, for instance, there were significant trade barriers between Catalonia and Castile, areas much smaller than the typical Chinese province (J. Elliott 1986; Lynch [1964] 1991). Despite a long-run process of political unification within European countries, many barriers persisted for half a millennium or more within what are now national entities, such as France or Spain. Trade barriers between national entities were first reduced in the middle of the nineteenth century and then were raised again starting in the 1880s. The process of creating a common market within Europe had to wait until the 1960s. In brief, Europe certainly had developed long-distance commerce, but its political fragmentation by Chinese standards of political integration meant that the expansion of long-distance trade suffered more challenges than it did in China.

Even with the development of ever more formal institutions for economic transactions after the Industrial Revolution, much long-distance European trade and international finance through the nineteenth century depended heavily on informal networks. These networks depended on ties of kinship, geographic origin, or religious affiliation. Hence China and Europe are less different from one another than some of the contrasts scholars have drawn would suggest. Transactions in both areas of the world respond to the same logic. In its starkest form, the model we propose suggests that cultural variation has little to do with differences in the demand for formal and informal institutions. Rather, the different kinds of economic opportunities available at either end of Eurasia are what count in explaining the formal and informal mechanisms for contract enforcement that became typical within each.

When late nineteenth-century conditions changed dramatically with the introduction of Western technologies and enterprise forms, the Chinese government began to create a new legal structure. Many of the ideas and institutions developed in late Qing China were selected from Western practices, much as when the Meiji-era Japanese elaborated economic institutions from Western models. The European origins of these formal institutions have conventionally been assigned a crucial role in bringing economic change to China. Certainly it is historically true that many of the concrete practices were first articulated in European contexts, but there is no logical need for these practices to have originated outside China. The very effectiveness of the reforms depended on the Chinese contexts into which they were placed. As we saw earlier, China had indigenous formal contracts of ship shares for overseas trade, as well as for joint-stock firms (Pomeranz 1997; Zelin 2004). Had there been many uses for other formal contracts, one would expect Chinese entrepreneurs to have developed more such forms. At the same time, importing well-developed formal institutional models in the late nineteenth century saved the Chinese much time and experimentation. Transposing these new models was rapid in part because of the earlier native experiences.

Still, foreign institutional models, including those promoted by the Chinese government, did not always fit the Chinese context very well. For example, many Chinese firms declined opportunities to incorporate when new company laws were first promulgated in 1904 (Kirby 1995). The costs of incorporation may well have weighed more heavily than the anticipated benefits, either because the government could not actually enforce the new property rights or because company owners feared that incorporation would expose a firm's financial situation and thus increase its tax burden. As the Tianjin Chamber of Commerce opined, the government promulgated a commercial code at odds with local commercial practices and largely imitated foreign ones instead (J. Fan 2007: 287). Although Western formal institutions could not be imported wholesale, Chinese institutions proved open and flexible enough to accommodate some new practices from the West. A better way to understand institutional change is to view it as Chinese expansion of practices that included selected Western practices, rather than a simple substitution of Western for Chinese ones. These changes suggest that we cannot take China's onset of industrialization after that in western Europe, and at rates slower than those in Japan, as a sign of institutional lock-in. There were more obvious factors that limited economic growth in the first half of the twentieth century, including a very difficult political situation. Political turmoil overshadowed any institutional change. The political disintegration started with the mid-nineteenth-century rebellions and then accelerated with international conflicts, resulting in the collapse of centralized political order in the first decade of the twentieth century. On balance, therefore, it seems reasonable to conclude that foreign models of formal institutions accelerated changes that would have occurred in their absence and that unstable domestic conditions slowed Chinese institutional change.

The existence of both formal and informal institutions for economic transactions in late imperial China implies that institutional imports were not necessary for growth to take off. The use of formal institutions would have increased when economic change made formal institutions superior to informal ones. The growing availability of foreign models did, of course, change the choice set available to Chinese policy makers and entrepreneurs. Not surprisingly, some Western practices were adopted. Equally sensibly, though less commonly noted by scholars, new practices were developed that drew on older domestic ones. As a result of both dynamics, a changing mix of formal and informal institutions emerged wherein formal practices grew in relative importance. Expanding our observations to look at the variable use of formal and informal institutions in early twentieth-century China and Europe, we argue that decisions about the relative attractiveness of formal versus informal institutions for similar kinds of transactions no doubt were influenced by earlier choices to use one set of practices rather than another. Thus the optimal mix of formal and informal institutions differed according to the path-dependent contexts of both China and Europe in the early twentieth century.

The rise of modern economic growth in western Europe has led many economic historians to posit the existence of a set of institutions that are optimal for growth, namely, those of eighteenth-century England. Because China's contracting institutions are quite foreign to the English common-law tradition, one might be tempted to conclude that absent major legal reforms, China's economy could not develop successfully. The past three decades of explosive growth question such conclusions, especially because a significant part of the growth in industrial output in the 1980s and early 1990s was achieved without formal courts and contracts.

An alternative argument would have it that although English institutions may work in Britain, they cannot be expected to have similar benefits in China or in other quite different cultural or geographic environments. In particular, different scholars have documented the importance of the conditions Europeans encountered for the kinds of institutions they set up in their colonies (Acemoglu et al. 2001; Engerman and Sokoloff 1997). Among their most startling findings is that within an ecological zone there was little variation among the different colonizing nations in the institutions they chose. This approach, like ours, takes geography quite seriously, but for our comparison it does not lead to strong conclusions. Indeed, the environmental variation across Europe is extremely large and is even greater in China, but the striking institutional differences are more between China and Europe than within each region.

In trying to account for differences in contract enforcement between China and Europe, we have relied on the observation that in some relationships formal enforcement is not very useful, just as in others it is the only way to make sure that parties adhere to contracts. From there we developed a framework of enforcement choice that showed that successful economies deploy a mix of formal and informal enforcement rather than relying solely on one or the other mechanism. The historical record is fully consistent with this view. Although merchant networks (organized around kinship or place-of-origin groups) seem to have been very extensive in China, they did not replace formal contracts. Further, in considering the relative importance of formal or informal contract enforcement, we found that the structure of the economy is likely to be key. Hence it is not surprising that Europe, a region where politics interfered with long-distance trade, saw more transactions that were local and formal than did China. Nor is it surprising that the trade resurgence of the late medieval period in Europe brought about a flowering of informal arrangements among merchants.

In many ways the argument we offer echoes the discussion of the theory of the firm we presented in Chapter 2. That theory says that whether an activity is structured by a firm's hierarchy or by a market mostly depends on the characteristics of that activity. In some cases it is best for these activities to be coordinated with a set of other activities in a firm; in other cases the market is more efficient. The argument in this chapter emphasizes that the division of labor between formal and informal enforcement depends on the nature of the transactions. But time and again the historical record forces us to concede that politics matter more than simple economics. That the Middle Kingdom had a large volume of domestic long-distance trade and a small volume of international trade (while Europe had the reverse) is a direct consequence of the imperial scale of the Chinese state. European governments competed to provide formal enforcement of contracts because they were after the revenues produced by contract registration and dispute resolution. Those revenues, in turn, were spent on military investments.

In this chapter we examined only the demand for formal contract enforcement (how individuals would want to structure their transactions); in effect we assumed that the supply of such enforcement mechanisms would respond to changes in demand both in China and in Europe. In many places in the world, the supply of courts to adjudicate cases is often wanting. Even in our two regions, rulers sometimes failed to provide needed formal institutions. For example, tenth- and eleventh-century Chinese policy makers declared government monopolies on many commodities, and foreign trade restrictions variously imposed, especially during the Ming dynasty, curtailed growth possibilities (P. J. Smith 1991; Wong 1994; J. Li 1990). Informal institutions (smuggling) arose as a result. In Europe, political intervention that wrecked the commercial networks of Antwerp in the late sixteenth century and the failure of the French state to reform its judiciary before the Revolution had even more serious political and economic consequences (Gelderblom 2000; Rosenthal 1992). But in Europe and China for most commercial transactions, governments were willing to provide enforcement services or to delegate those tasks to local authorities. In both regions formal enforcement was imperfect. There has never been a time when businesspeople have not complained of the cost, uncertainties, and delay associated with courts, but that has not stopped them from litigating. Imperfect formal enforcement does not make it valueless. In fact, both in China and in Europe, infrequent transactions like land sales were formalized.

Beyond these regions, however, there are numerous examples of states failing to provide the rule of law and instead structuring economic interactions to favor specific elites. The histories of Latin America and colonial Africa are often told in this light (Nunn 2008; Haber et al. 2003). In such places informal arrangements are the only ways for the disenfranchised to structure interactions. Those with political clout may have access to property rights and the courts, but such benefits are contingent on informal and unstable relationships. Developmental lessons have been drawn from such tragic examples as Zaire under Mobutu or Indonesia under Suharto (North et al. 2009). The histories of China and Europe alert us that these failures are political rather than economic or cultural. Further, differences in the extent of formal enforcement across societies may not be symptoms of pathology but rather the consequences of differences in economic structure.

Much like North, Wallis, and Weingast, we see politics as a critical variable in explaining differences in performance. Since Chapter 1, where we explored the spatial scale of European and Chinese polities, the theme of the impact of political structures on economic performance has loomed large in this volume. The burden of Chapters 2 and 3 has been to demonstrate that China and Europe were probably more alike economically than their institutions or cultures would suggest. Chapter 4 turns to the central issue of this book: the role of politics in explaining the great divergence in economic performance that could be observed by 1800.

4

Warfare,
Location of Manufacturing, and
Economic Growth in China and Europe

Our analysis of contracting arrangements put a significant emphasis on the size of the Middle Kingdom and the importance of long-distance trade in explaining why China relied on informal arrangements more than Europe did. That the size of the Chinese empire encouraged the early rise of long-distance markets is well established (Pomeranz 2000). Upon reflection this should cast doubt on a common thesis in economic history that political competition is directly beneficial to economic growth. Political competition historically has meant violent and expensive domestic and international conflict rather than well-ordered and cheap elections or even armed peace. Empires, such as China, have little political competition and, for a long time in the past, were rich. In contrast, regions with multiple polities bear the costs of war time and again, and even in peacetime they bear distortions to trade that reduce the volume of long-distance trade. Economists would do well to remember that most of the restraints to trade that Adam Smith or David Ricardo identified as reducing economic efficiency simply did not exist within Ming-Qing China. As Carol Shiue has shown this benevolent approach to internal trade fostered remarkably high grain market integration in preindustrial China (Shiue 2002, Keller and Shiue 2007). Central government officials collected few transit taxes and limited the ability of local authorities to do so; that policy gave China a quasi-free-trade zone the size of Europe.

In this chapter we explore the relationship between political competition and economic change further. In particular, we focus on the role of war in the rise of mechanical technologies in Europe starting at the end of the seventeenth century. Our diagnosis of the proximate source of divergence accords with a large literature (most recently Mokyr 2009 and Allen 2009a): England and later Europe's per capita income began to rise rapidly after 1750 because that part of the world was more successful in implementing mechanical technologies of production. However, we differ about the reasons that Europe sprang to leadership. Some have argued for environmental (Diamond 1997), cultural (Mokyr 1990, 2009), and political factors (E. L. Jones 1981). We believe that each of these arguments suffers from problems of chronology. Although it is romantically attractive, Mokyr's focus on the European Enlightenment and openness to new ideas seems to put aside the extensive religious and political conflicts that crippled many parts of Europe, including England, both before and after the Reformation. Enlightenment ideas may have sustained growth but certainly did not cause it. Much the same can be said of the natural-resource bonanza that Europe reaped from the colonization of America (Pomeranz 2000; E. L. Jones 1981).

We think that the causes of economic divergence between Europe and China emerged earlier. By 1500 the European and Chinese economies were on structurally different paths. Leonardo's sketchbooks may mostly contain drawings of machines that could not be built, but they represent an early manifestation of Europe's love of machines. The passion for mechanical innovation that blossomed in Europe over the next 300 years was far scarcer, if present at all, in China. The class of potential explanations is very large, but examining key facts about manufacturing before the Industrial Revolution helps us focus the analysis:

- It is now well established that China had an early lead in technology and that its technology continued to evolve long after the famed peak of the 1350s (Needham 1954–2008).
- By 1000, although low-skill, low-capital handicrafts were rural in both areas and high-skill, high-capital industries were urban in both areas, the range of manufacturing that was sustained in cities was much larger in Europe than in China (van der Wee 1988).
- By 1600 Europeans were developing and deploying machinery more intensely than the Chinese (Mokyr 1990).
- By 1700 the technology was such that it paid to adopt the new machinery only in a small area of Europe where particular relative price ratios favored capital over labor (Allen 2009a).

Rather than build a theory to explain the fourth or even the third of these points, as is common, we focus on the second and take the first as given. We do so because we want an argument that allows technological leadership to move from one location to another, say, from China to Europe or vice versa. We must allow both societies to be technologically creative to avoid developing a trivial theory in which Europeans will succeed from the outset. This approach therefore eliminates all possible arguments that make European cultural or political arrangements superior to those found in China. Indeed, if coastlines (Diamond 1997), culture (Landes 1998), or formal law (North et al. 2009) favored the West, why was Europe so poor a dozen centuries ago? It also eliminates all the arguments that focus on European institutions like the corporation, which diffused throughout the world but came to be important only after 1700. These include many arguments that focus on political and cultural developments like the Enlightenment or representative democracy (Mokyr 2002; North and Weingast 1989); although they may have provided a powerful boost to the process, they occurred too late to matter. Instead, we need to find a social process that first gives an advantage to China and then at some point allows Europe to take over.

Our argument has two parts: first, war was responsible for Europe's urban manufacturing; second, Europe's urban bias is precisely what produced the high rate of capital investment and the adoption of machinery in ever-greater areas of Europe. In contrast, China's peaceful economy experienced neither the pressure to protect its artisans behind city walls nor the consequent inducement to use machines to save on expensive labor. We highlight these long-term tendencies rather than a moment of critical invention, such as the appearance of the steam engine in the 1690s, because no single critical event in the seventeenth or eighteenth century propelled England or Europe toward mechanization. Moreover, in the fourteenth century Europe does not appear to have had much of a mechanical advantage over China, nor is there any evidence that wages were much higher there than elsewhere in the world. The urban bent of European manufacturing relative to its Chinese counterpart is, however, extremely old. What produced this bias is the focus of this chapter.

Cities and Economic Growth

Rather than ask what pushed Chinese manufacturing to be overly rural, we ask what pushed European manufacturing to be urban early on. Although the distinction appears academic, it has important analytical implications. In the first case, one sets up the European pattern as efficient and then looks for a Chinese pathology. This approach might be appropriate for the mid-nineteenth century when urban industries had clearly become a critical element of growth, but that was far from obvious in 1200. It is more historically relevant to seek out what pushed Europeans to choose urban locations for activities that could have been accomplished equally well in the countryside, where food was cheaper, raw materials were easier to access, and diseases were less prevalent. It has the additional advantage of allowing us to recognize that China's economic centers were likely more efficient and prosperous than were Europe's in the fifteenth and sixteenth centuries. This reorientation will prove quite fruitful.

The question of why Europeans had so much more of their manufacturing in cities than the Chinese did has three broad potential classes of answers. First, there are demographic and economic factors that could make cities more attractive in one place than another. Second, differences in political economy could have led rulers to favor cities at one end of Eurasia rather than the other. Finally, there are the consequences of regional differences in political structure, in particular, the spatial scales of polities. In our view it is this third set of explanations that is correct, but unlike earlier scholars, we do not view Europe's surge to mechanical leadership as the direct outcome of benevolent policies but rather as the unintended consequence of a regional political system embroiled in costly conflict.

Let us begin by dispensing with some simple answers that might explain why Chinese entrepreneurs might have preferred the countryside. The most obvious candidate is demography. In particular, urban mortality might be responsible for the lack of manufacturing cities in many parts of the world. Before 1800 cities everywhere had such high mortality rates that they had to import people from near and far to sustain their populations (Grantham 1993; Wrigley 1967). Artisans might have been tempted to choose rural locations for their shops simply to avoid the pernicious disease environment of cities. These mortality problems were perhaps more severe in warmer climates (where waterborne diseases tend to proliferate) than in colder ones, but then cities should have been larger and manufacturing more urban in northern areas of China and Europe than in southern ones. In fact, cities and towns grow more rapidly in the southern parts of China than in the north after 1100, while Europe's larger cities with more urban manufacturing were in the south rather than the north before 1500. This demographic argument does not lead to a divergence between China and Europe.

A second possibility for the lack of urban manufacturing in China was envisaged by Adam Smith and focuses on the poverty of China's larger population. In other words, capital was more abundant in Europe than in China, and because capital markets were more active in cities, the cost of capital was lower both in Europe than in China and in cities than in the countryside. To a large extent this is the argument developed by Robert Allen to explain the early adoption of machinery in England (Allen 2009a, 2009b). Although it is very appealing for England in 1730, it is more difficult to sustain for Europe before the Black Death, when interest rates were considerably higher than they would later become and wages were lower, but manufacturing was already very urban in Europe (Epstein 2000). Although there are few or no data on Chinese wages and interest rates for this early era, the qualitative evidence strongly supports the notion that the empire's manufacturing was already becoming increasingly rural after the founding of the Ming dynasty in 1368.

Beyond simple factor prices one could seek an explanation for the concentration of manufacturing in cities in Europe from economic geography. Research on urban systems has long emphasized the beneficial effects on costs and productivity growth of industrial clusters. In economics parlance, manufacturing derives increasing returns from network externalities (see Fujita et al. 2001). The idea is that production processes are more efficient when they are spatially concentrated. These externalities have been argued to come from thicker and more specialized input markets, greater competition among firms, and the willingness of workers to acquire job-specific skills because if their firm treats them badly, they can find another employer desirous of their skills next door. It is important to stress that the existence of such externalities alone is not sufficient for a divergence between China and Europe. In fact, if the returns from urban location are large and ancient enough, they should have been discovered at both ends of Eurasia, and the location of manufacturing should have been similar. Furthermore, given the existence of large cities in Asia and, in particular, in China by 1000, one would assume that China would have embarked on an urban path for manufacturing before Europe. To obtain a divergence that favors Europe, we need to differentiate across economic sectors in order to identify industry-specific externalities, with those industries that benefit from agglomeration economies accounting for a larger share of output in Europe than in China. The one industry that long differentiated Europe from China is probably weapons production (Hoffman 2010). But the scale of those activities was another consequence of Europe's troubled politics, which we will take up shortly. On the whole, economics alone is unlikely to explain this urban bias.

The second class of explanations comes from domestic political economy. The range of such theses is wide because either "bad" policies in China or "good" ones in Europe could be responsible for the European bias toward urban manufacturing. If we found Chinese emperors making it difficult for manufacturers to locate in cities (and thus preventing their subjects from taking advantage of the externalities associated with urban manufacturing), we could argue that Chinese entrepreneurs preferred to locate in cities. If we discovered that Chinese emperors suppressed capital markets, thus negating the possibly cheaper costs of capital in cities, then we could argue that bad policies hindered Chinese economic development. Chinese emperors did valorize an ideal of men plowing the fields and women weaving at home, but this political preference did not lead to real constraints on geographic mobility. Nor were people prevented from lending money; prohibitions on extremely high interest rates did not affect the cost and hence the availability of funds.

On the European side, medieval historians have long stressed the explicit policies of rulers of northwestern Europe that aimed to attract skilled workers to their territories and to their towns (e.g., Duby 1974, 1979). These policies surrendered some of the sovereign's authority to municipalities or more directly to groups of craftsmen or merchants organized as guilds. There is also evidence that cities and guilds actively attempted to limit the capacity of rural manufacturers to compete with urban producers (van der Wee 1988; Vardi 1993; Epstein 2000: chap. 5). Although one might make guilds responsible for the urban structure of production, one should bear in mind that each town had not one but many guilds, and even in a given industry they favored quite different policies. Towns were sufficiently small that no guild controlled the production of any good over any geographically significant market. As we shall see later, the boundary between rural and urban manufacturing was never fixed in Europe. Moreover, European guilds also served to protect their members from the rapacity of the ruler. Indeed, kings and princes were often tempted to confiscate the goods of merchants and craftsmen when they needed cash. As Greif (2006) notes in his examination of the conditions under which merchants might travel to distant markets, individuals have little power to resist rulers' temptation to tax or steal; in fact, only groups can stop such expropriation. A broader consideration of this matter leads us to the observation that both the relative scarcity of skilled workers and rulers' rapacity had their root cause, not in some flaw in the domestic political process, but in the ceaseless warfare that Europe experienced. Domestic political economy, like economics, drives us to consider international politics and, in particular, war.

The last class of explanations focuses on regional differences in political structure. For simplicity we take China to be a region of unified political control where war and civil disturbances were infrequent (except on the frontiers), and Europe to be an area of competitive politics where the likelihood of war and civil strife was much higher and more local. Even in peacetime Europeans and their rulers had to prepare for war; in China that problem was left to the emperor and his generals. Unlike other arguments that emphasize the benefits of political competition without measuring its costs, we recognize that political conflict was not a mere threat in a bargaining game, but something that happened and, when it happened, was expensive. In our view the primary reason for European manufacturing's urban bent was war. Although everyone wanted to escape war's ravages, farming was necessarily tied to the land and peasants to villages. Manufacturing, meanwhile, was both more mobile and more prone to pillage, particularly in activities that produced objects of high value per weight. European artisans therefore sought the protection of city walls rather than the more modest defenses available in villages. In China, by contrast, during the long centuries of dynastic stability the low frequency of warfare led manufacturers to choose their locations according to a different calculus. The relative prices they perceived were less affected by the anticipated ravages of war. The next section develops this argument and begins to trace the long-term impact of differences in the location of manufacturing.

Factor Costs and Manufacturing

We begin with the general observation that in most handicraft activity, firm size is tiny relative to the market, and thus competition prevails. As a result, over the long run enterprises will locate where the costs of production are lowest. Although the long run may not be a good way to analyze modern economies because factor costs and technologies are constantly changing, it will work well for our case because we are interested in secular tendencies in an era when technologies and factor costs generally changed slowly, but the latter could be subject to shocks that changed the relative costs of capital and labor.

Sixteenth- and seventeenth-century cities had advantages and disadvantages relative to the countryside. Urban dwellers faced increased risk of death and illness because concentrated populations are good loci for disease. People who lived in cities also faced higher food prices because staples had to be brought in from rural areas. Thus nominal wages had to be higher in cities than in the countryside. Consequently, an entrepreneur's cost of labor would be lower in rural areas than in urban ones. Evidence for such cost differentials is particularly abundant for the nineteenth century but can be seen in earlier periods from the correlation between nominal wages and city size (Ditmar 2009). If we consider capital, the reverse relationship holds: rural projects are more costly to monitor because they are dispersed and (we may assume) individually smaller in scale. Borrowers will bear the higher costs, and interest rates in the countryside will be higher than in cities. Evidence for these cost differentials is harder to find because in most preindustrial economies interest rates were not specified in contracts. One can turn to data about the geographic structure of credit markets: the systematic pattern of rural individuals going to towns and cities to borrow rather than to lend (and of city dwellers making more loans in the countryside than borrowing there) strongly argues that the cost of capital was lower in cities (Hoffman et al. 2011).

To evaluate the impact of these relative prices, we must define the production technology. To keep things simple, we begin with a production function where the ratio of capital to labor is fixed (in economists' terms, a Leontief technology, Varian [1978] 1984:10). For example, assume that there is one kind of loom and one type of worker; a Leontief technology arises if the only way to combine workers and looms is one worker per loom. In the case of fixed factor proportions, the entrepreneur who is seeking to minimize his costs simply picks the location where the input he uses most is cheapest: capital-intensive activities locate in cities, while labor-intensive activities are in the countryside. In fact, as the analysis in Box 4.1 shows, there is a unique level of capital per worker k^* such that all industries (or firms) that use more capital than k^* are in cities, while those that use less are in the countryside. This first step produces the classic differences in capital intensities between urban and rural areas, but the proposition on its own offers no help for understanding why China and Europe took different paths.

Warfare creates the difference in factor costs that can cause a divergence in the location of manufacturing between the two ends of Eurasia. War matters because rural projects are more likely to suffer from either civil disturbance or international warfare than urban enterprises. This is particularly true for capital invested in movable goods (equipment, tools, supplies, and people) because they can be appropriated by bandits, warlords, or foreign armies during unsettled times. Cities are not immune to warfare. Among other things, war disturbs the trade networks that are essential for cities, and of course, their wealth makes them attractive places to pillage. But cities can be fortified and resist redistribution through violence. To be sure, building walls and hiring guards were expensive, but many manufacturers found it preferable to locate behind city walls rather than in undefended rural areas. Our interpretation is that war increases the cost to capital in both cities and rural areas, but the rural increment is larger than the urban one. Although cities can protect capital, they are not as successful with labor because a disturbance of peace will hinder economic exchanges between city and countryside, further raising food prices.

In a region beset by threats of warfare, the entrepreneur decides where to locate according to a different set of relative prices, and thus a new critical level of capital per worker k_w^* decides what firms are urban or rural (see Box 4.1). Because war has made capital cheaper in cities than in the countryside, that threshold is lower than in the peaceful economy ($k_w^* < k^*$). Simply put, some industries, those with capital/labor ratios between k_w^* and k^*, are urban in the warring economy but rural in a peaceable economy. The industries remaining in the countryside during unsettled times are the least capital intensive of all.

Because China had few civil and international disturbances between the mid-fourteenth and the mid-nineteenth centuries, it gives us our baseline. All industries with $k < k^*$ are in the Chinese countryside. Because Europe had lots of war, only European industries with $k < k_w^*$ are rural. Because $k_w^* < k^*$, more industries in China locate in the countryside. Thus war produces the urban bias that characterizes Europe from the fall of the Roman Empire forward. If warfare is sufficiently severe, the bias will also be large. Although our model combines Leontief technology with war to explain differences in the location of manufacturing, it has limited implications for technological change. In such a technology, factor proportions are fixed (k, the capital per worker, describes the technology fully), and as a result, ratios of capital to labor in the same industry are identical in urban

Box 4.1. War and the location of manufacturing

Costs of production are $C = wL + rK$ if the entrepreneur hires L workers at wage W and K capital at cost r. The Leontief technology is linear, so the analysis can be carried out on a per worker basis. Costs are then $w + rk$, where k is capital per worker. As discussed in the text, wages are higher in cities, so $w_c > w_u$, where the subscript c denotes the countryside and u denotes urban areas. Capital costs are lower, so $r_c < r_u$. A manufacturer seeks the lowest-cost location. He compares $C_c = w_c + r_c k$ with $C_u = w_u + r_u k$. He picks the countryside if the fall in labor costs $(w_u - w_c)$ more than offsets the increased cost of capital $((r_c - r_u)k)$. This is equivalent to $k < (w_u - w_c)/(r_c - r_u)$. Let $k^* = (w_u - w_c)/(r_c - r_u)$. If capital per worker is less than k^*, then this manufacturer will operate in the countryside.

Denote the unit increment in rural capital costs due to war by Δ. Obviously, war raises costs everywhere, and cities' walls can protect both capital and labor. The model with fixed factor proportions considers the effects of war only on the relative price of capital thus understates the extent of the bias toward urban manufacturing. The rural capital cost in the warfare-prone economy will be $r_{cw} = r_c + \Delta$. Now the manufacturer who decides where to locate examines not $k < (w_u - w_c)/(r_c - r_u)$ but $k < (w_u - w_c)/(r_{cw} - r_u)$ or $k < (w_u - w_c)/(r_c + \Delta - r_u)$. This implies a threshold capital intensity of $k_w^* = (w_u - w_c)/(r_c + \Delta - r_u)$. Clearly, $k_w^* < k^*$.

and rural firms. If Europe's primary characteristic is that it is a warring economy, then relative to peaceful China it would be poorer and have less manufacturing over all.

The fixed-proportion production model is unfair to Europe because it does not allow entrepreneurs to substitute cheap factors for expensive ones, even though such substitutions are ubiquitous in reality. To return to the example of the weaver, it is in fact possible to employ more than one worker per loom (in particular, women and children as helpers), and it is also possible to have more or less capital per worker (because looms vary in quality). In each case the combination of labor and capital is different. The simplest class of production functions that allow such substitution have constant factor shares[1] (rather than proportions) and are known in economics as Cobb-Douglas production functions ($Q = K^a L^{1-a}$, where Q is output, K is capital, L is labor, and a is the factor share of capital). We will not carry out the mathematical analysis here, but the interested reader can find it in Box 4.2. Just as in the Leontief case, entrepreneurs locate their production on the basis of relative prices, and there is a unique factor share of capital a^* such that industries with larger capital-factor shares locate in cities and industries with lower capital intensity locate in the countryside. Similarly, the war economy has a smaller threshold factor share of capital a_w^* than the peaceful economy. So far, we have reproduced the substance of the lessons of the Leontief model. But Cobb-Douglas technologies allow us to go further. Indeed, when we allow for capital-labor substitution, more industries locate in cities in the warring economy. Box 4.2 provides the technical details, but the intuition for this result is that Cobb-Douglas technologies give firms two ways of mitigating the impact of war: choosing their location and adjusting their factor proportions.

The adjustment of factor proportions to urban locations is a general phenomenon. Any firm that locates in a city will operate with a higher ratio of capital to labor than if it had been in the countryside. Urban firms face cities' high labor costs and low capital costs, so they will want to substitute capital for labor. Thus when a firm locates in a city rather than in a

---

Box 4.2. War, manufacturing, and capital intensity

In Cobb-Douglas models, a, the factor share of capital plays the central role. It is a measure of the underlying capital intensity of the industry (if a is 1, then all expenses are made on capital, and if a is 0, then all expenses go to labor). If we look at entrepreneurs in a peaceful economy (labor is cheaper in the countryside, while capital is cheaper in cities), we again find a threshold value of a, a^*, such that industries with $a < a^*$ are in the countryside, and industries with $a > a^*$ are urban. We also find that industries with $a < a_w^*$ will be in the countryside in the war-torn economy, and $a_w^* < a^*$.

The first result follows by letting firms choose where to locate in the war-torn economy. If we then fix each industry's factor proportions to what they would be with rural relative prices, that determines a first threshold value ($a_w^{*\prime}$) for moving to cities. If we now allow firms to adjust their factor proportions when they move to cities, all those who already wanted to move to cities will still want to, and some who formerly did not will now want to; hence $a_w^* < a_w^{*\prime}$. The war-torn economy (Europe) has an even larger urban manufacturing sector than the peaceful economy (China) when factor proportions are adjusted to reflect relative prices than when they are not.

village, it uses more capital and less labor. In our model, because all firms in the same industry choose the same location, this pattern extends to the industry. Relative to the fixed-proportion model, the key difference is that industries pushed into cities by war become more capital intensive. If Europe is the war-torn economy, it has a more capital-intensive manufacturing sector than China because more of its manufacturing sector is imprisoned in cities by warfare. As we argue later, it was this capital bias that set Europe off on a different path toward machine-based innovation: urban manufacturers in Europe created more machines than their rural Chinese counterparts because they had more use for them.

The chain of causation in our model has two parts. The first is static and runs from war through relative prices and urban versus rural location and then to factor intensity. The second is more classic and dynamic; it runs from factor intensity to technological change, falling into the broad class of induced-innovation theories of technological change. The rest of this chapter defends the plausibility of this causal chain and, in particular, the static elements.

This defense is required because although our model is plausible, it is but one of many narratives of economic change one could construct. Moreover, the model's theoretical purpose is to produce the divergence we highlight. To do so, we need an appropriate friction in relative factor costs, and war is just one of the processes that can potentially produce such friction. Because there are many other differences between China and Europe, there are many candidates to act as friction, but we can eliminate all those that were of such long standing that they would have given a lead to Europe from the outset, because Europe was not always ahead of China economically. Similarly, we can set aside any friction that would have made it impossible for China to be ahead early on or to grow extremely rapidly later. Finally, sharp changes in Europe (such as the Glorious Revolution or the French Revolution) are of limited relevance because the process of technological divergence took centuries, not decades. We find that warfare has a singular advantage over other long-term factors: its intensity waxes and wanes, and if we are correct, the location of manufacturing in each region should reflect the ebb and flow of political disturbances—not just technology. The ebb and flow of warfare, in fact, turn out be just what we need to put our argument at risk of falsification.

Long-Term History before the Industrial Revolution

Here we focus on how war mattered to the location of manufacturing and its capital intensity, leaving its effect on technological change for the next section. Insecurity (to put war and civil violence in more neutral or euphemistic terms) is very costly. Indeed, as war costs increase and manufacturing shifts more and more to cities, the economy and the manufacturing sector also shrink because of the toll that warfare imposes. By implication, the economies of societies in which warfare is prevalent are smaller and have smaller manufacturing sectors. Thus up to the sixteenth century and perhaps beyond it, war should make Europe poor relative to China. For similar reasons China's manufacturing should be larger and more rural than Europe's after the Mongols reunified the empire in 1279. Conversely, in Europe, should the intensity of warfare decline, some manufacturing should move back to the countryside. Finally, should technology become more capital intensive, Chinese (and European) manufacturing should become more urban. In tracing the urban-rural competition for manufacturing location, we must explicitly deal with a comparison between China and Europe and a comparison between England (the cradle of industrialization) and the rest of the world. It would be particularly desirable for our model to have implications not just for the divergence between Europe and China but also for variations in the location of manufacturing within each region.

The accounts of early European travelers, as well as the flow of technology, suggest that early on, China was far more economically advanced than Europe, and that Europeans went to the Far East in search of manufactured goods, not raw materials or precious metals. That China was technologically ahead of Europe at the end of the first millennium A.D. is generally accepted in the literature and forms the core of the China puzzle—why an economy that was so advanced could fall progressively behind after 1300 (Elvin 1972). Could the connection between warfare and urbanization help explain this? In the mid-thirteenth century China's cities may have amounted to between 6% and 7.5% of the total population. The empire certainly had a number of very large cities. But by the nineteenth century a very small proportion of the population lived in walled cities, as little as 3%–5% of the total population (Skinner 1977a: 287, 1977b: 227). Over the same six centuries urbanization rates increased in Europe (de Vries 1984: chap. 2). But on its own, this contrast is insufficient. We must look more closely within the two regions.

Let us begin with a careful examination of urbanization and war in China. The Middle Kingdom certainly had its share of military troubles, for instance, in the mid-seventeenth century with the collapse of the Ming dynasty and the establishment of the Qing dynasty, and again during the mid-nineteenth century, when there were widespread peasant rebellions. But for most of the three centuries preceding the Ming-Qing transition, and for the two centuries before the mid-nineteenth-century rebellions, Chinese society was generally quite peaceful. Thus Chinese entrepreneurs did not usually need to anticipate that warfare would disrupt their production and distribution operations. They were spared the costs of warfare not only in the direct sense of having to pay taxes to support war-making initiatives, but also in the less obvious sense of not having to pay for protection from the threats of confiscation and destruction.

If we take a broader sweep of history, China's instances of political fragmentation show patterns of urban manufacturing similar to those of Europe. Recall that before its unification under the Qin dynasty in 221 B.C., China was the theater of severe political competition for more than two centuries. During this time China was divided into seven major warring states, each anchored around great cities that hosted both commercial and manufacturing activities. Rulers minted coins to facilitate trade, which they taxed in order to mobilize resources to pay for warfare. They expanded agricultural output through irrigation and improved iron tools in order to feed the cities that housed their governments and urban craftsmen. We lack adequate information on urban and rural locations of craft industries for the first twelve centuries of imperial rule that began with the Qin dynasty. The long stretches of political division and military competition between the periods of imperial integration and grandeur account for more than 40% of the entire period. It is therefore not likely that rural manufacturing enjoyed the kinds of advantages it had starting in the late fourteenth century. We do know that the commercial expansion of the Song dynasty (960–1279) was powered by a combination of improvements in agriculture, transportation technologies, and urban-centered craft production (Shiba 1970). This was also an era of great political insecurity for the regime, forcing a move in the early twelfth century from the north to Hangzhou, which became a great center of manufacturing and wealth (Gernet 1962). Thus through the fourteenth century it is likely that competition between rural and urban manufacturing was intense in China. By the fifteenth century, rural handicrafts began to play an increasingly important role in manufacturing. A clear contrast of relative peace in China and frequent warfare in Europe comes to characterize the early modern era at the two ends of Eurasia.

Although internal and international violence was less prevalent in China than in Europe, even a casual glance at early modern renderings of Chinese cities would convince skeptics that they were walled and gated. But relative to Europe, the number of such cities was limited, as was the size of their fortifications. Indeed, late imperial officials seem to have perceived investments in urban walls to demonstrate symbolic power more than to protect urban capital from physical attack (Fei 2009: 76–123). For their part, most people appear to have felt little need to locate within the confines of a walled city, because some 95% of the population lived in rural areas and some 97% lived outside walled cities as late as 1843 (Skinner 1977a: 287, 1977b: 227). Chinese with capital did not seek out cities to protect their investments in the same way in which Europeans did because of the threat of warfare. Instead, for most Chinese dynasties the threat of warfare came from the steppes; armies were routinely deployed along the northern frontier. In both early and late imperial times the fortifications collectively known as the Great Wall symbolized the state's commitment to assuring peace from foreign marauders and invaders for the whole of the empire—town and country alike. Before the tenth-century shift of China's population toward the south, what little industry existed seems to have had more urban locations, perhaps in part because the northern locations of industry made them more vulnerable to foreign military threats.

Within the empire, especially after 1000, domestic social order did not usually entail large investments in fortifications. Chinese officials pursued a variety of normative, material, and coercive strategies to promote and enforce both rural and urban social order (Wong 1997: 105–126). When growing numbers of bandits and rebels threatened domestic social order in the second half of the nineteenth century, increasing numbers of villages and towns built walled fortifications. In other words, the Chinese had no culturally based opposition to military defenses. Their response to insecurity was indeed very similar to that of Europeans in the waning days of the Roman Empire. They built fortifications when and where they deemed defense works desirable. For the vast bulk of the population across the empire between 1000 and 1800, city walls simply were not necessary for the pursuit of economic activities, including manufacturing.

Artisans in the late imperial empire chose to remain in villages with little or no defense. Doing so certainly did not prevent the rise of dense networks of markets for inputs and outputs. In fact, it appears that such markets were central to the functioning of Chinese handicrafts (Elvin 1973). It is also not the case that there was no manufacturing in cities whatsoever, for jewelry, silk, and other luxury products seem to have been urban activities. In the lower Yangtze region cycles of commercial expansion after 1000 created a sophisticated marketing network and considerable amounts of manufacturing, especially in cotton and silk textiles. The growth of handicraft production was largely a rural phenomenon. Goods were produced by agrarian households that also engaged in agriculture or by rural households that specialized in craft activities. Cities and towns marketed more craft goods with a rural origin than goods of urban origin (Elvin 1973: 268–284; Nishijima 1984; Tanaka 1984). As a consequence, increased manufacturing did not lead to a corresponding increase in urbanization.

The rural bias of craft manufactures does not mean that Chinese entrepreneurs disregarded urban technologies when clear advantages accompanied their use. Indeed, after the Industrial Revolution's technologies had diffused to East Asia, the Chinese predilection for rural manufacturing waned. Neither then nor in China's earlier history can we find evidence for cultural or political hindrances to locating enterprises in cities when new institutions and technologies made urban-based production more profitable. The growth of urban-based manufacturing in Shanghai during the first four decades of the twentieth century makes abundantly clear that certain areas of the country did shift from rural manufacturing to urban production. But in China, as in Europe, these developments were unanticipated—in 1500, much less in 1000, no one knew that mechanization would succeed. There were no reasons to create large industrial centers in China before the nineteenth century. Furthermore, as in continental Europe, rural manufacturing remained competitive, especially in labor-intensive activities and where entrepreneurs could respond to urban innovations. A good example of this phenomenon comes from the northern cotton-textile-producing county of Gaoyang, where rural weavers purchased iron-gear looms to install in their homes (Grove 2006).

In Europe the relationship between urban manufacturing and war is complex. At first glance, one might even think that the dominant chain of causation involves war causing destruction of both cities and manufacturing. After all, the Roman Empire was based on cities. In Gaul, Britain, and

Germania new cities grew under the imperial peace. These cities collapsed and many disappeared during the Great Invasions. The revival of urbanization in the Middle Ages was slow, in particular in northern Europe. It was during this revival that the pattern of urban, capital-intensive manufacturing became an integral part of the European economy. By the Renaissance the most urbanized areas of Europe were also those where conflict had raged most often: the band of territories from Flanders to Rome, including the Burgundian estates, western Germany, and northern Italy.

From Charlemagne onward, as cities slowly reemerged, rulers focused on providing security for skilled artisans. Continued strife, however, made rural manufacturing a risky proposition in Europe and thereby drove a larger range of manufacturing activities into cities where protection was available. In contrast, the countryside was open terrain for provisioning, thievery, and wanton destruction. J. R. Hale leaves little doubt that "in terms of personal impact the burdens of wars certainly afflicted the rural more than the urban population" (Hale 1985: 196). Although the images of towns sacked by conquering armies have a great hold on our imagination, we must bear in mind that all military campaigns ravaged the countryside, whether or not they succeeded in capturing cities. Evidence is abundant that in Europe the countryside was ravaged by warfare and that cities were relatively spared (Gutmann 1980). Although Parisians may have thanked Saint Geneviève for protecting them from Attila, it is more likely that the city was able to repulse invaders because of its walls. Paris maintained its walls, and they would also defeat the Vikings, Joan of Arc, and Henry IV.

The history of such Italian cities as Siena and Padua highlights the value of urban residence in times of conflict from the late Middle Ages to the Renaissance (Caferro 1998; Kohl 1998). Padua faced both civil war and the threat of outside invasion; Siena had to defend itself from the attacks of Florence and the raids of mercenary companies. In both cases strife devastated the countryside but typically spared the city (Siena was never conquered, and Padua fell only twice in 100 years of conflict). Each invading army seized whatever it could find in the fields and the villages. Historians have noted the deleterious effects of such raiding on agriculture because little could be done to protect farmland. In areas such as Italy, even villages were fortified in fear of localized raids, but walls that were not supplemented by a large body of soldiers did not afford much protection against a determined foe.

The siege warfare that prevailed in Flanders and the Low Countries more generally from the Hundred Years' War until the peace of Utrecht in 1713 also points to war's differential treatment of town and country. What made the sack of Antwerp in 1685 so surprising was that the Spanish armies visited the kind of destruction on an urban population that they and their foes normally imposed on peasants, but this was certainly not the first instance in that conflict of armies taking civilians' property. From the point of view of merchants, the sack itself was not a signal to give up trade or to set up in the countryside but rather to seek a new, safer location in the northern Netherlands (Gelderblom 2000). That location, Amsterdam, quickly became the largest city in the region. In manufacturing the movement was less concentrated, but what the southern Netherlands lost was gained by Dutch cities (de Vries and van der Woude 1997: 279–334).

The opposing forces of war acting to reduce the scale of the economy and of war pushing manufacturing to cities have made tracing the interaction between warfare and manufacturing difficult. In particular, Acemoglu, Johnson, and Robinson (2005) find no relationship between war and the growth of cities. That negative result provides support for the kind of balance our argument favors. Had cities provided superb protection or been systematically destroyed, one would have found either a clear positive or negative relationship. We are interested in a more subtle and slow-moving effect: how war reorganizes the supply of manufactured commodities. This process may well not affect the scale of cities.

If the general pattern of warfare and urbanization holds in Europe, Britain presents something of an anomaly. This anomaly is one that we must consider because, after all, that is where the Industrial Revolution occurred. With the departure of the Roman legions in 407, cities collapsed and did not reemerge for a long time. The Saxon period, as well as the two centuries when the Danelaw was in effect, could hardly be called peaceful. Although the Norman Conquest may have been the last successful invasion of England up to 1688, the throne of England was hotly contested (including landings from Normandy) throughout the Tudor period. Moreover, the borderlands to the north were subject to Scottish raids well into the seventeenth century. During this time England appears to have been a heavily rural frontier of Europe (de Vries 1984). It was not until the Tudors that English cities, particularly London, began to grow. Even then, as Wrigley has pointed out, urban centers were few and small (Wrigley 1985). They were largely administrative and commercial centers. Urban craft industries, by contrast, remained undeveloped because England was an economic periphery whose main export was wool. London's rise as the largest city in Europe can hardly be attributed to insecurity in England because there was little of it after 1600. In a country that was protected from its enemies by a fleet rather than a standing army, manufacturing did not have to locate behind city walls. The singular genius of the British navy may well have been its capacity to afford equal protection to city and countryside, thus destroying the long-standing advantages of cities. Therefore, London did not afford better protection from war than other towns or locations in Britain. Not surprisingly, much of the early growth of manufacturing in England was carried out in the north, an area favored by endowments of coal and where wages were lower than in London. The pacification of England did not set off urban industrialization but rather a dash for cheap labor. As many have pointed out, the early growth of manufacturing in England was as much a rural as an urban phenomenon. But by the mid-seventeenth century the technological impact of centuries of urban manufacturing was already large, and England's rural population was too small to alter the path of technological change.

Beyond England there is abundant evidence that in Europe the location of manufacturing was indeed a set of marginal decisions that varied over time. The key drivers of such change were the evolution of technology, changes in ratios of capital to labor, and changes in military technology. As a result, the history of manufacturing location is one that is different across the different polities of Europe. Before we review variations in manufacturing location across Europe, let us be clear that we are not claiming to explain Europe's urbanization processes generally. Cities grew for reasons beyond those of manufacturing; in particular, port cities grew in the early modern era as trade expanded. We are interested specifically in why manufacturing tended to move into cities in Europe more than it did in China.

Let us begin with the Low Countries. Although van der Wee does not detail the effects of the wars that ravaged that area from the Renaissance to the 1720s, he does identify urban and rural activities (1988). Three points are worth emphasizing: First, over time, urban activities tended to become rural as entrepreneurs made every effort to find methods of producing goods with fewer skills and less capital. New industries were therefore urban, but as they matured, they tended to become rural. Thus before the Industrial Revolution the urban nature of manufacturing was not a foregone conclusion. Second, in the absence of any urban response we would anticipate a fully rural manufacturing sector, and in some periods there were real declines in urban manufacturing. At other times urban workers reoriented their activities toward higher-quality goods (implicitly higher skill and higher capital). Third, during the period of the Dutch revolt, "the armies ravaged the countryside, occupying and sometimes plundering the towns and disrupting communications. For *reasons of security* and in order to have easier access to raw materials and markets, many rural industrial workers migrated to the neighboring towns" (van der Wee 1988: 347–348; emphasis added). This last point emphasizes both the negative impact of war (town and country suffer) and its differential effect (people seek refuge in towns).

In the northern Low Countries the spread of putting-out industries seems to have followed the vagaries of warfare. De Vries and van der Woude document the spread of rural manufacture in Holland after 1720. They view the near doubling of the proportion of nonagricultural households as a result of population pressure, but we think that the timing, after the end of the wars of Louis XIV, when the Low Countries had been under constant threat of invasion, is telling (de Vries and van der Woude 1997: 55–57). After peace "broke out" in the Low Countries, entrepreneurs could more easily rely on a cheaper rural labor force than in the uncertain times of the late sixteenth and early seventeenth centuries. The pattern we see both in the southern and in the northern Low Countries is not the inevitable march of manufacturing toward capital-intensive urban production. Rather, we observe a secular competition between two modes of craft production, one rural with low wages and low capital, the other urban with high wages and more capital intensive.

The same story can also be told for England. Although it may have been the cradle of the Industrial Revolution, it was first an area of widespread putting-out. Putting-out was an economic system whereby urban merchants advanced rural craftspeople raw materials and in return bought their output at a prespecified price. Rural crafts grew rapidly during the long period of internal peace that followed the end of the Civil War in 1651. Further, as shown by Berg (1994), the putting-out industry remained a strong competitor to urban, centralized manufacturing. In the case of textiles, at least part of the expansion of industrial manufacturing was a rural expansion, driven by the search for cheap waterpower and cheap labor. The long period of internal peace that began with the Restoration (1660) and of institutional stability that followed the Glorious Revolution (1688) reduced cities' security advantages so that the competition between urban and rural manufactures was quite fierce between 1730 and 1830. The first response was the rise of the putting-out industries. Later in the eighteenth century a similar phenomenon seems to have taken place in the Low Countries (Gutmann 1980: chap. 3) and France (Vardi 1993).

For many, the spread of putting-out industries in northwestern Europe was a precursor to industrialization. In fact, scholars have dubbed it protoindustrialization. From the technological point of view, however, putting-out was an altogether different path than the industrialization that followed. Putting-out relied on the spatial division of labor to produce large quantities of goods of moderate quality. The organizational innovations that allowed the putting-out industries to flourish were inherently labor, rather than capital, using and thus followed a path that was quite different from those that characterized the Industrial Revolution. Contrary to those who see protoindustrialization as a step toward modern manufacturing, in the light of our model, putting-out was making Europe more like China, not less so. Moreover, the Chinese evidence argues against any notion that sophisticated rural manufacturing networks (protoindustrialization) were critical precursors to sustained growth. Both China and Europe had a significant labor force in rural manufacturing, but only one region went on to develop industrial technologies (Wong 1997: 33–52).

The historical evidence strongly supports both the assumptions and the implication of our model: warfare mattered and made European manufacturing more urban. The effects of violence depended on its intensity, on technology, and on the urbanization of manufacturing. Thus although over the long term they pushed entrepreneurs into cities, these effects could easily be reversed. In the secular interplay between warfare and manufacturing a surprisingly subtle rule emerges: too much violence (as during the Great Invasions, the Thirty Years' War, and other brutal conflicts), and manufacturing collapses; too little violence, and manufacturing runs to the countryside.

Long-Term History through the Industrial Revolution

We must now move from asking how entrepreneurs adjusted to changes in violence to investigating the consequences of these adjustments for the path of technological change. So far, to keep the analysis simple, we have developed a model that is static; it takes technology in each industry as given and allows entrepreneurs to choose their input mix (how much capital per worker) and where their shop or factory operates. Now we turn to the consequences of choices of location for technological change. To do this, we borrow from the literature on induced innovation that has derived how factor scarcity might affect the pace and direction of technological change (Allen 2009a; Habbakuk 1962).

The argument is simple: where labor is relatively cheap (in our case, in the countryside), entrepreneurs will prefer to adopt new technologies that are labor using rather than labor saving. Thus the demand for new technologies that increase or decrease capital per worker depends on relative prices. To be sure, entrepreneurs are happy to adopt any input-saving technologies, but the relative demand will be greater for new technologies that accord with relative prices.

The relative demands for different technologies translate into technological change through one of two mechanisms. The first is learning by doing: in an industry that is capital intensive, entrepreneurs are more likely to discover new processes that improve the productivity of capital than that of labor. The second is conscious directed change: investments in research and development that lead to new machines are more likely to be undertaken where the price of capital is low relative to that of labor. That is not to say that in the process of industrialization there were no labor-using innovations; rather, in Europe a larger fraction of all innovations was associated with capital deepening than in China.

These two pathways are reinforced by external economies. Indeed, in economies in which the bulk of manufacturing relies on little capital, there are few capital-intensive industries from which entrepreneurs in other activities can learn about the value of machines. There will also be fewer skilled workers who can build equipment and deploy a varied set of solutions for adopting capital-using methods in a particular industry. On the other hand, in the same economy there are many industries that manufacturers can observe to develop labor-using improvements in their firms.

Many scholars have noted the importance of factor costs in inducing technological change. Kenneth Sokoloff's work on a radically different distortion—agricultural seasonality—is particularly relevant because of its spatial dimension. Sokoloff emphasized the importance of firms' incentives to adopt and create capital goods (Sokoloff and Dollar 1997; Sokoloff and Tchakerian 1997). He argued that the need to bring in the harvest created seasonality in rural wages as workers were drawn out of other activities to work on farms for a few weeks in the summer. Firms could either raise wages or shut down for one or two months. Where seasonality was intense, firms had little choice but to shut down. In turn, they avoided deploying costly machinery that would lie idle for part of the year. Seasonality in his framework increases the cost of capital in the countryside exactly as war does in our model. Because Sokoloff was primarily interested in the contrast between the U.S. and the British economies, he did not emphasize urban-rural issues, but other scholars (e.g., Postel-Vinay 1994; Magnac and Postel-Vinay 1997; van der Wee 1988) have done so and have noted the lower capital levels of rural firms even at the end of the nineteenth century and their close connection with the variation in rural wages over the months of the year. Sokoloff concluded that the United States deployed more machinery in manufacturing early on than England precisely because agriculture was less seasonal in America than in Britain.

More recently Robert Allen (2007) has put forth the argument that relative prices played a fundamental role in the development of the key machines of the Industrial Revolution. Only where capital costs were particularly low and wages high did it pay to invent machinery that would increase capital intensity several times over. These conditions, he argues, prevailed in England after 1650 or so but nowhere else. Allen demonstrates that after 1650 wages in England (and particularly in London) were the highest in Europe. Conversely, the cost of energy was remarkably low after 1700 because the English were reaping the rewards of several centuries of technological adaptation that transformed coal from a dangerous product into one that could be easily used for home heating and in manufacturing. Although differences in capital costs may have been less, they too favored England. Allen concludes that by 1700 the rewards for adopting mechanized technologies were highest in England, and that is why they were developed there.

Our question does not involve the path of technological change during industrialization, or why the key inventions were developed in England rather than some other part of Europe. Instead we consider the reasons why the structure of manufacturing was so different between Europe and China. In our view, differences in levels of warfare produced differences in relative prices, and the location of manufacturing. The structure of manufacturing then reinforced war's effects on relative prices. War's concentration of manufacturing behind city walls produced a series of biases that raised the cost of labor, in particular, unskilled labor, and in the long run lowered the cost of capital by making capital markets more efficient. These relative prices induced individuals to seek to substitute capital for labor. In turn, urban entrepreneurs provided a steady demand for specialized tools and later for machines. Thus cities' higher capital intensity was an important source of demand for machinery and provided incentives to make more machines. In the countryside these incentives did not exist.

Before 1400 the relatively high cost of capital throughout the world, combined with the limited supply of skilled artisans, made the path of innovation daunting because the machines many inventors imagined simply could not be built. In contrast, innovation achieved by transforming a production method from using skilled labor to less skilled labor and moving it to the countryside promised considerable savings (this dynamic remains an important element of economic activity to this day, as the migration of world manufacturing to China demonstrates). No one in China or Europe could forecast in 1400 the tremendous success humans have had at creating capital-using technologies. Thus the Chinese path of rural handicrafts is eminently reasonable, and it should be no surprise to see that much of Europe's manufacturing followed the same path. As we have seen, for a long time Europeans were attracted to low-wage/labor-intensive manufacturing; after all, the putting-out system is nothing more than outsourcing beyond city walls. Hence China's technological path is a very common process in economic growth; the deviation was that of Europe.

Again, the development of European manufacturing highlights the intensity and length of the competition between the two approaches. The best evidence for this comes from French industrial surveys carried out in the middle of the nineteenth century. At that time seasonal manufacturing was so widespread that the agents of the French Ministry of Industry gathered data about the phenomenon (Postel-Vinay 1994; Magnac and Postel-Vinay 1997). Here two facts stand out. First, urban manufacturers faced intense competition from rural firms. That competition endured into the twentieth century, particularly in labor-intensive product lines. Nevertheless, capital/labor ratios of rural enterprises were significantly lower than those of urban firms. Within France the regions where the seasonal variation in agricultural wages was largest had the highest share of rural industrial firms that shut down during summer months. It was also in those areas that capital/labor ratios were smallest. Over time, France saw a coevolution of agriculture and manufacturing as increased specialization in wheat in the eastern and central regions encouraged seasonal manufacturing to locate there, while in the west specialization in livestock did not provide many part-time industrial workers. Only when harvest tasks for France's very large grain production were mechanized could labor move into permanent industrial employment.

The second fact that stands out from the French data is that the rise of rural manufacturing antedated the advent of severe seasonality in agriculture. In the eighteenth century such seasonal labor migration was small and strictly local because local agriculture was quite diversified. Rural manufacturing may have begun to spread under Louis XIV. Such an early start suggests that for a large country like France, the location of manufacturing was more sensitive to internal disorder than to war. Indeed, the Sun King came to power after the last major revolt, the Fronde, had been put down, but wars with other countries raged almost continuously from 1620 to 1713. Those wars were mostly not on French soil, and internal peace was largely maintained until the Revolution. Interestingly, the number of rural weavers in northeastern France seems to have grown significantly as early as the 1690s, even though their expansion did not come into full bloom until after the Treaty of Utrecht (Vardi 1993).

Warfare thus proved to be a valuable irritant for economic progress. By changing the share of crafts that located behind city walls, war encouraged the adoption of production techniques that were friendly to further machine improvement. Cities also attracted skilled artisans capable of making parts accurate enough to avoid the crippling burden of friction (Landes 1983). For most of European history the center of these developments lay in the Continent. It began in Italy and over six centuries spread through parts of Germany and the Low Countries before coming into full bloom in England as the Industrial Revolution. To examine the conditions that prevailed in England after 1700 alone requires us to assume that the growth of skills and technological change that occurred before was somehow different. Only those who are terminally Anglophile would suppose that the forces behind improved waterwheels, the printing press, the pistol, or the knitting frame are somehow different from those that led to the spinning jenny or the steam engine. The key difference between these later developments and those that occurred earlier was economic value: the demand for cotton textiles or motive power is simply massively larger than that for pistols or woolens (Clark 2007). Although the magnitude of demand for coke or cotton textiles explains the visible success of the new technologies, it masks the fact that they developed in ways that were very similar to the development of older, less economically rewarding technologies.

The technological breakthroughs of the Industrial Revolution are but one step in a long process that was far more European than it was English. Thus the study of England will allow us to answer some important questions: for instance, why was it that technological leadership moved to England after 1650? But such a narrow inquiry will lead us astray in considering why Europeans discovered the importance of machines. In our view, the narrower question has largely been answered by Allen (2009a). As Allen has argued, the relative price context goes a long way toward explaining the specifics of the miraculous inventions of the Industrial Revolution. But high English wages in 1650 do not seem likely to explain structural changes whose most intensive locus varied over time and that began in Italy in the late Middle Ages.

We think that Allen's analysis of the sources of high English wages indicates politics and warfare as major forces explaining capital-intensive technological changes. Two key elements in his account, the rise of the new draperies (a more versatile and lighter wool fabric) and the massive expansion of English trade, were in fact the result of political change. The rise of the new draperies in England did depend on a series of technological changes (which moved from carded to combed wool to produce a lighter fabric), but one wonders why this industry grew up in a land-abundant, labor-scarce economy that before this period exported most of its commercialized wool to the Low Countries. Given that the Low Countries were the dominant producers of woolens and had all the infrastructure to weave and finish cloth, one would have expected the new technologies to be deployed there rather than in England. But as John Munro has observed, an English industry arose because wars interfered with the market. On the one hand, wars on the Continent tended to reduce the demand for English wool while at the same time reducing the supply of high-quality textiles in Britain. The Crown had long relied on taxing English wool exports, in effect protecting English artisans (Munro 2005). Finally, the move of artisans from the Low Countries and northern France to England in the late sixteenth century is likely to have been spurred by the instability provoked by the Dutch revolt and the French Wars of Religion. Had England and the Low Countries been in the same polity (as would have been the case in a China-like empire), the rise of the new draperies in England would have been unlikely at the very least.

The second key element of Allen's explanation is the capture of an ever-increasing share of international commerce by the English commercial fleet. But the economic logic of London becoming Europe's entrepôt seems far fetched because any goods unloaded there would have to be reloaded onto a ship to cross the Channel. Amsterdam would seem better located. Of course, the competition between Amsterdam and London was not simply economic but also political. That there were two Anglo-Dutch wars precisely at the time at which London forged ahead is not mere coincidence. That Rotterdam rather than London emerged as the largest port in Europe after World War II is simply further testimony to the distorting impacts of political competition on the economics of geography. Rotterdam (like its forebears Antwerp and Amsterdam) is simply much better situated to serve the European hinterland than London. It is not a great surprise that the city on the Thames declined as a transshipment point once the Royal Navy lost its relevance.

In fact, one would do well to ponder just how long high English wages would have persisted if politics had not made it difficult for English entrepreneurs to locate their enterprises on the Continent rather than in northern England. It is not much farther from London to Mons in Belgium or Maubeuge in France than it is from the same city to Manchester or York. It seems doubtful that English entrepreneurs would have deployed their textile devices in high-wage northern England rather than in the cheaper continental settings had they had that option. Even more likely, they would have avoided the costs of developing such devices if they could have relied on the cheaper wages that prevailed on the Continent. Such traitorous outsourcing was precluded by politics.

Just as one should not take the English pattern of technological change in the eighteenth century out of its longer, European context, one should be wary of lessons learned by restricting the comparison of political systems to China and Europe exclusively. Although there is no doubt that political competition altered the location of manufacturing in Europe, it is also abundantly clear that reaping the benefits of this alteration was difficult. In most times and in most places, the destruction brought about by war simply outweighed the positive benefits from either war's relative price implications or government spending on technology. A glance around the globe will find many places beyond Europe where political fragmentation endured and warfare was endemic. Southeast Asia, Mesoamerica, and Africa between 500 and 1500 all come to mind. Yet by 1500, when European contact occurred, none had embarked on the transformative process that would produce the Industrial Revolution. On the contrary, although they were abundantly endowed with valuable resources, most of these territories were relatively poor. For Southeast Asia, at least, the evidence is consistent with the notion that when warfare occurred, it was very intense and very destructive of both persons and private capital—much like the periods Europeans know as the Dark Ages (Andaya 1999, Taylor 1999). We should also bear in mind that the expansions centered in Italy and the Low Countries were brought to a halt by warfare and that the Thirty Years' War so devastated Germany that its economy spent much of the next century and a half in recovery. We conjecture that further research may make more precise just what kind of political competition is tolerable if one seeks to produce economic change.

Coda: China and Europe Diverging Greatly

The model of economic change analyzed in this chapter is not the first to argue that political economy is essential to understanding why the structures of the European economy departed from those of China starting in the Middle Ages. Many authors (Deng 1993; Mokyr 2002; Diamond 1997; E. L. Jones 1981; Landes 1998) favor Europe because political competition there avoided costly and abrupt policy reversals, such as those that occurred under the Ming. They also put politics before economics. Our conclusions are starkly different: political competition, unlike economic competition, is no panacea; the benefits of warfare were indirect, contingent, and secured at tremendous cost.

The narrative we construct from the model has several advantages over traditional narratives. Because it is based on a very small number of parameters, investigating whether its assumptions are reasonable and its implications are consistent with the historical record is easy. For instance, if the cost of capital in cities and in the countryside were the same, we would have been hard pressed to maintain the argument. But as we have seen, such cost differences did exist, and war exacerbated them.

From a dramatic narrative point of view our approach has severe drawbacks. It fails, for example, to point to specific actors as responsible for failure or success: neither culture nor politicians are responsible for China not taking the path toward mechanical innovation. Indeed, in our view China failed to do so because its entrepreneurs had no reason to forgo the advantages of handicraft labor in the countryside. Similarly, Europeans can take little credit for the countless discoveries that led up to the Industrial Revolution. Ours is a tale without heroes or villains, in which the unintended consequences of political conflict are what matter most. A second drawback of our narrative from a dramatic point of view is that it is not deterministic. War made it more likely both that Europe would be poor (if war was too destructive) and that it would embark on the path toward capital deepening earlier than China. In contrast, China was more likely to remain an agrarian handicraft economy but less likely to experience the Dark Ages or the devastation that followed the Hundred Years' War, for instance. As Needham (1954–2008, vol. VII part 2) and many others have shown, technology was far from static in China, and it may well have been that given another several hundred years or so, machine invention would have sprouted there too. From our point of view, the political economies of the far ends of Eurasia made it significantly more likely that such processes would emerge at the western end of the landmass than at its eastern end.

What makes for poor drama, though, might actually make for good economic history. Indeed, it would be remarkably unjust to expect Chinese governments of the early Qing to implement policies promoting a kind of economic change that Adam Smith, the foremost economist of the eighteenth century, did not even perceive. *The Wealth of Nations* is not an ode to the Workshop of the World; it is far more an apology for light taxes and unfettered trade in an agrarian economy. Those are precisely the policies pursued by the Qing emperor. They were not those of European rulers because the fiscal requirements of war interfered with trade, an issue we will take up in Chapter 6.

If removing lead actors makes sense, so does accepting contingency. This would be true not just for us but also for authors who advocate the importance of endowments (Pomeranz 2000; E. L. Jones 1981) or culture (Landes 1998). Consider culture. The same social norms, religion, and ideas that first made China the most advanced economy by 1300 and then held China back before 1900 must be permitting its growth since Deng-era policies undid so much of what the Mao-led government had created. How can a culturally deterministic approach account for all this change?

This chapter has linked political economy with relative prices over the very long term. There are other accounts of the impact of politics on relative prices that also focus on the long term. Unlike our framework, which emphasizes differences in relative prices within a particular geographic area, these tend to focus on differences in relative prices across regions. The most eloquent exponent of these arguments has been North (North 1981; North and Weingast 1989). In his view capital costs were lower in certain parts of Europe than elsewhere on the Continent and the globe because political arrangements like representative government reduced the risk of expropriation. The idea that growth was precluded in China by the cost of capital has such a long lineage and its interaction with political economy runs so deep that we devote the next chapter to this problem.

5

Credit Markets and Economic Change

By 1700, as we saw in Chapter 4, the seeds of a capital-intensive, machine-using economy were sprouting in Europe. Although this new sector remained small through the eighteenth century, it was growing, most notably in England. For the next 150 years China, unlike North America or the European continent, made little effort either to adopt or to develop capital-intensive methods of production. By the eighteenth century divergence had clearly set in and would grow for a long time. Some readers may be willing to grant that differences in political structure played some role in moving Europe toward machines and keeping China focused on its rural labor, but more would invoke differences in capital markets to explain both the divergence and its persistence. As we shall see, although there were and remain important differences in financial institutions between the two regions, there is little evidence that credit-market failures were responsible for the path of the Chinese economy.

This thesis may strike the reader as folly. After all, China has been either unwilling or unable to develop financial institutions that resemble those of the West (e.g., banks and equity and bond markets), and the Chinese approach to financial institutions has often been invoked to explain the Middle Kingdom's failure to sustain the catch-up process in the waning days of the Qing dynasty or in the Republican period. Regarding more recent history, some scholars have laid the blame for the failure of the command economy under Mao on centralized capital allocation and the consequent inability of anyone to discipline firms. Since the reform period Westerners have forecast the collapse of the growth process because of looming financial problems several times. In contrast, Europe's early affection for such institutions provided an infrastructure that was critical to the spread of the new technologies. Hence even if capital markets were not responsible for the onset of divergence, their abundance in the West and their scarcity in the East mattered beyond divergence. A careful look at these arguments will help us focus our inquiry.

Economic historians, most recently Robert Allen, argue that differences in the cost of capital were important in understanding the location of innovative activity within Europe. As many have noted, by the 1750s England had the most developed financial system in Europe. Financial economists and economic historians have long argued that differences in financial institutions imply differences in the cost of capital. To understand the evolution of China and Europe before the nineteenth century, we must consider three possibilities. The first is that the cost of capital was lower in Europe because of the early development of a specific set of financial institutions whose ideal manifestation flowered in England after 1700. The second possibility is that capital costs were lower in Europe than in China because the region as a whole had developed a cornucopia of financial institutions, starting in the Middle Ages, that lowered the cost of securing investment resources. The third is that the cost of capital depended simply on the high rate of savings in Europe. In each case the cost of investment resources would be low enough in Europe that it would pay to deploy labor-saving/capital-using technologies. The institutions that affect the formation of capital thus represent the primary alternative to our political economy thesis in explaining both the rise of the divergence between China and Europe and its persistence.

Of course, it could also be that the cost of capital was rather similar in the two world regions. Certainly China's ancient and extensive water-control projects are consistent with a long-standing willingness to make and sustain long-term investments. Moreover, one should bear in mind the past thirty years' record of massive rates of investment and savings in China—a period during which Chinese financial markets have certainly not taken a form that Westerners recognize as their own (Brandt and Rawski 2008: chaps. 1 and 14). These kinds of facts serve as warnings to anyone who would accept the capital-cost thesis without careful inquiry.

At this stage of research, our knowledge of the institutions governing capital in Qing China is at best embryonic. This is in part because until recently, scholars seem to have been content to document that China either lacked some specific Western institution or that it failed to deploy such institutions efficiently and speedily once they became available for adoption from abroad (e.g., Ma 2006; Goetzmann and Koll 2006). But new evidence about Chinese methods of capital formation has come to light when scholars have been willing to look closely at firm-level financing. Nowadays, as we shall see later, scholars are looking far more broadly than before. In this chapter we will review that evidence and suggest that the capital-cost thesis lacks much basis in fact. We will begin by examining the cost of capital, including what seems to be damning evidence against China. The key, we argue, is to compare the same kinds of transactions across regions because the rates we observe involve costs to borrowers rather than returns to lenders. We examine the diversity of credit-market institutions in Europe to show that they responded to changes in the demand for capital. We then turn to China to show that similar patterns held there as well. In particular, the second half of the nineteenth century saw the rise of a variety of credit institutions. Having considered supply, we turn to demand to show that, consistent with Chapter 2, we expect demand for credit transactions to be lower in China than in Europe and the borrowers to be systematically more risky. We then return to political economy because one major source of credit demand in Europe was public agencies (sovereigns, sovereign bodies, and other public institutions), but in China such organizations played virtually no role in credit markets until the mid-nineteenth century. We look both at the positive benefits of government demand and at its costs. Government borrowing was costly because sovereigns were risky borrowers and spent the resources they received on war. In closing, we return to a broader set of questions and suggest that absent political constraints, growth drives capital deepening rather than the other way around.

Credit Markets and the Price of Capital

According to most accounts, interest rates in Europe were high in the Middle Ages, when credit markets were small. Over the long term European credit markets grew, and interest rates fell. The best evidence comes from very long-term mortgages variously known as rentes, renten, rent charges, or perpetual annuities (Schnapper 1957; Epstein 2000; Clark 2007; van Zanden 2007). The decline that we can chart from the Black Death onward led to a rough halving in the interest charge on long-term annuities (from about 10% to 5% per year or less). This trend began long before Europe industrialized and continued into the nineteenth century, when mortgages could be had for as low as 4% and for terms of more than a half century.

There are few data on interest rates from the late imperial era in China; historians of China often refer to conditions in the early twentieth century to make more general claims. In this era pawnshops and moneylenders typically charged between 2% and 4% a month, although examples of far higher rates have also been noted. The absence of cheaper credit was cited by R. H. Tawney in the 1930s as a major cause of indebtedness and the ruin of peasant families (Tawney 1966: 58–63). More recently, Philip Huang has echoed earlier concerns about high interest rates, saying that peasants engaged in borrowing to ensure survival and thus tolerated far higher rates of interest than any capitalist would. He further suggests that modern enterprises paid higher rates of interest because of the situation prevailing in the countryside of both northern China and Jiangnan (P. Huang 1985: 189–190, 301; 1990: 108–110). Rates of 2% to 4% a month made borrowing money extremely expensive, some ten to twenty times higher than the costs of credit at the same time in Europe. If these rates held throughout the economy and over time, then the conclusion is inescapable: China was starved of capital, and as a result, the path taken by Europe was closed.

But one should not accept these conclusions at face value. In a market without transaction costs, the price paid by any buyer is the same as the per unit income of any seller. But, as we know, there are no such markets, and what a farmer earns for a pound of rice is a far cry from what we pay for it. Credit is no different. There are transaction costs, and they matter. Consider first what we might learn from the data just cited if there were no transaction costs (in this context that would mean no asymmetry of information and no differences in default rates across borrowers, and that competition prevails). Then from the demand side we know that the price of capital must equal its marginal product. Thus a very high rate of interest implies that capital is extremely scarce and thus productive. From the supply side an individual who makes a loan forgoes using the resources, and thus the interest rate must be related to his impatience. If interest rates are very high, then individuals are very impatient.[1]

For Europeans, the decline in interest rates to 5% corresponds to a period of significant increase in durable goods in probates (de Vries 2008) and in the capital stock of the economy (livestock, buildings, and so forth). Thus the quantity of capital seems to increase as its price declines. For China, the evidence on quantities of capital does not match the putative high-price data. In a context of no transaction costs, high Chinese interest rates (100% a year) would imply massive capital scarcity, but such scarcity is not consistent with the observed patterns of consumption or of investment. On the consumption side China did not lack in the production of luxury goods, and elite households, at least, could have redistributed some of their consumption to the future to take advantage of a doubling of their wealth each year. Moreover, we know that the Chinese made large-scale long-term investments. Water-control expenses were large. Beyond the costs that local officials and people bore to keep irrigation networks in repair, larger efforts were needed to maintain canals and major dikes. In the mid-eighteenth century the government turned to the salt merchants and expected major "contributions" (*juan*) to pay for especially large repairs (Z. Zhou 2002: 22). More general efforts to solicit contributions for water-control repairs were made in the 1820s (Tang 1987: 35–37). Amounting to several million taels on occasion, these costs could reach some 2% to 5% of the normal annual expenditures of the government. Such persistent investment suggests that the interest rates quoted earlier are not a good indicator of the impatience of society. Even if interest rates in credit markets were as high as 100% a year, making borrowing very unattractive, there were other ways to invest. In particular, families would invest their own resources in their own enterprises. If individuals were not very impatient, then capital accumulation would proceed no matter whether formal credit institutions existed. To be sure, investment would be larger with capital markets than without, but very high rates of interest should not have persisted for centuries unless there were fundamental threats to the security of property.

Once we abandon the idea that there are no transaction costs and allow transaction costs to be present, the interest rate received by the lender becomes the interest paid by the borrower minus the transaction costs. In this case high interest rates paid by some borrowers can persist even with large-scale investment and low rates of social impatience (consider interest rates on credit cards as an example of such high rates). This is no surprise, as we can see in credit markets in modern economies where scholars measure spreads: the difference between the price at which a bank borrows (what the lender receives) and the price at which it lends (what the borrower pays). A bank charges different interest rates for different types of loans to different types of borrowers, but it is making these different kinds of loans from the same pool of money. Hence the expected return across types of loans must be relatively similar. We can extend these ideas back into history to better understand credit markets.

Interest Rates Reconsidered

To explain why historical interest rates quoted for China were about ten times higher than those quoted for Europe, we need to understand differences between markets and differences among borrowers within markets. Here what we mean by a market involves a particular type of loan defined by its collateral, duration, and any other characteristic that might affect returns. Borrowers within a market will differ primarily in their risk of default. Let us start with the last factor because it is necessary to understand it before we move on to look at different, more complex kinds of markets.

Consider, for instance, a lender in a given credit market who knows his potential borrowers quite well, as might be the case in the countryside or in a small town in China or Europe. Some of these borrowers are in safe activities, and their current indebtedness is low. Hence they are extremely likely to make loan payments and to repay. Others are engaged in riskier but more profitable activities and thus, with some probability, may be unable to pay off their loans. As Box 5.1 shows, the lender will charge these riskier borrowers a higher interest rate than the safer ones. More generally, the lender will increase the interest above what he would charge a perfectly safe borrower to offset any cost or losses that he incurs or expects to incur as a result of default. Because part of the lender's costs is independent of the transaction's size, smaller loans will face higher interest rates and costs of capital than larger ones even if they are no more risky. This will be true whether or not the market is competitive.

This is exactly what occurs in the contemporary mortgage market, and it is also something we observe in early modern Europe (Rosenthal 1993). Hence one possible explanation for the differences in interest rates between China and Europe is that the Chinese borrowers we observe were riskier than those we observe in Europe. That is certainly so because the rates we have been comparing are those paid for pawnshop loans in China

Box 5.1. Pricing credit

Individuals are different, and borrowers know that. Therefore, it is interesting to ask what kind of interests might prevail in a market.

On the lender's side we assume risk neutrality. On the borrower's side we assume that each individual has an idiosyncratic risk of default, and Q is the probability that the loan is repaid, while $(1 - Q)$ is the probability of default. Some individuals will warrant larger loans (because they have more collateral or businesses with a higher expected cash flow). The lender has access to a low-risk borrower (the state or some local institution that serves as a reference point). Thus he can invest L in a loan that has an expected net return of r_s. In dealing with a borrower, he must invest $C + \Delta L$ to learn about the borrower and what she is going to do with the loan. In other words, the borrower's expected return is $Q(1 + r)L - c - \Delta L$.

Because the market is competitive, the lender is indifferent across investment opportunities, so $Q(1 + r)L - c - \Delta L = (1 + r_s)L$. The interest charged is then

$$r = \frac{(1 + r_s)L + c + \Delta L}{QL} - 1,$$

or

$$r = \frac{1 - Q + r_s + \Delta}{Q} + \frac{c}{QL}.$$

In this context individuals who are more likely to default or who get smaller loans will pay higher interest rates. It is easy to show that individuals who borrow for longer terms also get lower interest rates.

Lenders all get the same expected rate of return independent of whom they lend to. Borrowers pay different interest rates depending on their qualities. Those are the interest rates in the contracts. If in a given market Chinese borrowers take out smaller loans and are riskier, then they will have higher interest rates than their counterparts elsewhere.

and mortgage annuities in Europe. In Europe individuals who resorted to pawnshops were those who did not have access to alternative sources of credit, while getting a mortgage required real assets. That borrowers in pawnshops are riskier than borrowers in mortgages stands to reason, and that must be part of the explanation for differences in interest rates between China and Europe. More important, these are different types of loans, and we must consider the impact of such differences on interest rates charged.

Recall from the introduction of this chapter that until the past decade or so the assumption that interest rates in China were extremely high was received wisdom, and no one particularly bothered to ascertain what kinds of credit markets existed there. If these pawnshops and moneylenders were in fact the most important sources from which farmers secured new capital, then the Chinese credit market could not have been large, and investment would have been severely restricted. The argument about China's financial market failure seems complete even before we consider any further historical evidence. Recall that in Europe, by the eighteenth century rates were between 4% and 8% a year, and loan costs of 1% a month were often cited as prima facie evidence of usury. Those few observations that had been gleaned from pawnshops seemed sufficient to verify the general thesis.

From our point of view, that is simply inadequate. Historically and in contemporary Europe, the fact that different credit markets charged different average interest rates was accorded little significance. Indeed, economic historians have focused more on the long-run decline in interest rates and the differences in interest rates charged for the same type of loan across locations; very little has been done to examine differences across credit instruments. Nevertheless, European economic historians would not dream of using pawnshop rates as an indicator of the cost of capital. Doing so would seem absurd because that is the type of market where the spread between the lender's return and the borrower's cost is largest— most borrowers and investors could get resources for less. If we accept for now that there are different kinds of credit markets, we will have to be careful to distinguish between them. Box 5.2 sketches a model in which borrowers choose to enter one of two markets, one with collateral (mortgage) and the other without (short-term credit), depending on what kind of loan they need. As we saw in the case of borrowers with different risk profiles, interest rates vary systematically between the two markets because they saddle borrowers with different types of transaction costs. In our example mortgage markets have lower interest rates because the collateral insures the lender in case of default (in other words, he does not have to impose higher interest rates to recoup his losses from a default from those projects that succeed). However, there are fees required to place a lien on the collateral, so for small loans the borrower will prefer to pay the high rates in the unsecured market *even* if he has collateral.

Now let us return to our two examples: pawnshops and mortgages. For China, we lack interest rates for credit instruments that look like mortgages.

Box 5.2. From one market to many

Assume that an individual has a project for which he needs a loan of size L and that he will succeed with probability Q. In this case his return gross of capital costs is R. He has a choice among several sources of credit (family, network of friends, pawn, mortgage, bank) and has to decide where to get financing. The borrower considers that each market is defined by five characteristics $(L_i, r_i, P_i, c_i, Q_i)$. L_i is the maximum loan he can get in that market, r_i is the interest rate, P_i is the penalty he faces in case of default, c_i is the transaction fee he faces, and Q_i is the exogenous probability that his project will succeed if he gets a loan of type i. The borrower defaults only for unanticipated reasons (the project fails) with probability $1 - Q_i$. The borrower may be shut out of a given market (for instance, because $P_i = 0$ in a mortgage market when the borrower has no collateral).

For simplicity, we consider a borrower who faces a choice between two markets. One has no up-front fee because it is a reputational market (a family or network of friends); the other is a mortgage market where lenders must verify the collateral. When the borrower chooses to fund his loan in the reputational market, he will face the following expected profit:

$$\Pi_r = Q(R - (1 + r_r)L_r) - (1 - Q)P_r.$$

If instead he gets a secured loan, he faces a different expected profit,

$$\Pi_m = Q(R - (1 + r_m)L_m) - c_m - (1 - Q)P_m.$$

It is immediately obvious that because there are no information costs in the reputational loan market, for the borrower to enter the mortgage market, one of three things has to be true: $r_m < r_p$, $P_m < P_r$, or $L_m > L_r$. Because the penalty in the mortgage market is the loss of the asset that is transferred to the lender, interest rates in the collateral market will be lower than in the reputational market. Second, the rich borrowers who can post high collateral can get bigger loans in the mortgage market than in the reputational market. Hence different borrowers will sort themselves among the different markets.

What about differences between China and Europe? They all depend on who shows up in what market. The logic of Chapter 2 suggests that in China larger households and, in particular, lineages would function as internal capital markets, while in Europe the more limited extent of kin would make more individuals dependent on kin. Thus individuals whose families have fallen on hard times or whose projects are viewed as too risky to fund would be the dominant participants in China, and therefore, market interest rates in China should be higher than in Europe even though average returns, including projects funded by lineages, are the same.

For Europe, however, we have evidence of both going back to the Renaissance. Borrowers tended to turn to pawnshops only when they had exhausted alternative sources of credit, such as mortgages or reputational credit. The reason was their high costs: not only did pawnshops carry a high interest charge, but pawnbrokers also added fees that made the annualized cost of short-term loans extremely high. These fees were required because the lender also assumed control of the pawn, which was then stored, and no one could use it. Should the borrower want to retrieve the pawn, the lender had to find it in his storeroom; otherwise it would have to be sold. All the costs that involved handling the pawn did not depend on its value. As a result, pawnshop loans were always very expensive, and consequently, few investment projects could be plausibly funded with such loans.

In Europe pawnbroking was an opprobrious and regulated activity precisely because everyone knew that interest rates were massively higher than for other types of loans. In Renaissance Italy, for example, Jewish pawnbrokers regularly charged an interest rate twice as high as the legal rate for perpetual annuities (Botticini 2000). High pawnshop interest rates sparked debate, and in many places pawnbroking was taken over by regulated municipal organizations, such as Italy's Monte di Pietà (Delille 2000) or Paris's Crédit Municipal (Hoffman et al. 2000: 255). Where such lending was left to the market, interest rates were quite high. As late as the 1870s, interest rates for pawnshops in England were well above 20% when mortgages were being had for less than 5%. The cost of a pawn loan taken out and repaid within a week was far beyond the contracted 20% interest rate because of the fixed fees that brokers charged. In fact, they were just as exorbitant as they are now on payday loans in the United States (Great Britain 1870). All of a sudden, interest rates in China look quite similar to those in Europe. Most likely the remaining differences in interest rates came from variations between rural and urban pawnbroking. The rates we have for Europe all come from urban areas, where unredeemed pledges were easy to sell and there was more competition among pawnbrokers. The rates we have for China come from more rural settings, where pledges were likely more difficult to sell and competition was lower. When we compare pawnshops with pawnshops, differences in interest rates are less substantial.

Pawnshop loans in late imperial China were not a standard credit agreement for production and trade. Borrowers tended to turn to pawnshops when they had exhausted alternative sources of capital, in particular from kin and associates. What then of more normal loans? We do not have data on the interest rates implied by the sale of repurchase loan contracts or other loans backed by real assets in China. We do have some evidence for commercial debts; interest rates again appear to be in a range near, although not equal to, European rates. Huang Jianhui has documented the loans made by native banks *(zhangju)* in 1844 in three northern cities. These banks charged monthly rates of 0.38%, 0.4%, 0.45%, and 0.55%. He also suggests that Suzhou rates (without specific years) were in the range of 0.6% to 0.9% per month. He argues that Jiangnan and the south of China had higher rates than in the north (J. Huang 1994: 38–39). The range of these rates, once annualized, runs from 4.5% to 11%. We can compare these rates with interest rates in England and France in the 1840s. The long-term rate on public debt was about 3.2% for the United Kingdom and 4.59% for France (Homer and Sylla 1991: 197, 222). The discount rates set by the central banks were 4% and 4.1%, respectively (Homer and Sylla 1991: 209, 230). Both of these rates were below the Chinese commercial rates, but they refer to the safest long-term bonds and the rate afforded to the very best commercial paper in either country (the Bank of France required that all commercial paper presented at its window be endorsed twice as added security). The rate on letters of exchange between London and Paris was also in the range of 4% to 4.5% (Boyer-Xambeu et al. 1995). If Huang's data are to be trusted, they suggest that interest rates in Chinese cities were up to twice as high as in Europe, but most likely a good deal closer to those in Europe. It is important to note that although Huang's data come from the 1840s, well after the onset of industrialization in Europe, China remained relatively untouched by economic change at that time. Hence it is credible that interest rates in this period were similar to those that might have prevailed during much of the preceding century. These years were also the last in China before the onset of a long period of institutional instability that came to a close only in 1949; hence rates may well have been relatively low and have risen significantly afterward. At the very least, these data beg to be supplemented by future research because they no longer allow us to be comfortable in assuming that China had dramatically higher interest rates than those prevailing in Europe once we control for types of loans.

Interest-rate data available at present are doubly inadequate—there are not enough Chinese data to support any serious assessment of the cost of capital for investment purposes, nor do the rates themselves tell us much about the institutional contexts in which credit transactions were made. Thus the interest-rate data are clearly inconclusive. As was the case for wages in Chapter 2, we cannot make the assumption that markets are perfect; interest rates must be placed in a context. To do so, we divide the effort into two parts: first, we consider the supply side of the market; second, we assess demand. The supply side will borrow heavily from the ideas of Chapter 3 because we will eschew the simple idea that one set of institutions is optimal. Instead, we argue for the importance of diversity and change over time. Understanding differences in demand for credit will take us back to issues we encountered in Chapter 2. We move our argument beyond those in Chapters 2 and 3 by focusing here not just on sources of divergence but also on what happened beyond the initial parting of ways between China and Europe.

From Interest Rates to Credit Markets in Europe

We start with Europe because of its vast literature on credit markets before, during, and after the early phases of industrialization. Much of that literature focuses on the slow diffusion of modern financial institutions and blames government agents for failing to provide the prerequisites for financial development: safe property rights, sound public debt, a central bank, easy incorporation of private companies, and low barriers for new financial players. But much of that literature forgets that these modern institutions were not put in place instantly. Credit markets have an old history that long antedates the rise of even the simplest banks. As we review that history, we will emphasize the diversity of financial institutions, the adaptation of credit markets to local political and economic circumstances, and their capacity for change. Although there are vast numbers of examples of political intervention to limit the spread of "modern" financial institutions or to dampen competition, there is a veritable cornucopia of examples of local markets expanding with economic activity. Such examples abound in Europe, dating back to the Middle Ages.

Credit contracts are both ubiquitous and elusive in European archives. They are ubiquitous because as early as the Middle Ages, they clog the archives of notaries, and disputes over their execution crowd the rolls of lower courts. They are also elusive because not all credit transactions were preserved. In many cases only fragments of the original body of contracts remain for historians to pore over—discharged contracts were often discarded. Moreover, as we shall see, well into the nineteenth century European credit markets were characterized by a bewildering diversity of institutions and contracts, and much the same can be said for equity markets. Here we focus on credit because such contracts were far more prevalent than stocks in households' portfolios and because European loan markets were large before the divergence set in. Equity markets grew over time, but most of their development follows industrialization (before that time the bulk of equity was not tradable). Thus although stocks and their markets may be valuable institutions for growth, they cannot help us solve the riddle of why Europe's economy forged ahead of China's.

Europeans' debts can be broadly classified into four groups that correspond to different legal categories. The importance of each of these categories has varied considerably over time and space, but evidence for each of them can be found all over Western Europe as early as A.D. 1000. The first and simplest consists of private IOUs. These were unsecured loans between private individuals, and the conditions upon which recalcitrant borrowers could be made to pay varied greatly. In England a variety of means, including debtors' prison, aided enforcement, while in France and other southern European countries such extreme measures could not be used as easily (Luckett 1992). These types of debts are very easy to find in probates and merchants' accounts and were a necessary lubricant of economies in which the local supply of physical money was both limited and highly uncertain (Brennan 1997). Because farmers fell under the civil law rather than the commercial law regime, their notes were considered private unsecured IOUs, and thus this part of the credit system was important. If we trust merchants' accounts, these types of debts appear essential to their business. When we look at probates or loan-registration documents, such debts are quantitatively numerous, but their value pales compared with that of mortgages.

The second type of debt was commercial debt. Although most European countries gave debtors some protection from creditors who had lent them money in an unsecured transaction, there was an exception: merchants. Commercial debt was the realm of commercial law rather than civil law. It generally emphasized the rights of creditors and speedy resolution. Merchants who did not pay their debts were typically imprisoned until they came to some agreement with their creditors. Even so, institutional variation was extensive, with dramatic differences in the extent of endorsement, the standing of noncommercial creditors in courts, and the share of such instruments issued by formal financial agents (banks). This type of credit has received a great deal of attention both because it was key to the commercial expansion of Italy, the Low Countries, and England and because it was closely associated with the development of merchant banks that would give us the commercial and investment banks of the contemporary era (de Roover 1953; Muller 1997; Neal and Quinn 2003). The maturity of the instrument (inland bills, letters of exchange, local commercial IOUs) was typically quite short (one to three months), and many of these loans were small. Starting as early as the thirteenth century, commercial loans included letters of exchange. These contracts allowed a merchant to purchase a note in one city payable in another, thus avoiding the costs and risks involved in carrying cash from one location to another. Depending on whether the merchant paid for the note upon receipt or upon his return from his travels, credit was extended either to the banker or to the merchant. Letters of exchange were accepted at distant locations because wholesale merchants and banks formed networks that spanned Europe. Nevertheless, merchant banks tended to concentrate in the most economically active areas, thus creating a correlation between banks and economic change. Again, before concluding that banks caused economic growth, one must consider the fact that many of the merchant banks were simply the result of the increased specialization of wholesale merchants into credit operations. A bank was born when someone shifted his primary focus from commodities to finance. Such specialization depended on the existence of sufficient demand for financial transactions. Commercial debts were not registered at issue; thus it is difficult to form an estimate of the size of this market. Nevertheless, what documentation has survived in insolvency proceedings and the collections of commercial families makes it clear that such credit existed throughout Europe by 1700 (Kindleberger 1984: chap. 3).

The third type of debt, collateralized debt (mortgages), generally composed the largest set of loans by value. These could, of course, be used for the purchase of land, but often the funds raised were used for other purposes. The institutions that made these types of loans possible were also quite varied. In some places, at some times, mortgages were drawn up by notaries; in others they were registered by town secretaries or manorial courts; and in still others they were prepared by attorneys as purely private arrangements (Hoffman et al. 2000; Anderson 1969a, 1969b; Gelderblom and Jonker 2006, 2008; Servais 1982; Pfister 1994). In some places, even before 1800, information about land ownership and liens on property could be recovered from public registries. In others, this information remained the private property of intermediaries. The legal consequences of default also varied considerably. In England title to the pledged land simply passed to the lender, while in the parts of the Continent where the Roman law legacy was strongest, complex and expensive procedures of expropriation and auction were required to punish borrowers. Although the geographic reach of the mortgage market increased with city size, lenders and borrowers did not live far from each other. More than 90% of all loans linked borrowers and lenders living less than 20 kilometers apart (Hoffman et al. 2011). In western Europe, at least, the density of small towns meant that these markets overlapped, creating, in effect, an integrated market for mortgages. Despite (or perhaps because of) all this variation, the sums that could be raised with collateral were significant, and terms were typically quite long. In the case of annuities they were indefinite and on average were paid off after fifteen years or so, but some endured for several centuries. Thus these markets involved far more credit than unsecured debt, and the amounts grew where land was valuable and cities were large (Hoffman et al. 2008; Brennan 2006). They were also responsive to change—when economies boomed, so did mortgage markets. There is no strong evidence that large mortgage markets initially accelerated growth (Hoffman et al. 2008). Nevertheless, in many economies mortgages and other secured debts form the largest stock of outstanding obligations in any economy after public debt. The reason it outweighs commercial debt is simple. Commercial debts are used to facilitate transactions related to current economic production on a basis of less than three months, so they are a fraction of national income. Mortgages, however, are a fraction of national wealth because they are based on the value of real assets. Those differences were even larger before 1800 than later because on the Continent, at least, agriculture lay outside the realm of commercial debt. This part of the credit system has been understudied, first, because sources for England are scarce and it is the English financial system that has served as the reference point, and second, because it can promise neither the roguish adventures nor the transformational investment of commercial or public debt.

For the private sector of the economy, the existence of these different types of loans meant that rich Europeans had access to a variety of credit markets even in the seventeenth century. To be sure, the scale of each market varied from place to place. So did the specific legal rules and information techniques that constrained and sustained these markets. From the perspective of the Dutch, most of seventeenth-century Europe may well have seemed underserved by credit intermediaries, and they would not have recognized the legal practices that surrounded mortgages in England (where they were privately drawn up and not registered), in Spain (where they were drawn up by notaries but not registered), or in parts of Germany (where they were notarized and also registered with lien authorities). Nevertheless, all these markets were ubiquitous: absent political constraints and absolute poverty, they were set up everywhere in Europe.

At any one time the map of European credit markets had one or two sinks where capital was relatively abundant and interest rates were low. These were also the most economically dynamic areas within the subcontinent. Thus in the late Middle Ages northern Italy was both the most advanced economy in Europe and the most innovative area for finance. Later both leaderships passed to the Low Countries and later still to England. This evidence has been taken as confirming the hypothesis that good credit markets are a source of growth. Although it is obvious that the absence of credit markets would have slowed growth, a careful examination of what actually happened typically shows that except where politics constrained finance, private credit markets evolved in response to economic change rather than caused it.

The fourth and final important kind of European credit involved the debts and financial assets of the public sector, by which we mean cities, provinces, corporations, religious institutions, including the Catholic Church, and, most important, sovereigns (Tracy 1985; Potter and Rosenthal 1997; Altorfer 2004; Courdurié 1974; Epstein 2000). Except for sovereigns, almost all the debts issued by public actors were long-term annuities, most often with an indefinite term (the borrower could repay at any time). Sovereigns dabbled heavily in both the short- and long-term debt markets (Drelichman 2005; Pezzolo 2005; Epstein 2000; Quinn 2004; Gelderblom and Jonker 2006, 2008; Hoffman et al. 2000). As was the case with the other three types of loans, these debts also had medieval origins. The primary motivation for borrowing was the prosecution of warfare or the raising of defenses around cities. Public institutions, such as religious institutions or guilds, relied on the capital market either as lenders investing donations from the public or as borrowers when they needed to meet a demand from the sovereign.

Public borrowers were innovators in the long-term debt market. Even before the advent of public debt markets, rulers relied on credit to fund their political-military competition with one another. This competition involved extremely expensive warfare that they could not easily pay for because they controlled only a small fraction of their economies, and their peacetime budgets were limited relative to the expenditures that rulers wanted to devote to war (Hoffman and Rosenthal 1997; Dincecco 2009). The way in which sovereigns managed their finances, as Epstein has argued, was deeply entwined with their decisions to enter or exit international competition. As long as they perceived that their participation in international affairs was temporary, they tended to rely on expedients such as short-term finance and made little effort to develop long-term financial markets, with the consequence that their long-term cost of finance was high (Epstein 2000). Over time more and more rulers came to the conclusion that conflicts in Europe were long, and they thus took measures to create institutions that allowed them to borrow (Pezzolo 2005; Velde and Weir 1992; for an exception, Drelichman 2005). These institutions included central banks (which initially acted to provide short-term funds to the state), long-term bonds and bond markets (Dickson 1967; Muller 1997), and life-contingent claims and underwriting (Hoffman et al. 2000), as well as debt-for-equity swaps (Quinn 2008).

One important theme in the history of these markets has been that only some political and financial institutions allow sovereigns to borrow long term at low cost (North and Weingast 1989; Dickson 1967; Neal 1993; Epstein 2000). For England, it is argued that the political changes of 1688 secured a political equilibrium between the Crown and parliamentary elites (North and Weingast 1989). This was followed by a series of financial innovations (a central bank and long-term bonds traded on an exchange) that by the 1730s allowed English monarchs to borrow at the most favorable interest rates in Europe. England has often served as the model, leading scholars to ask why other countries failed to do the same (e.g., Stasavage 2003). Recent research, however, again emphasizes institutional variety and suggests that the English model was far from the only path toward a large, low-cost public debt. Most startling is the province of Holland, where debt-management practices followed a path almost opposite to that of England.

At the start of the struggle with Spain, Holland primarily issued annuities. Over time, however, it developed a market for short-term obligations that by the mid-seventeenth century made up the bulk of its debts. Furthermore, the primary actors in this market were the province's fiscal receivers, not bankers (Gelderblom and Jonker 2008). Like private debt markets, European public debt markets seem to have developed in response to the demands of war. The arguments made by North (1981) and North and Weingast (1989) about the importance of representative government in securing the property rights of bondholders should thus be placed in a larger context. In particular one should consider the impact of international politics and the rise of the fiscal state on the success of representative government and the rise of financial capital. Returning, to public debt markets, their particular structures reflected political constraints, but by the eighteenth century few states could do without issuing bonds to the public, and few did.

Precisely because some important innovations in debt markets began with public bonds, it has been argued that public debts, and in particular those of sovereigns, were an important element in fostering the aggregate growth of credit markets for several reasons (Neal 1993). Their huge scale favored the rise of intermediaries who saw to the short-term needs of the king, found individuals willing to hold the long-term bonds, and created markets where these long-term debts could be traded. Later the same intermediaries expanded their activities to cover the private sector. Although we could simply accept this argument as an additional element of a broad thesis that political economy drove the divergence between China and Europe, we want to be more cautious. To be sure, cheap credit from modern intermediaries may have been important to the continued development of the European economy after 1750, just as cheap American cotton favored English factory production in the late eighteenth and early nineteenth centuries. One would have to carefully quantify the costs of sovereigns' interventions in credit markets before the mid-eighteenth century and include the diversion of more resources to warfare before coming to any conclusion.

This account has emphasized institutional variation and change over time. This variation complicates the task of a comparative analysis in several ways. To begin with, governments were not concerned with establishing statistics about private credit transactions. What data were preserved depended on the legal requirements for registration (either at the time of

signing or when the debt entered a judicial proceeding). These requirements weighed unevenly across space and time. As a result, we must be
careful to avoid problems of sample selection. Comparing the size of markets (say, the value of mortgages per capita in England and France) is difficult because of differences in registration practices. We have good information about some markets (in particular, public debt and mortgages) in
some places at some times. For many other markets, we have only qualitative evidence and are tempted to use differences in prices to come to conclusions about markets.

The second difficulty is one we have already encountered. One cannot
equate information about interest rates with capital abundance, because
we most often observe rates charged on specific instruments to specific
groups of borrowers. The market interest rate thus depends both on the capital abundance that drives the riskless rate and on whom the market allows
into these particular loans. More specifically, it could well be that England
had lower interest rates than France for mortgages around 1700 because
capital was more abundant in England and the mortgage market was more
efficient. The difference in interest rates, however, could also be due to entirely different reasons. It is quite possible that at least part of the difference
could come from the concentrated property structure of England (Allen
1992: 102–105, 199–200). This structure meant that little capital would
involve mortgages to small farmers. Because such small farmers have higher
risks of default than large ones, interest rates would be higher for them,
even if they were to draw on the same pool of capital (Rosenthal 1993). Lest
one think that this is a purely theoretical concern, the range of interest rates
charged to different borrowers in one town in the south of France (4.5% to
7%) was larger than the average differences between England and France
(4% to 5%) in the same period (Clark 2001; Hoffman et al. 2000). Moreover,
when tenant farmers wanted to borrow in England, they could not pledge
land and thus never appeared in the mortgage market. Thus the riskier part
of the French mortgage market simply had no counterpart in England. That
interest rates would be lower in England is thus not much of a surprise
and tells us little about the supply of capital.

The third difficulty we also encountered when trying to account for differences between China and Europe. It comes from the fact that different
types of instruments play different roles in different economies. The relative importance of annuities and short-term obligations in English and
Dutch public finance is an example of this phenomenon, but the problem

is quite general. Consider the more rapid development of merchant banks in England after 1660 relative to its continental rivals. This is precisely the period of London's rapid commercial growth and the spread of putting-out in England, to be followed by the development of manufacturing (Neal 1994). Entrepreneurs who wanted to raise capital could not rely on the mortgage market because few of them owned any land. The alternative was to use short-term debt to fund firms, including some long-term activities. Contrast this situation with that in continental countries where agriculture remained more important and landholdings were more dispersed; under these conditions there was a smaller demand for commercial debt and a greater supply of mortgages—including mortgages to manufacturers. As a result of these differences, should we expect interest rates for mortgages or commercial debts to be similar in England and in continental Europe? If we want to make the comparison on the basis of prices, we must compare like with like, and that is a much harder comparison than has been undertaken to date.

Rather than conclude that Britain owes the Industrial Revolution to its capital market, we might consider an alternative. Perhaps Britain owed its capital markets to the combination of its initial distribution of land and its process of economic change. In any case credit markets did change and grow over time. For instance, the City banks of London of the eighteenth century were preceded by seventeenth-century goldsmith bankers. The kinds of business enjoyed at a later date by country banks were most likely taken up initially by merchants. In each case we can point to causes of change. The City banks arose in response to the greater role of London in public finance and international trade (Neal and Quinn 2003). Many of the organizational and institutional changes that we associate with financial development occurred concurrently with industrialization rather than before. Notably these included the spread of a network of banks throughout the country linked to the key merchant banks in London after 1750. Industrial equities were quoted on either regional or national exchanges only after their firms had achieved substantial scale: the key investments had already been realized (Michie 1999). To argue that financial innovation caused the Industrial Revolution is hard to support empirically. At the same time, it is equally clear that had financial innovations not emerged, the Industrial Revolution could hardly have proceeded as swiftly as it did.

Absent major political obstacles, we observe responsiveness to changes in demand for credit across Europe similar to what is first seen in Britain.

As industrialization spread to France, the country's network of banks grew (Hoffman et al. 2008). The banking network did not approach British density, but only because notaries provided important alternative services— the value of outstanding loans mediated by notaries was between a fifth and a quarter of French gross domestic product in the nineteenth century. Although it is true that there were strict restrictions on formation of joint-stock banks into the 1870s and on listing on the Paris stock exchange (Bourse), there were important escape valves. Individuals could freely enter into private banking, and there was an active curb market for shares. If France did not have the best financial institutions, it certainly avoided the worst, and when demand for finance increased, there was a significant supply response. Much the same tale can be told for the Low Countries, Germany, and Italy.

But the remarkable variation in financial institutions has provided fodder for inward-looking narratives of national economic success. Germany, for example, has been said to have caught up with England at the end of the nineteenth century because of universal banks (Gerschenkron 1962; Calomiris 1995). Although it is true that this statement cannot be refuted because England did not have universal banks and Germany caught up, it overlooks other salient facts. That these banks were a rather small fraction of the whole credit system should have raised some questions (Guinnane 2002). Similarly, France's failure to build a large stock exchange and the slow diffusion of banks there has been taken as a good explanation of its slow industrialization. However, that there were no real obstacles to the creation of private commercial banks in France and that there was a rather low demand for their services in the countryside must be neglected for this narrative to be persuasive. Fortunately, recent research has been more nuanced, uncovering ways in which two very different systems actually provided resources to enterprises. Thus the English equilibrium of merchant banks and stock market was just as capable of providing resources as the German equilibrium of universal banks, but it did so in different ways (Collins 1991). To be sure, for a given industry or a given firm, one of these two solutions may well have been preferable to the other, but the optimum is unlikely to have been the same for every industry. Similarly, at any one time one of the two equilibria may have been more efficient. Growth occurred in Europe because each country's system evolved to meet new demands, not because any country was able to consistently achieve the most efficient practices.

Rather than the national comparison so sharply focused on drawing out the responsibilities of any particular financial system to economic success, we prefer a different perspective. We believe that in a world of intense competition, the survival of different institutions over centuries should induce scholars to consider that they are probably equally efficient or, at the very least, useful. Moreover, the institutional differentiation of Europe did not peak in the 1750s on the eve of industrialization but more likely in 1913 on the eve of World War I. As financial systems became larger and added savings banks, curb and formal stock markets, central banks, pension systems, mutual banking organizations, insurance companies, and other financial intermediaries, each country chose its own path. Some were very centralized; others maintained multiple exchanges. In some cases the share of the financial sector under public control was larger; in some countries the nonprofit sector was important. Hence element-by-element comparisons are easy but rarely informative, because what one part of the system could not accomplish, another likely did.

Financial markets grew with demand; thus the level of credit activity at any one time actually says little about the future capacity of the system to provide loans when needed. What was true before 1700 was also true after 1850. Industrialization was capital deepening, and it did make new demands on the financial system. The response in terms of new financial organizations was slow but steady. It was not until the 1820s, and by accident, that the Dutch king founded what came to be known as the Belgian Société Générale—the first financial institution designed to promote industrial development (van der Wee and Verbreyt 1997). But when industrialization began to raise capital requirements for firms, a variety of formal capital markets was already present. Thus although before the 1850s few firms took on the joint-stock form and even fewer raised capital through public offerings, European manufacturers could rely on traditional financial intermediaries (merchant or commercial bankers) for short-term loans. They also raised both equity and long-term loans from more traditional sources of capital (business associates, friends, and family). As Gerschenkron (1962) noted, firms were small in the early phases of industrialization, allowing the financial sector to grow with economic development. Because a large fraction of the flows of capital went unrecorded before industrialization, focusing only on formal institutions such as banks will tend to overstate the growth of credit.

Finally, national politics played a critical role in shaping the contours of a country's financial system. In western Europe, at least, that influence led to a diversity of institutions that was far greater than their differences in efficiency. As we prepare to turn to China, we must be careful not simply to search out organizations that we can compare with a German universal bank or an English country bank. Instead, we must examine whether mechanisms existed whereby individuals with excess capital could make it available to individuals with demand for resources, whatever form these mechanisms may have taken.

China: Do Credit Markets Exist?

When we turn to Chinese credit markets, we wish to see how economic actors similar to those we have encountered in Europe financed their activities (e.g., production and trade) in quite different social and institutional environments. To begin with, we must ascertain what kinds of credit transactions and institutions existed. As we shall see, an important difference from Europe was the absence throughout China of any systematic registration of debt or equity contracts at the moment of their execution. In that sense late imperial China was more like early modern England, where debts are visible only in the archives of some long-lived organizations or when they entered the courts. Investigators of credit in China initially largely confined themselves to studying the twentieth century. Indeed, scholars could not imagine that there was any economic growth of note before nineteenth-century Western merchants began to connect China to large-scale inter-oceanic trade. But in the past two decades considerable new material has emerged that challenges such simple assumptions. As this section shows, there is no longer any reason to doubt the existence of a variety of private financial transactions in China before 1800.

That said, scholars have found far less evidence of financial markets and credit institutions in late imperial China than in early modern Europe. Nevertheless, if we reprise our typology from Europe, there is abundant evidence that private debts (between two individuals) were ubiquitous. Work on Qing-dynasty legal sources suggests that debts are one of the main categories of disputes brought before county magistrates by people, along with disputes over land transactions and marriage (P. Huang 1996; Macauley 1998). The large number of cases relating to debt in the Chongqing municipal archives for the early twentieth century confirms that such debt relationships continued to be important (Dykstra n.d.). Beyond private debts we come to those between merchants. Institutions to provide credit in long-distance trade also developed early on, although along different lines than in Europe. As we discussed in Chapter 3, the spatial scale of the empire gave an early impetus to long-distance trade, particularly along the coast and the major rivers, but also along the Grand Canal and over land. This trade expanded after the fifteenth century through the formation of complex merchant networks. These networks fulfilled multiple functions, but one of the most important ones was to provide institutions to facilitate trade in an environment where space alone made the formal enforcement of contracts quite difficult. Merchant networks, which overlapped with kin networks, functioned as internal capital markets and thus dramatically reduced the demand for formal debt contracts between relative strangers. This hardly means, of course, that formal debt arrangements did not develop in China, but only that they would, in relative terms, be less important than in Europe.

In both China and Europe long-distance trade in the late medieval era began with merchants traveling with their goods over long distances. Those who achieved some measure of success established resident operations in several of the cities where they did business. In Chinese cases there was a head office (*zonghao*) and branch offices (*fenhao*) (Niu 2008: 251–260). Each had its own management team and could raise its own capital through issuing shares. In what ways the accounts we have of their transactions included either a calculation, or even a recognition, of implicit interest costs associated with the gap between the time at which money was spent on purchases and when it was received following sales remains unclear. In contrast to Europe, for which detailed studies of account books are quite common, far less has been published on this matter for China. Firms were composed of people sharing native-place and often kinship ties. Therefore, it is likely that they relied on informal and poorly documented mechanisms to support the credit required for their transactions. This is a second important feature of the conditions for Chinese commercial credit that deserves consideration.

In the eighteenth century Chinese merchants used promissory notes drawn up in one city that could be redeemed at another location after a specified duration of time, exactly like European inland bills. Typically, these appear not to have been taken by strangers but by people who were part of the regional merchant networks defined by native place (Ye and Pan 2004: 148–152). Some notes were issued by what we call "native banks" in English (*qianzhuang, piaohao*); some of them were redeemable on demand, while others had a specified duration. A group of twenty-three such notes dating from the 1680s was discovered in 1985; their stipulated lengths were as short as 20 days and as long as 210 days. Almost all the notes were between one family and three other families of merchants from their locale doing business in different parts of the empire (J. Huang 2002: 7). Huang Jianhui posits the possibility of more of these credit instruments existing but notes the absence of direct evidence, which he suggests means either that knowledgeable scholars of the era did not bother to write about such practices or that we simply have yet to discover further examples of still-extant notes (J. Huang 1994: 21). At a minimum we know that the Chinese did have ways of providing credit for long-distance trade, even if we cannot say how widely used such practices were. Arrangements for credit were even developed between Chinese and Western merchants in eighteenth-century Canton (Van Dyke 2005: 150–156).

By the nineteenth century we have considerable evidence of native banks in China. They took deposits from merchants, officials, and other wealthy people and arranged fund transfers and credit for both commercial transactions and consumer loans. The literature suggests that these networks of banks spread after the 1840s to more and more localities, but what is not clear is how the same transactions were carried out in earlier centuries. These financial intermediaries were also needed to facilitate exchange of copper coins for unminted silver of varying degrees of purity, which together made up the empire's bimetallic monetary system. When foreign banks entered the scene in the second half of the nineteenth century, they worked successfully through Chinese native banks to put their capital into the Chinese financial market. At the end of the nineteenth century, however, Chinese financial institutions became increasingly vulnerable to pressures in the political and fiscal turmoil preceding the collapse of the dynasty in 1911 (Ye and Pan 2004: 190–203).

When we turn to our third category, evidence of mortgages is, to be blunt, nonexistent in China. This does not mean, however, that legal mechanisms for either full or partial alienation of real assets were absent. As we observed in Chapter 3, there was active buying and selling of land. Land was traded most often in rent-to-buy contracts. These transactions allowed both the seller and his heirs to repurchase the sold land provided they paid fair value for improvements, making the transaction equivalent to a loan secured by the land. This type of transaction was open to opportunism when land prices changed abruptly because the terms upon which the land could be repurchased were ambiguous, and buyers at times found themselves making subsequent payments to sellers. Qing law tried to make a clear distinction between sales that were final and sales that were subject to repurchase in order to simplify and bring order to the diverse practices that began to multiply after distinctions between conditional sales and outright sales of land began to be made in the tenth century, if not before. Local officials ruled on disputes between buyers and sellers of land regarding the conditions upon which the land could be redeemed and the amounts of additional money required from the buyer to terminate the seller's claims to the land. Between the sixteenth and the eighteenth centuries disputes over additional payments to original sellers increased. These cases were especially common in the lower Yangtze region, where commercial expansion was greatest. They can also be found in other southern locales. When a contract did not stipulate the finality or completeness of a transaction, it was possible for the seller or his heirs to redeem the land with some additional payment that represented the market value of the land. For the buyer to complete his purchase, he would have to make some supplemental payments. Problems emerged among parties regarding the period during which such redemption could take place, as well as the number of supplemental payments to be made by a buyer seeking to gain complete ownership. Magistrates sometimes resolved these disputes by getting the buyer to pay the seller a small sum, apparently in recognition of the increased productivity of the land and the commercial value of crops, even when there had been a contract of outright sale. In such cases the magistrate aimed to promote local social harmony and order and called on the party benefiting from market prosperity to share his good fortune with the person who had previously sold him the piece of land (Kishimoto 2007). Scholars offer different views on the coherence and effectiveness of eighteenth-century legal efforts to adjudicate disputes over land transactions (Zelin 2004; Bourgon 2004), but for our present purposes the key point is that these disputes affirm the existence of intertemporal markets for land.

Lest one think of these contracts as utterly foreign to Europeans, one should remember that as late as the nineteenth century across a large swath of Europe, the land market also included a right of repurchase of land that had been transmitted through the line of descent. In France this was known as *retrait lignager* (Diderot and D'Alembert 1751–1772, Vol 14: 211; Dyson 2003). To the narrow-minded, these contracts appear inefficient, but are they any odder than leases based on three consecutive lives, or the ninety-nine-year leases with subtenants that were, until recently, common practice in urban Britain? Cash rent on short leases (three to nine years) replaced life tenancy in England only after the structural transformation of the economy was well under way (Allen 1992: 87–102). Other contracts seem to have functioned as a sale, with a repurchase option known in France as *vente à réméré*. The seller transmitted his land to the buyer for a fixed number of years in return for a capital sum. If the capital sum was not repaid in time, the buyer became the owner. Whether one considers these contracts sales or loans, they are intertemporal contracts. Customs such as *retrait lignager* may have raised transaction costs, but they did not eliminate the market for land. The reader will surely notice that such contracts are not as effective as mortgages for several reasons, the most important being that the borrower had to give up control of some of his or her assets to secure credit. Thus if credit markets aim to augment able entrepreneurs' capital resources, contracts with repurchase options are worse than mortgages. In a mortgage the farmer can combine his entire holding with the cash he raises from the loan, while in a contract with a repurchase option he loses land as he adds capital.

Our fourth category of credit also shows major differences between China and Europe. Before the 1840s one would be hard pressed to find much evidence of public credit in China. Except for episodic loans from salt merchants, neither the emperor's central treasury nor local administrations had much recourse to credit markets. When a region was in need of resources for infrastructure projects, the imperial bureaucracy simply changed tax flows. Part of a province's taxes could be redirected from Beijing to another part of the empire, or adjoining provinces could be asked to transfer resources to a needy neighbor. Before the nineteenth century even military expenditures were met from current revenues. As we shall discuss later, China's capital markets did without the gains (and losses) from sovereign debt.

Although the evidence from China remains far less abundant than that for Europe, it also shows that credit transactions were long standing and diverse. Future scholarship, less beholden to theories of economic development that require European-style finance, is likely to add more dimensions to Chinese credit markets. With the exception of public credit, it is clear that in China and in Europe there were firms that distributed their equity claims in a manner more complicated than small simple partnerships. The evidence is presently still thin, but if subsequent research includes more systematic study of these markets, we can expect that markets once thought not to exist or to exist solely to channel land from marginal peasant households to rich people will prove to have broader functions. We should also get a sense of how these markets evolved over time as the economy changed. Thus in the absence of the political problems that sprang up in the nineteenth century, it could be that China would have found indigenous financial institutions to speed its industrialization in ways complementing those it might have adopted from the West. Certainly, in the late twentieth century China experienced a massive rise in domestic investment with capital markets that were quite different from those in North America, Europe, or even other parts of Asia. Therefore, we should seriously consider the possibility that in the past, as in the present, the Chinese met investment demands through markets of their own design.

The view that the Chinese could develop capital markets in response to demand is bolstered by taking into account evidence from after 1850. To be sure, before the 1890s there were no banks in China, at least banks that a European could recognize. There was no obvious mortgage market or securities exchange, and the multiowner firm had dubious legal standing. These absences could well have been major stumbling blocks to growth because by the 1880s, when industrial firms began to form, their scale was radically larger than that of private firms in earlier centuries. Here the reader will notice an important distinction between credit markets and labor markets as discussed in Chapter 2. In that case industrialization simply made household structure irrelevant as an ever-growing fraction of the population became employees rather than entrepreneurs. All this could occur with traditional labor markets. For capital, however, entirely new structures were needed if China's firms were to grow in response to technological change.

Despite the political difficulties of the late nineteenth century, China did create such credit markets in some locations, most notably Shanghai. Some of the new organizations closely copied Western examples, but others reflected the importance of institutional adaptation. Chinese financial institutions both emulated some foreign traits and remained different from European practices. Beyond new institutions, not all traditional structures of investment were incompatible with the development of industrial production.

An obvious place to begin our inquiry is with textiles, the dominant industry in terms of employment in most developing economies. Chinese textile mills, at first spinning and later weaving, were owned under a variety of legal devices. One form involved corporate charters granted by special decree similar to those granted European firms before the 1850s. Other firms were owned in more straightforward ways as sole proprietorships or corporations. In the latter case, however, much as in Europe, a single family tended to exercise control over the business (Goetzmann and Koll 2006). From 1890 to 1922 (after that date Japanese investment in Chinese textiles surged, and the data no longer represent domestic initiatives), the number of Chinese textile firms grew from 1 to 95, and capacity expanded from 35,000 to 1.2 million spindles. The story for weaving factories is similar: by 1922 there were 27 factories operating more than 7,000 looms (Ding 1987). More than half of these factories were Chinese owned. One might think that the textile industry developed rapidly because of legal innovations that transplanted the corporation to China, or because of the rise of new financial institutions (Ma 2006). Indeed, Shanghai, the center of the textile industry, in the late nineteenth century looked a lot like an emerging market. As in many other places in the world, a stock market opened in the 1880s. Its growth was hampered by a crash following a bubble, and the market did not reopen until the 1920s. The failure of the Chinese stock exchange echoes the failure of the first São Paulo exchange. Both institutions were created in a boom, but shares were so closely held that when the boom collapsed, there was no business on the exchange (Hanley 2005). The São Paulo market reopened within a decade as shares and, in particular, bonds became more widely held, but the Shanghai market remained shuttered for three decades. Ma and others are right to point out the failure of some European institutional transplants. The massive growth of the city, however, suggests that there were likely Chinese alternative institutions and means of securing finance.

Similarly, both native and foreign banks provided short-term loans to manufacturers during this period. The introduction of modern banking, in particular, has been claimed to be of great importance for economic growth in early twentieth-century China (Rawski 1989). The importance of imported financial institutions has been supplemented by arguments that Western law and the more general institutional environment for economic growth in Europe were needed to create modern growth in China (Ma 2006; Goetzmann and Koll 2006). But there are reasons to be skeptical. First, a corporate code was enacted in 1904. Although the number of firms in the industry was growing and so was their use of finance, the corporate code provided little stimulus to the creation of new corporations (Kirby 1995). The failure of the corporate code to have much impact may have Chinese explanations, but in a comparative framework it is not surprising. Unlike in the contemporary period, when entrepreneurs rely heavily on incorporation, in the early twentieth century many firms in many countries opted not to incorporate. Limited liability was not a major issue for several reasons. For one thing, the desire to retain control tempered the temptation to issue stock to raise capital. In addition, there may have been far less need for the new form because the well-established partnership form may well have made access to loans easier (Lamoreaux and Rosenthal 2005; Guinnane et al. 2007).

The crucial importance of Western institutions for twentieth-century economic growth is also brought into question by the financial practices of firms outside Shanghai before the twentieth century. Shanghai may be a good locus to study how the Chinese adopted European technologies and how they adapted native institutions, but the important role of foreigners begs the question of how industrialization might have proceeded in areas less affected by the presence of foreigners. It implies that such possibilities were few, if not absent altogether. Beyond Shanghai we have two excellent examples of industrial development. The first is in salt mining. The industry required digging deep wells (a form of fixed capital) to collect brine; it also required much working capital to evaporate the water from the brine and still more capital to market the salt. The industry also required some skilled labor and management services. Nevertheless, these firms appear to have been relatively small. In this industry the Chinese deployed partnerships with shares (Zelin 2005: 342) that resemble private limited companies in many ways. These organizations were first enacted in Europe in the early nineteenth century (Lamoreaux and Rosenthal 2005). European private limited companies had joint-stock attributes, but because they were not traded on exchanges, their bylaws typically included additional provisions about control and income. Chinese salt enterprises were strikingly similar. Because the specific contracts that have come to light in China are

‚heavily concentrated in the last decade of the nineteenth century and the early twentieth century, it is not clear to what extent the clauses they contain draw solely on native legal tradition or rely on legal imports to deal with the changing circumstances in China. Nevertheless, it seems that such multiowner firms, often lineage based, had been in existence at least since the eighteenth century. Moreover, the technical nature of salt making seems to have changed little. The Zigong salt-making firms were very successful—they endured, they invested, and their output grew rapidly (Zelin 1990). There seems to be little specific to salt mining that would explain the choice of organizational form, save that the investments were durable and large. To the extent that industrial investments were of the same kind, lineage-based firms were an available response; neither the corporation nor capital markets were necessary. This industry also demonstrated an ability to bring in Western steam-engine technology within the management and financial practices that had existed before (Zelin 2005: chap. 7).

The second non-Shanghai case of adaptation also took place well outside the lower Yangzi region. It is the remarkable tale of the Yutang pickle factory in Jining, Shandong (Pomeranz 1997). Like the Zigong salt mines, it was initially a family firm. Like the salt mines, it was remarkably long lived, having been founded in the 1770s. Unlike many eighteenth-century condiment makers, it grew to be very large by the early twentieth century. Its history, as recounted by Pomeranz, contains much valuable detail that allows us to push the analysis beyond what the Shanghai textile mills or the salt mines of Sichuan have established. Founded by migrants from Jiangsu, it was sold to a partnership of locals in the early nineteenth century that grouped individuals from at least two lineages. Further, in 1827 management was turned over to an employee, and it remained managed by a person who was not a family member for the rest of the century. In the 1870s the general manager had to find new equity partners and issued interest-bearing notes to raise capital when one of the lineages decided to reduce its investments in Yutang in order to buy some land. Around 1900 the two original lineages took the firm private by buying out all other investors, and one lineage assumed control. The firm then branched out of the pickle business into local finance. If we replace all the Chinese location names with English or French ones and pickles with textiles, the Yutang story suddenly looks unexceptional in a European context. From Shanghai to Jining, what we know of the history of Chinese manufacturing leads us to conclude that absent the political difficulties that engulfed China in the first half of the twentieth century, the financial system would have evolved to fund its manufacturing growth.

There is, of course, an alternative reading of each of these three cases, one that puts more emphasis on the political connections of the players. Such connections were important both for early textile mills and for the Yutang company. One could also point out that nearly half of all investment in Chinese industrial textiles was foreign by 1922 and that these investments were heavily concentrated near Shanghai, where foreigners had both the financial might to make the investments and the military might to enforce their property rights. Only those (foreigners or Chinese) with proper political connections could and did invest. But such qualifications could lead us to miss the central point of the examples for our topic of financial markets. China was not an enterprise desert, nor was the legal structure truly limiting to the formation of large enterprises. It may not have had a capital market before the 1880s, but each of the preceding examples suggests that there were important pathways for investment. As has been the case in the past three decades, these pathways can act as very powerful motors for investment when politics allow. We can see, however, from the very troubled history of China from the 1850s to the 1940s that circumstances were rarely favorable to capital-market development. That Chinese entrepreneurs accomplished as much as they did in the decades between the Opium War and the Japanese invasion is quite astounding, given the political weakness of their governments.

Since the mid-1970s another transformation has been taking place, one that again features financial markets that most Western scholars view as unstable, if not outright dangerous to China's growth. We refer, of course, to the massive expansion of investment since the liberalizations of the late 1970s. The critiques are multiform, but the most damning involve excessive control over access to credit and the inability of banks to discipline borrowers who do not perform. But during the same time the Chinese government has created equity markets and consumer banking and has allowed nonbank intermediaries to play an important role in the provision of credit. China is entering its fourth decade as the fastest-growing economy in the world, fueled by extremely high savings and investment. We might want to balance our concerns about these credit institutions with some consideration of the speed of their evolution. Clearly, what was suitable for the economy in 1980, when most manufacturing remained state owned and rural reforms had just begun to pay off, is radically different from what China needs today. Even today it is not obvious that China needs a financial system that replicates the American, the British, or any other Western model.

A Key Difference between China and Europe: Levels of Demand for Credit

Our analysis of Chinese credit markets suggests that we have yet to uncover the full range of credit markets in preindustrial China. The most recent scholarly research is nonetheless striking because it has stopped seeking European forms in preindustrial China and has started to find the indigenous solutions to common economic problems. Some demand for credit was met informally within business forms and networks that did not calculate interest rates as a basic part of their business-making practices. It is even more likely that much of the demand for credit in the early modern Chinese economy could be satisfied within social institutions and networks that did not require new specialized institutions with particular efforts to document credit transactions. It is also clear that investment resources flowed in other ways. The state, as we will consider more fully in Chapter 6, took a much more proactive role in infrastructure investment than nearly everywhere in Europe. The economic cost to the Chinese of not developing more formal credit markets was likely quite small, especially when we recall that much of the resources raised in early modern European credit markets went toward improving the arts of war rather than economic development. Nevertheless, as European economies began their structural transformation away from agriculture, the role of capital markets increased. If capital markets are not responsible for the initial economic divergence, could they nevertheless be responsible for China falling further behind in subsequent decades?

China had credit markets, but its formal markets were less developed than European ones. We believe that a key reason for this state of affairs was a difference in demand for credit despite comparable levels of economic development. Demand for credit was lower in China for both political and economic reasons. In this section we consider briefly why the Chinese state did not accumulate a public debt before the nineteenth century, as

European states did (we will return to the subject of public finance in Chapter 6). We then look more closely at economic sources of demand for credit.

European empires were founded and survived on oceans of finance, but the Chinese empire was largely debt free until the intrusion of Europeans into its internal affairs. The empire had three kinds of expenses, all of which might have led to borrowing: expenses to fund military campaigns to preserve or enlarge the borders of the realm, domestic administration, and economic development projects. All of these would have led to debt in the European case, but none of them did in China. Over two millennia Chinese rulers faced two sets of military expenses, steady ones that involved the defense of the empire and extraordinary ones that arose when the empire had to be defended from an invader or reassembled after a collapse. Most of the time, the empire was able to maintain a distinct military advantage with current levels of spending, in part because outlying populations were thin and not organized to put serious pressure on the empire. Periodically, however, the people living beyond the Great Wall mobilized armies that could threaten major disruptions. These types of threats typically brought dynasties to their knees, but they occurred very infrequently and were separated by long periods of stable rule. The incentive to turn to credit was probably quite strong when regimes were tottering, but in such dire circumstances few would have been willing to lend, and there was no credit-market infrastructure. Hence Chinese rulers who were in need of quick revenues resorted to actions similar to those of "despotic" rulers in Europe. They manipulated currencies and preyed on individuals who had large amounts of liquid wealth (Von Glahn 1996: 175–178).

When the state was challenged by internal disturbances in the nineteenth century, the "contributions" (*juan*) it had long extracted from wealthy people to fund public improvements were both increased and shifted to meet military expenses (Tang 1987: 35–37; Y. Zhou 2000: 41–42). When a dynasty was stable, however, the value of credit for military affairs was small. Then the Chinese emperor, like his Roman, Ottoman, or European counterparts (Charlemagne, Napoleon, Mehmed II), preferred to run his campaigns out of current revenues.[2]

Not surprisingly, domestic administration in China was also funded out of current revenues. Given that these costs over the whole of the empire were likely to be quite stable, there was no reason to shift their burden over time, especially given the glacial pace of growth. As long as episodes of civil unrest, environmental catastrophe, or other types of disturbances were local or provincial rather than empirewide, borrowing made little sense. Instead, the empire's officials could easily shift resources from peaceful or prosperous provinces to unstable or famished ones. Using space (transfers) rather than time (loans) as a means of providing insurance was sensible and had the desirable goal of binding the provinces together.

Overall, the history of the Qing offers a caution to the theses of North (1981) and North, Wallis, and Weingast (2009) that representative government is necessary for a broad security of property rights. The Chinese emperor, unless compelled by very serious challenges, did not undertake policies of confiscation nor did he distort markets for personal gain. As we saw in the case of Europe, this benevolent despot could change his tactics radically when threatened by exterior forces. War, however, does seem to be a universal impetus for fiscal and financial recklessness.

When we turn to the demand for credit for private investment in China, there are two aspects to highlight. Let us first consider agriculture. Irrigated rice was probably as capital intensive as any farming activity undertaken in Europe, but most of the capital was in improvements to water control and thus in a mix of public and private hands. Although Chinese farmers may have contributed all the labor for maintaining ditches and dikes, they did not have to make all the financial investments. Draft animals, the major investments in Europe, were actually less prevalent in China. This is not to say that Chinese farmers had no demand for credit.

A final difference between Chinese and European demand for credit lies in handicraft production. As we saw in Chapter 4, rural locations figured more prominently in China than in Europe. Until the very late eighteenth century rural sites of production were typically more efficient than their urban counterparts. Rural industries in China were typically pursued by households also engaged in farming; they were therefore both very small scale and labor intensive. In some cases the income from craft pursuits could equal or exceed that from farming, but across much of the empire craft production was a supplement to farming income. Some of the craft production was processing crops, such as curing tobacco and tea, refining sugar, extracting the blue dye from indigo plants, or tanning leather from animal hides. But much production involved handicraft production of final goods, mainly textiles and housewares (Zheng 1989). These were labor intensive and appear to have required little capital investment in tools. For silk production, where we know that rural households likely needed credit to purchase needed inputs, Ming-te Pan has carefully constructed a plausible household scenario based on available data to suggest that even if a peasant family paid high rates of interest, it was likely to be better off engaging in sericulture than in its next-best alternative (Pan 1996). For cotton textiles, we know that the division of labor meant that weaving households could buy their needed thread and sell their finished product at local markets (Elvin 1973). The efficiency of these markets for small-scale transactions meant that credit transactions were less necessary for cotton textile production than for silk. The rural location of craft production also affected capital/labor ratios. Beyond the fact that Chinese putting-out markets may well have been dense enough to minimize the capital invested in inventory, the structure of Chinese manufacturing also reduced demand for capital. Indeed, as we have argued in Chapter 4, the overwhelmingly rural nature of manufacturing in China encouraged labor-intensive methods of production. In China, as in Europe, rural manufacturing was less capital intensive and thus less likely to be a source of demand for the credit market than urban manufacturing. As we noted in Chapter 3, the Industrial Revolution made it clear that capital-intensive methods of production had a much greater potential for raising productivity in the long run than labor-intensive methods of production, but this was not obvious in 1650 or even in 1700. In any case, the demand for credit was low because rural production took place near sources of input supply (so inventories were limited), because all workers were family members (so no wages were paid), and because rural artisans used less capital than their urban competitors.

Both in agriculture and in handicraft production, individuals who needed a loan for productive purposes could either turn to the market or rely on their lineage connections. If, as we expect, kin members were well informed about one another, they would have been happy to fund promising ventures. In this context the large kin groups in China (seen in Chapter 1) would be superior to the market as sources of capital for most individuals. Within these kin groups the ability to enforce contracts (including implicit expectations of future contributions to group activities) tilted capital flows away from the market and toward less formal intragroup, intergenerational transactions. As long as the scale of activities remained relatively small, the costs of using kin groups rather than credit markets could not be very large.

Because there was little public credit, lineage groups and clans provided investment resources to their members, and the structure of manufacturing reduced the demand for capital, credit markets were smaller in China than in Europe. This would have been true even if China had had the same credit institutions as, say, England or the Low Countries. But making such a large investment in financial services when demand was low would have been inefficient.

We began this chapter by considering the commonly held view that capital-market structure is critical to economic outcomes, and we have now come, in effect, full circle. Rather than finding that structure is paramount, we advocate instead greater recognition of different types of markets in different places and different mechanisms for producing investment. Although it is likely that some financial structures are more efficient than others, the lens of history is not clear enough to allow us to discern which ones these are. To the extent that we have wanted to explain the key differences in capital markets across space, we have had to move to more fundamental processes, including differences in politics. For example, the fact that traditional empires do not borrow has important consequences. But there is also inequality in the distribution of wealth—highly unequal societies are unlikely to create mortgage markets and more likely to create reputational debt markets. Equally important are relationships between households; extended kin groups can and do act as internal capital markets. Finally, demand for credit is very important. The Chinese empire with its internal peace and agrarian emphasis did not have much demand for credit markets. Europe, whose violent politics drove governments into debt and pushed manufacturing into cities, had a higher demand for capital markets. When industrialization began, Europe's advantage over China would most likely have been shorter lived except for the tragically difficult dozen decades from 1850 to 1970 that China experienced. This is in part because China could and in many ways did imitate the West, and it is also in part because China could deploy different mechanisms to create structural changes in the economy, none of which depended on capital markets. Although it may be that (as Robert Allen would have it) the relatively higher price of capital in China discouraged machine invention and innovation in the eighteenth century, it did not stop the adoption of these machines at a later date (Allen 2009a). Thus the explanation of a difference at one time in the economic histories of China and Europe may or may not have significance for explaining changes at a later time.

To conclude, financial structure seems to have been of limited importance to economic growth, at least before industrialization. Whether one has large or small banks and large or small capital markets, what matters more is the aggregate size of the financial market. Moreover, finance most often follows rather than leads growth. When processes of structural change arise, they create demands for financial services, and where political constraints are not overwhelming, these demands are met either because old intermediaries adapt or because new ones arise.

Autocrats, War, Taxes, and Public Goods

In literature and social science the rapacious despot is hard to kill. In fiction he survives countless defeats because the hero demands a nemesis. In the social sciences the despot endures because he serves as a perfect foil for the virtuous political regimes that allow their people representation. Indeed, the despot's rapacity leads to leaving his subjects destitute, while more liberal regimes promote the material well-being of their citizens. It is no surprise, then, that the despot is regularly pressed into service to drag absolutist France and Spain down behind the Netherlands and England (North 1981; De Long and Shleifer 1993; Acemoglu et al. 2005). He is also enrolled to explain why China fell behind the constitutional monarchies and republics of Europe (Mokyr 1990; Diamond 1997).

In each case the argument is the same: autocrats levy far more taxes than are necessary to provide public services. Relying on the despot is tempting. For at least the past two millennia, European fiscal institutions have more often than not involved formal constraints on the executive's capacity to raise taxes. The most famous of these are various assemblies of subjects that have come to be known as representative institutions. To be sure, European rulers repeatedly attempted to throw off their fiscal yoke, and in many places they succeeded for long periods of time. Nevertheless, the contrast with China is striking; its emperors never faced formal limits in fiscal policy. Much the same can be said of the half century of Communist Party rule. It is thus tempting to ascribe differences in economic performance both across Eurasia and within Europe to the fiscal consequences of political regimes (North et al. 2009). We often imagine that only representative regimes have the light taxes that liberate growth, while the economies of autocrats are hobbled by high taxes and low infrastructure. The despot lives on.

It is time to bury the despot. Indeed, little of the evidence about fiscal regimes unearthed in the past quarter century is consistent with the comparative perspective just outlined. China did not fail because of avaricious emperors, and Europe succeeded despite a public finance system that was onerous and distorted economic incentives. We do not take issue with the logic of the traditional argument; in fact, it will form the core of our exploration of comparative public finance. But our review of the history of China and Europe requires us to impose additional constraints on both representative government and autocrats. As we shall see, those additional considerations will first moderate and in the end reverse the comparison so that China's emperors may well have enacted more favorable tax policies than any European ruler and his or her representative institutions. To carry out this analysis, this chapter departs from the analytic mode we have used so far, whereby a single central theory is used to reconcile what are initially disparate and contradictory pieces of evidence. Instead, this chapter unfolds as a dialogue between theory and history in which the model evolves through three stages.

We begin by reviewing the basic logic of a heavy-handed autocrat. We then compare that model with the historical evidence to conclude that two critical political elements—war or international relations and the capacity of the disenfranchised population to resist taxes imposed from above— need to be added to the model. Rather than take both of these elements on at once, we start with the more essential one: international relations. The traditional model focuses heavily on domestic spending, but historically international relations often swallowed the bulk of a sovereign's expenses. War, in particular, proved extraordinarily costly. Because rates of conflicts were radically different in China and Europe, war cannot be subsumed into a general public expenditure. When we include war in the analysis, fiscal differences across political regimes do decline; nevertheless, autocrats still extract the most from their subjects. War will, however, prove to be an important force in moderating the public spending of nonautocratic states.

Limiting how much revenue autocrats want to raise implies changing not just their demand for revenues but also supply (the political costs they face when they raise taxes). This leads us to think explicitly about how subject populations can resist arbitrary taxation. We borrow from and elaborate on Albert O. Hirschman's important insights into exit, voice, and loyalty. Among the strategies the subject population can deploy to limit taxation, we distinguish exit from voice. In exit, individuals affect the fiscal system because they either migrate out of the polity or move to the informal economy if taxes are too high. Exit combined with war can indeed lead unfettered rulers to moderate their taxes, particularly when the international scene is peaceful. But this mechanism is inefficient when fiscal needs change abruptly. We also consider voice, in which the population influences the ruler's fiscal decisions either through revolt or formal institutions. We show that if exit and voice are effective, then peaceful autocracies can have lower taxes than any regime in a war-torn region. We then use the lessons of theory to understand how the fiscal structures inherited from the Middle Ages evolved in China and Europe.

The Long March of an Idea

Throughout history, thinkers have considered and analyzed the nature of despotism. By the era of the Enlightenment, Europeans had come to characterize the type of despotism practiced by Asian rulers as repressive, backward, and heavily burdensome to their people (e.g., Montesquieu [1748] 1951: bk. 13, chap. 13). The philosophes also entertained the notion of an enlightened despot who wisely made his subjects' well-being paramount, an ideal with which to criticize their own rulers. But by the beginning of the nineteenth century, Europeans had conceived an alternative to despotism (enlightened or otherwise). According to the new thinking, "modern" and good regimes were parliamentary monarchies that gave voice to some of the ruler's subjects. The rise of twentieth-century totalitarian regimes breathed new life into the study of despotism. In a comparative context Karl Wittfogel's (1957) hydraulic societies may well have had the most impact. Wittfogel's despot owed his power to the environment, especially its water resources. Wittfogel argued that in economies whose prosperity depends on water control, politicians can amass unbounded power because they alone can guarantee the smooth flow of water. This efficiency of rulers comes from fundamental features of water control. This activity has extensive economies of scale and economies of scope. The cost of water control does not rise with the amount of area covered, and it is best for the same agency to organize its different facets: irrigation, drainage, flood control, and waterpower. According to Wittfogel, providing water control requires a bureaucracy that can efficiently decide where new investment is needed and where maintenance is required. This bureaucracy then becomes the primary mechanism for repression because it is both well informed and designed to detect deviations from normal behavior. The ruler can thus extract massive tribute as long as life in the hydraulic society remains at least slightly preferable to life on the unirrigated periphery.

Economic historians have reprised Wittfogel's arguments and have extended them to cover cases of despotism not created by environmental conditions. Douglass North (1981) famously argued that despotism could arise simply because the technology of violence privileged specialists who could use their weapons to gain control of productive assets. Given this danger, one of the key purposes of representative government in Europe was to force rulers to respect property rights and refrain from confiscatory taxation. Hence despotic Spain and France were fiscally more oppressive and irresponsible than England or the Netherlands. Comparative scholars, such as E. L. Jones, concurred with North when they ascribed much of the differences in economic performance across Eurasia to the failure of emperors to provide adequate public goods (E. L. Jones 1981). Jones and more recently Jared Diamond have stressed the abrupt halt of Chinese maritime voyages in the 1430s because of a single central government decision (Diamond 1997). In these various accounts each author comments on the power of the emperor and of the central Chinese government and offers a variant of the imperial despot thesis, as if they had each penned a different episode of a serial novel. The emperors in these accounts all tax excessively, fail to invest in useful public goods, and greedily divert public resources to their own purposes, such as building palaces, enjoying luxury goods, and enriching favored friends—all of which can simply be called private consumption.

Although there are many comparative models of public finance, one formulated by McGuire and Olson (1996) is particularly suitable to our analysis because it is framed around a dictator who is both rational and rapacious. Rather than simply model a dictator and his polar opposite of democracy, McGuire and Olson start with a simple premise: political regimes can be analyzed by examining the size of the faction in power. A dictator is a faction of one, and regimes become more liberal as the faction becomes larger. The faction in power wants to maximize the private returns to its members. In the extreme of a faction of one, this model thus features a despot maximizing the net revenue from taxation. The dominant group has the same two instruments with which to achieve its goal: taxation and investment in public goods. Citizens' incentive to work in the formal sector declines with taxation. In the most pessimistic case, when taxes increase, individuals will simply consume more leisure; a slightly more optimistic scenario has individuals evading taxes by moving to the informal sector. In either case the economy suffers. Public goods make the economy larger. It is important to note that the size of the faction in control affects the trade-off through a single channel: as the size of the faction increases, it owns more of the economy and thus bears more of the distortional costs from taxation and gets more of the rewards from public goods. All regimes thus face the same decline in the size of the economy as tax rates increase and the same growth of the economy as more public goods are provided.

The details of this model are provided in Box 6.1. The key results are, first, that given any public good expenditure, a dictator will choose the tax rate that maximizes revenues (the rate at the top of the Laffer curve). The intuition for this result is straightforward: the dictator's return is earned through the difference between his expenditure on public goods and his total tax extraction—all else being equal, the dictator wants to maximize tax revenue. As the size of the faction that is in control increases, taxes fall because members of the faction bear more of the cost of taxation (reduced total output). The second conclusion involves how much to spend on public goods. For the dictator, the last dollar spent on public goods must do much more; it must increase the size of the economy to such an extent that it generates another dollar in tax revenue. As the size of the faction in control increases, it realizes two gains from more public goods, increased tax revenue and a larger private economy. Thus public goods increase as the size of the faction increases. Corruption (the difference between what the government takes in and what it spends on public goods) must fall as the size of the faction increases. McGuire and Olson further showed that once the faction's share of the economy reaches a critical point, it spends all the tax revenue on public goods (corruption is eliminated). Increasing the size of the faction beyond that point has no effect on taxation or public goods. Because autocratic societies have higher taxes and fewer public goods, their economies will also be poorer than those of democracies.

The contrast suggested by this theory fits nicely with the eighteenth-century evidence of the prosperous economies of England and the Netherlands relative to the poverty of Austria-Hungary, Spain, Naples, or France

Box 6.1. Taxation and public goods

This box reproduces McGuire and Olson's results in a simple setting. Let $Y(G)$ be total income, given investment in public goods G. $Y(0) = 0$. Let t be the tax rate and the resulting size of the economy be $R(t)$. There is a faction that controls the net proceeds from taxation. That faction accounts for F of the economy ($F = 0$ corresponds to a dictatorship).

The faction must decide the tax rate and public goods. To do so it maximize the return to taxation and public goods

$$\Pi_D = (1-t)R(t)FY(G) + [tR(t)Y(G) - G] \text{ subject to } G \geq tR(t)Y(G).$$

First assume that the constraint does not bind. Then

$$\frac{\partial \pi_D}{\partial t} = F\left\{-R(t)Y(G) + (1-t)\frac{\partial R}{\partial t}Y(G)\right\} + \left\{R(t)Y(G) + t\frac{\partial R}{\partial t}\right\}Y(G) = 0,$$

$$\frac{\partial \pi_D}{\partial G} = F\{(1t)R(t)FY(G) + t(Rt)\}\frac{\partial Y(G)}{\partial G} - 1 = 0,$$

$$F\left\{1R(t) + (1-t)\frac{\partial R}{\partial t}\right\} = -\left\{R(t) + t\frac{\partial R}{\partial t}\right\},$$

$$t^* = \frac{R}{\dfrac{\partial R}{\partial t}} - \frac{F}{1-F}, \text{ and}$$

$$\frac{\partial Y(G)}{\partial G} = \frac{1}{(F + (1-F)t)R(t)}.$$

Thus starting with dictatorship ($F=0$) and as F increases, t declines and G increases. There exists an $\hat{F} < 1$ such that the constraint binds ($G = tR(t)Y(G)$). In other words, the controlling faction finds it inefficient to redistribute income to itself:

For every F greater than $\hat{F}$,

$$t^*(F) = t^*(\hat{F}), G^*(F) = G^*(\hat{F}).$$

Past that point, political structure no longer matters.

(North 1981). It also fits nicely with the nineteenth-century evidence of the prosperous economies of Europe and the poverty of China. Finally, it fits nicely with an ideology that more representation reduces the extent of confiscation by elites to the extent that taxes can fall at the same time that public goods spending increases. But the theory's predictions are certainly not consistent with current evidence where repressive regimes have under-developed fiscal capacities and prosperous democracies have very large public sectors. It also does not fit as we move backward in time. Nor does the theory account for the range of historical evidence we consider in this book. In brief, China has not always been poorer than Europe, and the economic rise of both the Low Countries and England seems to have begun long before their political transformations in the late sixteenth and late seventeenth centuries, respectively. Furthermore, as we shall see shortly, the rulers of the Middle Kingdom seem to have spent considerably more resources on public goods than any European ruler.

History Strikes Back

McGuire and Olson's model is a mathematical exposition of the received wisdom of political economists from the philosophes to the 1980s—but it is wrong. When scholars have investigated either tax rates or expenditures on public goods, the model has simply failed to stand up. Attacks have come from all sides. China scholars have radically revised Wittfogel's thesis in favor of a Qing imperial bureaucracy that sought legitimacy in the provision of key public goods. European scholars beginning with Mathias and O'Brien (1976) discovered that taxes were actually lighter in countries such as France and Spain than they were in England and the Netherlands. While taxes likely amounted to more than 10% of GDP in mid-eighteenth-century England and the Netherlands, they were about half this level in Austria and France (Bogart et al 2009). Their findings conformed with another observation of Montesquieu: "Taxes may be heavier in proportion of the liberty of the subjects" ([1748] 1951: bk. 13, chap. 12). In this light the confiscatory behavior of absolutist monarchies is an expression of their lack of power to tax. Had despots had full capacity to choose their own fiscal rules, they would not have resorted to inefficient confiscation. Because the evidence about the burden of taxes is very often forgotten and some of it is poorly known, it is useful to review the history at some length.

Here is what we know about taxes and expenditures before 1800. Government expenditures by states of the early modern era can be divided among military expenditures, civilian administration, public goods, and sovereign consumption. Although the costs of the sovereign's consumption could look dramatic from the perspective of a single household or an extended family, these costs never loomed large enough in any of the major European states or the Chinese empire to exert a significant effect on fiscal decisions. Nor did the costs of civilian administration weigh heavily, even though officials often used their offices for their private gain. Public goods caused little fiscal distress in Europe because they were few, and almost none were financed from central government revenues. In China, as we shall see, there were more public goods, and more of them were funded from the imperial purse. These expenditures, however, were financed in ways that made costs bearable and thus acceptable.

Chinese rulers viewed public goods as an important element in maintaining social order and control. They were well aware that social stability translated into political longevity. Social order, in turn, was understood to depend on popular material security. These criteria for political success made more sense in a large polity where external enemies were few relative to the domestic challenges of sustaining social order. In contrast, European criteria for political success made sense because the spatial fragmentation of the region produced relatively more external threats. Despite their understanding of the value of domestic social order, European rulers had to face the fiscal consequences of war. The costs of competition with other states occupied a proportionally larger amount of government finances than domestic rule.

The Chinese logic for successful state maintenance in the centuries under consideration in this chapter was quite different from that necessary for successful state formation in Europe. At heart it emphasized light taxation and generally tried to avoid interfering with commerce. For instance, there were few, if any, transit taxes or other tariffs within China. Although the state nominally regulated international trade in a restrictive fashion (leading to implicit if not explicit tariffs), the reader should bear in mind that China's internal market dwarfed those of Europe as a whole for millennia. States do, of course, need taxes to survive, and in 1500 the Chinese central government levied taxes on peasants in two main forms, grain and labor service. Over the next three centuries both of these were converted into monetary payments, which made the movement and spending of revenues far easier and more flexible.

Under the Ming Empire agricultural taxes were divided into two main categories, those that remained in the county to meet local administrative expenses and those that were forwarded to the capital or diverted to another part of the empire. Taxes sent to the capital paid for central administrative costs; they were joined by additional levies in grain from the rice-rich provinces along the Yangtze River that were sent up the Grand Canal to help feed the capital. Despite the lack of a comprehensive accounting system, officials were able to keep track of most of the revenues sent to the capital and those that were left at local levels. Moreover, Ministry of Revenue officials were able to move revenues around the empire among locales in order to meet extraordinary needs, thereby reducing the need to tax at higher levels within locales to provide resources (Wong forthcoming).

During the eighteenth century officials collected routine taxes amounting roughly to some 5% to 10% of agricultural output, but the Chinese state managed to help maintain waterways, manage water-control works for irrigation, and build massive granary reserves and other projects that helped promote material security and economic growth. To achieve these goals, the Qing dynasty forged a more tightly integrated bureaucracy to improve the flow of information up and down the official hierarchy. In 1766 land taxes collected in monetary form accounted for some 68% of routine revenues, salt revenues about 12%, commercial taxes 11%, and miscellaneous sources the remaining 9%. If taxes collected in grain are expressed in terms of their monetary value and are added to these totals, land taxes account for 73%, salt taxes for 10%, commercial taxes for 9%, and miscellaneous sources for 8% of total revenues (Z. Zhou 2002: 29). Land taxation rates were higher in the richer provinces, and portions of the revenue raised in these provinces were sent not to the center but to poorer provinces. The two provinces of Jiangsu and Zhejiang, within which lay the Jiangnan delta, the empire's wealthiest region, accounted for roughly a quarter of the total agricultural tax revenues of the empire but had probably less than 20% of the empire's population (Wang 1973: 89–90). These revenues were used to support military operations, build up granary reserves, establish schools, and pay for general civilian administration expenses. Although exact figures are hard to come by, the limited rate of taxation of agriculture and the even lighter taxation of commerce and handicraft production makes it likely that revenue, even in the most heavily taxed provinces of China, did not approach the 7% of GDP that France was raising in 1780. The reader should bear in mind that this was a much lower rate than that of Britain or the Netherlands.

If the Chinese empire can be characterized as one of restrained taxation and limited fiscal innovation, nothing of the sort can be said for European polities. European rulers were always eager to increase their income; they relied on an amazing array of taxes and ceaselessly invented new ways of squeezing revenue from their subjects. Before the Dutch revolt, direct taxation, as in China, may well have been the backbone of most European sovereigns. By the seventeenth century, however, in France, Spain, and England revenue growth came from indirect taxes (duties, excises, and stamp taxes). In fact, European sovereigns were ceaseless taxation innovators. One striking European innovation was public borrowing. Indeed, European rulers were never content to live off current revenues; rather, they sought to escape the unpleasant consequences of balanced budgets by bringing forward future revenues. Here we will explore the fiscal consequences of rulers' desires for credit, having already explored the consequences for credit markets in Chapter 5. We must emphasize that as economists know well, more borrowing requires more tax revenues. Thus the long-run development of public debt was undergirded by the growth of public revenues. To take but one example, that of France, the rate of growth of tax revenues per capita was extraordinarily steady over the centuries from 1550 to 1850. Hence tax burdens that may have started out as modest levies rose inexorably over time (Bonney 1995, 1999).

Beyond these generalities, one critical point stands out: taxes were generally higher in regimes with representation than in regimes that called themselves absolutist (and are generally understood as dictatorships). Since Mathias and O'Brien's 1976 seminal article focusing on the comparison of England and France in the eighteenth century, other scholars have verified this finding for a broader set of countries and longer periods of time. The essays in Hoffman and Norberg's 1994 volume, for instance, make this point for the main participants in the wars of the seventeenth century (England, France, Spain, and the Netherlands) from 1600 on. Richard Bonney and others have assembled much more detailed fiscal data from a large set of countries and have come to quite similar conclusions (Bonney 1999). More recently the focus has moved back to the early Renaissance, in particular because of the work of Stephan Epstein (2000). Epstein downplays the achievements of parliamentary England by noting that Italian republics had achieved remarkably good public finance by 1300. The reason for this, of course, was that these republics had been remarkably innovative in finance *and* in taxation, even though representation was often limited to a very select few. European economic historians have found, time and again, that representative governments simply taxed more than authoritarian ones. Representative governments were also more innovative in public finance: they extended taxes beyond traditional sources like land and moved aggressively into indirect and commercial taxes; and they were pioneers in issuing long-term debt and creating markets where their bonds could be traded. Many of these innovations were imitated by absolutist regimes so that the advantages of any particular innovation dissipated over time. Nevertheless, the fiscal inventiveness of smaller, more representative states gave them an important advantage over their larger rivals.

China's less aggressive fiscal policies do not mean that the emperor and his staff were content to sit in some isolated palace and let the population fend for itself. On the contrary, the central government aimed to influence local conditions through policies implemented by both provincial and county officials. Within each of more than 1,300 counties in the eighteenth century, officials depended on local elites to help them implement a neo-Confucian agenda for local social order, which included the repair of roads, bridges, and temples, the funding of granaries and schools, and in some areas an even broader spectrum of benevolent activities, such as orphanages and the care of widows. At the core of the local elites were individuals who had studied for the civil service examinations and had consequently learned the same principles for promoting social order as those advocated by state officials. Because local elites made significant contributions to local welfare, taxes could be collected in smaller amounts, and only a fraction of these were kept at the local level. Considerable services were nonetheless provided when elites met their Confucian duties to fund and manage various local institutions (Wong 1997: 105–126). On occasion it seems that local elites preferred to manage local welfare efforts without official participation (Mori 1969), but the more common norm appears to have been a mix of official and elite efforts and a joint shouldering of expenditures. In some cases imperial officials monitored local activities in a routine fashion, for example, community granaries, but in other cases there was little direct oversight (Will and Wong 1991: 63–69).

The Chinese attention to local public goods was rarely found in western Europe. At their best, European states allowed local agencies the capacity to raise resources in order to improve communications or aid public welfare (Bogart et al. 2009). But European states were rarely at their best. From the end of the Middle Ages to well into the twentieth century, rulers waged a relentless campaign to limit local freedom to tax and to borrow, and to appropriate as many local revenues as possible. The rise of a parliamentary regime in England after 1688 did nothing to loosen the power of the center to control investment in local public goods, such as roads, docks, and canals (Allen 2009a). Even after 1688 local parishes had to seek parliamentary approval to change their tax rates. Hence higher central government taxes did not translate into higher rates of public goods provision. The only exception is the Netherlands, where the political structure allowed cities and provinces to promote water control without much interference (to be sure, this is in part because there never was much of a central government in the Netherlands). If public goods had been any indication, taxation should have been higher in China than in Europe, but taxes were lower in China. As we shall see, the contrast is not due to European kings thirsting for more palaces and personal consumption than their Chinese counterparts, but to military expenditures.

International Relations

In our first model, taxation serves two purposes: increasing the incomes of the faction in power and producing public goods. One can think of these two activities separately because their only interrelation comes from the fact that they share a common revenue source. When we consider war, the problem is rather different. On the one hand, war involves consumption for the sovereign; up to the French Revolution kings liked to fight wars (Hoffman and Rosenthal 1997). On the other hand, war has dramatic effects on the size of the economy independent of the fiscal burden it imposes. The economies of the losers in war tended to shrink, while those of winners tended to expand. The other reason to take war seriously is that the military dominated public expenditures everywhere, but to an extent that was radically different in China compared with Europe

To bring a framework like McGuire and Olson's closer to the fiscal histories of Europe and China, we must take account of the extent of war, which, as many before us have observed, explains Europe's high taxes (Bonney 1999). A less obvious consequence of war also matters: war breaks the independence of the public finance decisions of different polities. We can make the assumption that welfare spending in France, for instance, is independent of that in England, but when we are considering war, that is not possible. Indeed, a despotic regime fighting a representative regime must raise approximately the same amount of resources. Thus we cannot assume that France's taxation evolved independently of that of Spain or England (its key rivals); we also cannot assume that the Netherlands' fiscal system provided no incentive for innovation in Spain when the two polities were at war with each other. As we shall see, war created pressures on regimes of all types to raise taxes in Europe. In other words, the contrast between Europe and China is twofold. On the one hand, there was a millennium of different experiences in the extent of warfare that explains why, in general, taxes were lower in China than in Europe. On the other hand, there is a contrast between representative and absolutist regimes independent of war. How do these two realities come together?

We can begin to answer this question by considering that war is a public investment to which states seem to have had to devote some minimum of resources in order to continue to exist. The technical details are exposed in Box 6.2. When there is no investment in the military, the economy simply disappears (it is taken over by someone else). An economy with no public expenditures on roads, schools, or welfare still has some level of output, but, as the history of Poland makes clear, a state without an army is doomed to be absorbed by another regime. As military investment increases, the economy first shrinks less, and with some sufficiently high investment it may actually grow. Of course, investment in the military also affects individuals' willingness to pay taxes and the returns to public goods investment. What happens to the property of the inhabitants varies. In some cases, such as colonial America, conquest was associated with very high levels of confiscation by the conquering population. In the case of Poland, however, the redistribution of private property was not nearly as severe. Local elites who accepted their Russian, Prussian, or Austrian rulers kept their estates. In any case, because we find few instances of conquest by popular request, we can assume that both rulers and subjects would prefer to conquer than to be conquered.

Paying for the army requires that the faction in control adjust its spending on other priorities. First consider an autocratic government. Recall that in a peaceful economy the autocrat is already maximizing tax revenue. When war becomes an important consideration, the tax rate does not change. Investments in public goods, however, will decline from their already-low levels in polities where war is not profitable, and they will increase in economies where war is profitable. Nevertheless, the autocrat's net diversion of public money declines. In our model, as many others have

Box 6.2. Adding war

Let war be a gamble $W(w)$ such that $W(0)=0$. The function W is increasing and concave. If F is sufficiently small, then the faction in power sets taxes exactly as if there were peace: it funds war and public goods out of the fraction of revenue that it would have confiscated.

$\pi_w = W(w)(1-t)R(t)FY(G) + W(w)tR(t)Y(G) - G - w$ subject to $G + w \geq tR(t)Y(G)$,

$$\frac{\partial \pi_w}{\partial t} =$$

$$W(w)F\left\{-R(t)FY(G) + (1-t)\frac{\partial R}{\partial t}FY(G)\right\} + W(w)\left\{R(t)Y(G) + t\frac{\partial R}{\partial t}\right\}Y(G) = 0,$$

$$\frac{\partial \pi_w}{\partial G} = W(w)\{(1-t)R(t)F + tR(t)\}\frac{\partial Y(G)}{\partial G} - 1 = 0,$$

$$\frac{\partial \pi_w}{\partial w} = \frac{\partial w}{\partial w}\{(1-t)R(t)FY(G) + [tR(t)Y(G)]\} - 1 = 0,$$

$$t^* = \frac{R}{\frac{\partial R}{\partial t}} - \frac{F}{1-F},$$

$$\frac{\partial Y(G)}{\partial G} = \frac{1}{W(w)(F + (1-F)t)R(t)}, \text{ and}$$

$$\frac{\partial w}{\partial w} = \frac{1}{R(t)FY(G) + [tR(t)Y(G)]}.$$

Again there exists $\hat{F}_w$, such that the constraint binds $(G+w=tR(t)T(G))$. In other words, the controlling faction finds it inefficient to grab tax revenue for itself when it includes more than $\hat{F}_w$ of the population. As in the peaceful economy, taxes are highest and spending on public goods is lowest in the dictatorship ($F=0$). War expenditures rise with F.

Public goods spending depends on the returns on war. Thus for a given F, they may be higher if war is very profitable ($W(w)>1$) or lower if war is very costly ($W(w)<1$).

If wars are an even bargain (at $\hat{F}_w$, $W(w^*)=1$), then public goods spending is the same as in the peaceful economy for all political regimes where $F < \hat{F}_w$. For regimes where $F > \hat{F}_w$,

$$t^*(F) = t^*(\hat{F}_w), G^*(F) = G^*(\hat{F}_w).$$

It also follows that for all regimes where $F > \hat{F}_w$, taxes are higher and public goods spending is less than in the peaceful economy.

also argued, political competition does reduce corruption, but only to the extent that resources are diverted to the military. Beyond the case where there is a dictator, we must consider regimes where a fraction of the population is in control. As in the initial model, increasing the size of the faction in control still leads taxation to fall, while public goods spending and war spending increase. Finally, the critical size of the faction such that private diversion is eliminated declines relative to an economy without war. Indeed, for any faction size, the sum of resources devoted to war and public goods is larger in the war economy than it is in the peaceful economy, and thus the total-expenditures curve must intersect the tax-revenue curve (which is still declining with faction size) earlier than it did in the peaceful economy. For all regimes in which expenditures on public goods and war are equal to tax revenue, war increases taxes; its effect on public goods depends on just how effective the military is at protecting the private economy.

War offers the first avenue for thinking about the fact that a peaceable autocrat might provide more public goods than a more liberal regime. Because wars are very costly and unprofitable (war-torn economies must spend a lot just to survive), investment in public goods will be very low. This helps explain why the Chinese state could devote a larger fraction of its budget to public goods than governments in Europe did. In Europe military expenditures were always a very important element of the budget, consuming anywhere between 70% and 90% of the government's revenues (Hoffman and Rosenthal 1997). The reason is simple: major European powers were about equally as likely to be at war as at peace. Even peace was uneasy and required significant military expenditures. In fact, the history of the rise of the state in Europe is written against a backdrop of military expenditures. In particular, the fiscal innovations we discussed in the previous section were largely motivated by the relentless drive of rulers to secure the resources necessary to pay their armies. European rulers were granted tax increases and new sources of revenues for specific military campaigns but then did their best to turn temporary (extraordinary) taxes into permanent (ordinary) sources of income. War not only explains high taxes in Europe but it is also the central force behind fiscal change.

Although imperial China was more peaceful than Europe, it was not without its foes. Consequently, the emperor fielded an army that may well have been the largest in the world for centuries. Under the Qing the military continued to consume a very large share of total public revenues. The celebrated Great Wall was clearly a military expenditure. The late imperial Chinese state maintained a military presence along its borders and within parts of the empire. Moreover, the eighteenth-century campaigns that took the armies of the Manchu rulers into inner Asia and led to the incorporation of far more territory than the previous Ming dynasty had held were expensive. As a result, the central government may have devoted a bit more than 50% of its routine resources to the maintenance of its army. Figures are difficult to assemble, but in the mid-eighteenth century total annual military expenditures were around 23 million taels and annual revenues around 41 or 42 million taels (Y. Zhou 2000: 36–38). The lax principles under which fiscal accounts were maintained all across Eurasia mean that we must take these figures as indicative rather than as exact numbers, but they do suggest that the fraction of a sovereign's resources that were devoted to the military was much higher in Europe than in China and that the differences as shares of national output were larger still.

Although half of a government's resources going to the military may seem large in today's world, at least it left a considerable amount to be spent on domestic public goods. That was more than what Europeans managed, and indeed, the contrast between fiscal resources available for public goods in China and in Europe was significant in the centuries we consider in this chapter. While European rulers had to fund all nonmilitary activities out of less than a fifth of all tax revenues, China's emperor had a full half of his revenue to devote to public goods, his bureaucracy, or his personal welfare. Moreover, until 1830 at least, China did not experience Europe's ever-increasing military needs. In fact, for long periods dynasties faced few outside rivals. If Chinese subjects came to expect a relatively high level of public goods, trouble on the frontiers could cause problems of domestic unrest. War therefore seems an essential component of the comparison.

It is also important to note that early modern European rulers' thirst for higher taxes did not come from a difference in ideology. Ideas of good governance in Europe, as in China, emphasized low taxes, balanced budgets, and the provision of public services. Henry IV and his prime minister, the duc de Sully, attained a hallowed mark of good governance in seventeenth-century France for restoring public order, encouraging the revival of economic activity, guaranteeing the property rights of religious minorities, and, most amazingly, keeping taxes light. A century and a half later the Burgundian estates attempted to decline requests for further resources from Louis XV's minister by gently reminding the powers at Versailles that the only reason the Crown's finances were precarious was that it had gotten involved in wars and that prudent economy was the only proper way to run the country (Potter and Rosenthal 1997).

But these French attempts to live up to ideas of good governance were frustratingly rare. European rulers craved revenues because they wanted to fight wars. To raise the resources for war, they had to confront the opposition of their subjects. Subjects had local allegiances and were not always easily persuaded that defending some other of their ruler's possessions was in their interest. More important, as Hoffman and Rosenthal (1997) emphasize, rulers seem to have been the primary beneficiaries of successful wars, while their subjects bore most of the burden of unsuccessful ones. The absence of an imperial peace in Europe therefore meant that military expenses and their attendant taxes were a continuous source of tension between rulers and their subjects.

Nevertheless, the existence of an empire with low taxes and low levels of military effort is neither particularly nor intrinsically an Asian trait. Southeast Asia, in particular, remained a competitive and unstable system well into the seventeenth century. Thai, Vietnamese, Malay, and Burmese rulers fought with one another, as well as with smaller groups of people across mainland and island Southeast Asia, into the early modern era. China's equilibrium was only one among many in Asia. Conversely, European kings were hardly the only rulers to depend greatly on military activities. Empire builders like the Ottomans and the Mughals conquered additional territory through military force and organized their territories in ways that allowed them to support substantial armies. In fact, one could argue that the political organization of these empires gave strong priority to continuous political expansion. To be sure, the Qing, like other dynasties before them, expanded the territorial reach of China, but their true genius lay in improving the system of internal administration they had inherited to provide a broad range of public goods at low cost.

European rulers were also well aware of the principles that promoted good governance in China, even though they did not associate them with the Qing dynasty. As noted in the French case earlier, such ideas had a good deal of currency in Europe. Had European rulers followed the policies recommended by the early economists, of whom Adam Smith was the most famous, they would have taxed their subjects at far lower rates and thereby met some of the goals more actively pursued by Chinese policy makers. They would also have eliminated many of the impediments to trade so as to extend the market, and such reforms would have made their domains more like China. Unfortunately for European rulers, the revenue they needed to finance military and bureaucratic expansions, which were basic to state making of the period, meant that meeting Smith's hopes for low taxes was impossible. Perhaps the best that could be done was what Smith proposed: in short, recognize that rulers need ever more revenue and think of ways to raise unavoidable taxes with as few negative impacts on the economy as possible.

Moving from a comparison of political regimes whose sole priority is domestic spending to one in which they also face external competition offers several general lessons. To begin with, including war in the analysis helps explain why European rulers persistently spent more than Chinese emperors. Taking the despot as a fiscal maximizer implies that tax rates should be higher in authoritarian regimes like China than in representative governments like the Netherlands or Britain. Indeed, as long as we assume that autocrats' greed for revenue is unchecked, and that they perch at the top of the Laffer curve, democracy should levy similar taxes only in the most extreme circumstances. Having maximized tax revenue in a peaceful economy, the despot must fund war out of resources that would have gone to private consumption, and the tax rate will be similar in peace and war. A second lesson concerns spending patterns. In any political regime, war reduces spending on domestic public goods. Thus that China's emperors may have allocated more of their revenues to domestic public goods than European rulers becomes more understandable. But one final and major fact conflicts with the argument: China's autocratic rulers simply taxed less than their European counterparts. Our framework will accommodate this fact if we introduce additional costs of raising revenue. We will do so in the next section, but first we want to detail some additional implications of interest.

The first of these implications is that political competition as it played out in Europe in the early modern period was extremely costly. Very little, if any, of the higher tax revenues in Europe relative to China went into useful infrastructure before 1700.[1] In particular, the beneficial effect of contemporary domestic political competition mentioned at the start of this chapter cannot be assumed to carry over to international relations. In fact, the very political competition that was supposed to align rulers' incentives had very large military budgets as a first-order consequence. To be sure, political competition creates a check on rulers because inefficient politicians will be replaced or their polities will be conquered, but it also requires resources. Although the number of independent polities in Europe shrank over time, the size of the major powers, Great Britain, France, Spain, Portugal, the Netherlands, Florence, Venice, and the Ottoman Empire, changed very little between 1500 and 1789. Central European powers (Austria-Hungary and Prussia) did grow some, and other countries expanded their territorial reach outside Europe through colonial empires. Nevertheless, within Europe few rulers were eliminated despite the fact that political-military competition grew more intense over time. To the extent that we can find a return to political competition, it can only be indirect, say, in the development of capital markets, or external through colonial empires. War in Europe was expensive and offered little gain.

The second implication concerns democracies, or rather polities with representative institutions: their freedoms came at the considerable price of very high taxation because they were small and because they had to face larger, absolutist opponents. Before 1800 the time and expense of travel meant that regular representative assemblies could be sustained only in small polities. It was easy to have regular meetings of assemblies in Venice, harder in a French or Spanish province, England, or the Netherlands, and virtually impossible for the whole of Spain. Given the limited variation of population density and per capita income, small states had to levy high taxes just to field armies that could hold their larger enemies, such as France, Spain, or the Hapsburg Empire, in check. If we measure a country's economic success by the amount of resources available per person, military success, to a large extent, depends on the absolute level of resources one polity can bring to the field. Consider the case of England and France at the beginning of the eighteenth century. The population of the British Isles (England, Wales, Scotland, and Ireland) was about 9 million, while that of France was twice as large (de Vries 1984). It may be that the British fiscal system was more efficient (Brewer 1989) and British incomes were higher, but those two effects were not sufficient to overcome the built-in advantage of the larger but less representative territory. As a result, in England, as in the Netherlands or Venice, tax rates were driven by war, and the tax decisions were made by autocrats who ruled large territories, not by any domestic calculus. Even if their fiscal institutions had wanted to be light, they could not but be heavy.

Considering war as an important element in the evolution of fiscal institutions helps us understand a final contrast in public finance between China and Europe: public credit. China had, for all intents and purposes, no public debt until the disastrous treaties that followed the Opium War. Most of the money raised by Chinese debt issues between the 1850s and World War I went toward paying war indemnities; thus it had few benefits for the economy. In contrast, European countries have been addicted to debt since the Middle Ages. Overwhelmingly they turned to credit markets, not to finance public infrastructure, but to pay for military expenditures. Debt was attractive because it allowed rulers to bring forward future expected peacetime surpluses and thus increase the scale of the military at the time at which it mattered most. This was particularly important for the smaller representative polities that fought bigger foes. Without credit markets it is unlikely that the Netherlands would have prevailed against Spain or England against France. The credit market also allowed absolutist rulers who had complete discretion in spending but limited leeway to increase revenues on their own to circumvent constitutional limits on taxation (Drelichman 2005). As a result of these differences in the importance of public debt, there clearly was more financial innovation in Europe than in China. But war-driven financial innovation was double edged. War no doubt encouraged the monetization of economies (simply because sovereigns preferred to get their revenue in cash so as to pay for a professional military rather than rely on feudal services). Such monetization certainly assisted the spread of markets. War also no doubt encouraged the growth of a market for public bonds and the shares of corporations whose primary assets were also government obligations (e.g., the Bank of England) or government-granted monopolies. Given the importance of scale in the efficiency of financial markets, there were likely positive externalities for private financial actors. But the downside of war-driven financial policy is simply stunning. Europeans states engaged in trade-distorting taxation on a scale unimagined in China. They also quite frequently debased their currency and in other ways reduced the security of financial contracts denoted in official units of account. Many of them also defaulted and engineered some of the most spectacular financial crashes of all time, as occurred under Philip II in Spain or under the Regency in France in 1719–1720.

Constraining the Despot: Exit and Voice

Although the development of credit markets can help us understand the persistence of smaller, richer polities in Europe, these markets are not much assistance if we want to explain why taxes were low in China. In fact, economic forces alone are likely to be only a minor obstacle to rulers who want to behave as revenue maximizers. Thus the willingness of individuals to take political action plays an important role in limiting despotic taxation. Indeed, contemporary evidence suggests that one can sustain hefty rates of taxes on labor (on the order of 30%) without a huge effect on formal work (in the United States the income-tax rate is above 20%, state taxes are often on the order of 7%, and Social Security and other taxes add another 4% or 5%; although European rates are different, they add up to a similar magnitude). If the formal economy does not start to shrink much until taxes surge past 30% or 40%, then, absent political constraints, a dictator would choose rates of taxation at least that high. But except for resource-rich economies today, where dictators can tax heavily because they control exports, rulers make do with much lower rates of taxation. In societies like China and Europe before 1800, the bulk of revenues came from internal sources, and the cost of increasing taxation was substantial. The need to secure at least the grudging willingness of the population to pay taxes has profound implications (Levi 1989). Transferring Albert O. Hirschman's important insights about firms to government, we argue that subjects and citizens can influence the fiscal plans of rulers and officials in two broad ways that we call *exit* and *voice* (Hirschman 1970).

Exit, for our present purposes, refers to a variety of strategies that deprive the ruler of revenue without confrontation when individuals decide that they do not like their leaders' behavior. It includes people migrating to another country that might offer a better mix of public spending and private opportunities. It also includes moving into the informal economy. A household might undertake either of these moves simply to escape the burden of taxes, but it might also do so if spending on public goods is too low. This kind of passive resistance is unlikely to break a regime, but it proves costly in resources and may be enough to persuade rulers to keep their rapacity in check and provide more than the bare minimum of services.

There are also other ways, more effective and more expensive, to get the attention of the ruler; these we will call *voice*. They include both institutions whose assent is required for new taxes, such as the Spanish Cortes or the French Estates General, and organized protest and revolts. To the extent that these kinds of mechanisms are effective, tax collection and spending cannot get too far out of line with the expectations of the population, regardless of whether the regime is democratic or autocratic. The critical issue is that individuals' willingness to pay taxes depends not just

Box 6.3. Adding exit and voice

The key in establishing the results obtained in Boxes 6.1 and 6.2 is that taxes damage the formal economy at the same rate independent of political regime or what they are used for. In this context, where the dictator is a tax maximizer, he will always choose the highest tax rates of all. But we know that the extent of evasion depends on whether people feel that taxes are raised for legitimate or for corrupt purposes. Judgments about the legitimacy of taxation concern both the degree of representation *(F)* and the level of diversion that the controlling faction carries out.

These considerations mean that the share of the economy that is lost to tax avoidance $(1 - R(t))$ depends on *F*. In other words, *R*(t, F) such that

$$\frac{\partial R}{\partial t} < 0; \frac{\partial R}{\partial F} > 0; \frac{\partial^2 R}{\partial t \partial F} > 0.$$

The faction in power continues to maximize the same objective function:

$\pi = W(w)(1-t)R(t)FY(G) + W(w)tR(t)Y(G)$ subject to $G + w \geq tR(t)Y(G)$.

We claim that if the willingness to pay taxes increases sufficiently rapidly with $F(\partial R/\partial F > 0)$

then $\frac{\partial t^*}{\partial F} > 0.$

Clearly, as in the earlier cases, there must exist $\hat{F}$ such that $G + w = tR(t)Y(G)$. For any $F > \hat{F}$, the constraint will continue to bind, but because the taxation is less costly, taxes will be increased to produce more public goods or spending on the military.

For $F < \hat{F}$, because the constraint on revenue does not bind, spending on the military and public goods will expand as it did in the earlier cases.

The key, therefore, is the comparative effect of changes in *F* on changes in *t**:

$$\frac{\partial \pi}{\partial t} = W(w)F\left\{-R(t)Y(G) + (1-t)\frac{\partial R}{\partial t}Y(G)\right\} + W(w)\left\{R(t)Y(G) + t\frac{\partial R}{\partial t}Y(G)\right\} = 0,$$

Because W(w)Y(F) appears in every term, the equation simplifies to

$$\frac{\partial \pi}{\partial t} = F\left\{-R(t) + (1-t)\frac{\partial R}{\partial t}\right\} + \left\{R(t) + t\frac{\partial R}{\partial t}\right\} = 0, \text{ and}$$

$$\frac{\partial^2 \pi}{\partial t \partial F} = -R(t) + (1-t)\frac{\partial R}{\partial t} + \frac{\partial R}{\partial F}(1-F) + \frac{\partial^2 R}{\partial t \partial F}(F + t - tF).$$

The first two terms in the equation $(-R(t) + (1-t)\partial R/\partial t)$ are negative, between 1 and 0, and involve the standard tax-avoidance response of the population. The third and fourth terms $\left(\frac{\partial R}{\partial F}(1-F) + \frac{\partial^2 R}{\partial t \partial F}(F + t - tF)\right)$ are positive and relate to the greater willingness of individuals to pay taxes as the franchise expands. When no taxation without representation holds, these two terms dominate the first two.

on the tax rate but also on the political regime. In Box 6.3 we model a situation in which the decline in economic output due to increased taxation depends directly on the size of the faction that controls the economy (the dictator is a faction of one person, and full democracy involves a faction that includes at least half the population). Although there are many ways to model the impact of exit and voice on a fiscal regime, this turns out to be the simplest. It also has the advantage that the gains from political change are not exhausted as soon as the size of the group that controls taxation and spending is large enough that it ceases to steal part of the tax revenue. In doing so, we forgo the analysis of a possibly more subtle political interplay whereby autocrats may secure more revenue by promising and delivering more public goods. If the willingness of individuals to pay taxes rises sufficiently fast as the political regime becomes more inclusive, then revenues, public expenditures, and war expenditures will all rise with the size of the faction in control. Still, taxes will be higher in war-torn economies than in peaceful ones, as argued in the previous section. Our iterative approach to theory has produced a different model with which to compare China and Europe. It is kinder to China than the simple dictator approach because it recognizes that peaceful economies can provide more public goods than war-torn ones (even today the rate of infrastructure spending would surely slow in China if it were to spend a fraction of national income on the military equivalent to that of the United States). It also reaffirms our understanding that the European political and fiscal innovations associated with representative governments were important.

For some, implicit threats of exit were precisely what persuaded the Chinese emperors to show restraint in taxation, and it was the same threats that dissuaded them from raising the revenue to meet the political challenges of the nineteenth century (M. Li 2003). In China a combination of low taxes and provision of public goods defined good governance. By the Qing dynasty the imperial bureaucracy devoted considerable effort to advertising its adherence to this standard and, in particular, to ensuring that the population understood that any deviation from these principles was undertaken to fulfill a public need. These efforts are easiest to see in expenditures for water control. These expensive infrastructure projects would have been ideal arenas for corruption if the government had been capable of diverting resources gained from expanding public spending. Instead, the empire organized water-control efforts as campaigns. Major problems were addressed by bursts of bureaucratic energy and resources. Zhichu Zhou estimates that routine river-conservancy and water-control projects cost more than 2 million taels annually in the eighteenth century (at a time when routine revenues were roughly 41 to 42 million taels annually). Special projects of extraordinary repairs amounted to another 1.5 million taels annually. Finally, he estimates that the combination of routine and extraordinary repairs needed for the seacoast waterworks in Jiangnan cost another 500,000 taels annually, for a total of some 4 million taels annually, nearly half of which was nonroutine expenditures (Z. Zhou 2002: 27). Campaigns had advantages over routine projects. They allowed the emperor to mobilize additional resources, while his subjects were comforted by the fact that the resources raised would go to a very specific purpose rather than be swallowed in the mysteries of the public treasury.

Campaigns were, in fact, used for several purposes. The expansion of the granary system depended on periodic campaignlike efforts to mobilize and store additional amounts of grain. Between the late seventeenth and the late eighteenth centuries these succeeded in amassing hundreds upon hundreds of tons of grain (Will and Wong 1991). Unlike water-control issues, the granary system's expansion created no ecological dangers, although some officials pondered the possibility that public operations would interfere with the market. As for water control, creating routine maintenance and supervision could prove more challenging than mobilizing men and resources in campaignlike efforts to establish granaries or augment their reserves.

The long periods of quiet in the Chinese empire enabled rulers and subjects to rely heavily on such strategies. At the other end of Eurasia, kings' extraordinary revenues showed some similarities to what was raised in China as campaigns. Every early modern European potentate filled his coffers with both ordinary and extraordinary revenues. Extraordinary revenues were earmarked for specific purposes and were set to expire at some prespecified time. But any resemblance to China's campaigns is deceptive. European rulers failed to develop a workable fiscal system based on an understanding that the funds subjects provided would be allocated to useful purposes. This failure had multiple causes, starting with the fact that extraordinary revenues rarely went to public goods provisions rather than warfare.[2] Kings could not keep their promises to spend money on domestic public goods because they were at war with one another so often. The high cost of war constrained their behavior to the extent that the resources they allocated to the military and basic administration always dwarfed even their private consumption. Even such a sumptuous monarch as Louis XIV could have afforded Versailles ten times over and cut taxes had he avoided the wars of the League of Augsburg and of the Spanish Succession.[3]

Moreover, resources did not go to any special administration but rather flowed into the public treasury. It is not surprising that populations were loath to consent to significant taxes for public goods because they were well aware that these would likely be appropriated for military purposes whenever war broke out. Furthermore, given the already-high levels of taxation in these poor economies, the bulk of the population may well have preferred to keep what income it had for basic necessities rather than for better roads or, later, schools. The surprising fact about European history is how little rulers were punished for redirecting resources to their preferred activity: war.

Consider that rulers tended to expropriate part of the resources of welfare providers (the most famous example is Henry VIII's nationalization of church wealth in England). For instance, in France, by the seventeenth century the primary provider of education and charity, the Catholic Church, had been induced to assist the treasury by granting subsidies (called *dons gratuits*). These resources were supposedly designed to assist the Crown in fighting infidels (Michaud 1991). When the Crown reallocated the resources to the general budget, the church did not cease to pay. Although the negotiations had the trappings of an equilibrium based on exit, the church failed to punish the Crown. Clearly, then, Europeans had plenty of occasions to practice exit on misbehaving rulers, but the resulting equilibrium was not the same as in China: revenues grew ceaselessly, and expenditures on war were rarely popular.

The likes of Louis XIV were not kept in check by the threat of exit. Instead, Europeans relied heavily on voice, and ideas about good governance became linked, not to low taxation per se, but to "no taxation without representation," as it was famously put in the context of the American Revolution. European monarchs, even the most absolutist ones, were not fiscal dictators, because elites had voice. Rulers faced serious constraints on raising revenues and in some cases on how money was spent. In some domains they could set taxes with little restraint, but most tax rates had to be decided in consultation with representative assemblies. Although rulers could govern for long periods of time without consultation, they found it extremely difficult to expand their revenues without calling an assembly. In fact, revenue and expenditure institutions are remarkably important if we want to understand early modern European public finance.

To raise money, early modern European sovereigns relied on a variety of strategies. At first, taxes were collected by individuals who were required to provide services in kind to the state. Theoretically, in this initial feudal equilibrium the king's sole revenues came from his own estates, and he could call on his vassals to perform periodic military service, most often capped at sixty days a year. This arrangement proved unsatisfactory because military campaigns tended to last longer than military obligations, and vassals had limited incentives to provide high-quality services. Rulers were thus soon hunting for more effective sources of revenue. They could obtain these by special arrangements with some of their subjects or, more practically, by bringing together the important players in the polity to discuss fiscal matters. These discussions were institutionalized as Parliament in England, the Estates General in France, the Cortes in Spain, the Diet in the Holy Roman Empire, and other bodies. Henceforth we will refer to these institutions as estates. Although there was tremendous variation in who was represented in these meetings (e.g., mostly cities in Spain and mostly barons in England), one thing is clear: these institutions had important constitutional privileges regarding tax revenue. When representative institutions perceived that the policy objectives of the Crown coincided with their own, they could loosen their purse strings.

In authorizing new taxes, representative bodies could grant either ordinary revenues (taxes that could be levied as long as the ruler lived) or extraordinary revenues (taxes that would expire after a war ended, after some specified period of time, or after some specified revenue was raised). These revenues could include either direct taxes on land, people, and capital or indirect taxes (sales or transit taxes). Once taxes were granted, a variety of systems were used to collect the attendant revenue. In some places and at some times, taxes were collected by salaried government officials; in others they were collected by private firms that bought the right to collect revenue. In either case the investment in fiscal infrastructure throughout Europe was nothing less than astounding, a testimony to rulers' dedication to secure additional revenues (Tilly 1990; Hoffman and Norberg 1994).

Despite the institutional investments of rulers, taxes rose slowly because they faced a number of problems. To begin with, sovereignty was a personal matter in Europe. As a result, when two independent areas came to be ruled by the same person, this did not necessarily mean fiscal unification of the areas. Although Castile and Aragon were united by Ferdinand and Isabella, for instance, that action committed the sovereign only to a common line of inheritance. When their successors wanted to raise taxes, they had to negotiate separately with the assemblies of the different provinces—not only with the Cortes of Castile and the assemblies of Aragon, but with those of Catalonia and the northern provinces as well. The process of fiscal unification was slow. It was not completed in many parts of Europe until the nineteenth century (Dincecco 2010). This was not a problem only of southern or continental countries. The same ruler reigned separately over the kingdom of England and that of Scotland until 1707. Unification with Ireland did not occur until 1801. The result of this divided sovereignty was twofold. First, it created a problem of free riding— each territory wanted others to shoulder the cost of the common good. The best the Crown could hope for was to negotiate with some large entity and then persuade the other ones to go along with proportional increases. Success depended on strong popular support for the Crown's fiscal aims. The second consequence of divided sovereignty was that it raised the cost of negotiations with outlying areas. The basic constitutional principle was that the sovereign had to travel to the province and meet with its estates to request revenues. Obviously, if the Crown's goals were popular, then such meetings were unnecessary. But most often some, if not many, of a ruler's subjects had sufficient reservations to refuse to provide funds. Then the ruler faced a stark choice: travel to the recalcitrant province or make do with a smaller grant. As a result, there was wide variation in the fiscal burden across regions (Hoffman and Rosenthal 1997; Beik 1989; Elliott 1986; de Vries and van de Woude 1997; van Zanden and van Riel 2004).

The fiscal equilibrium of divided sovereignty coupled with a requirement of consultation of elites was very unappealing to early modern monarchs. They resented the time it took to negotiate tax increases, as well as the oversight it implicitly gave to other groups in society. In each country the Crown attempted to change tack and sidestep estates. Whenever it succeeded, an absolute monarchy was established. Under absolutism the

Crown did without estates and thus could spend its resources with complete discretion. Doing without estates was feasible because their meeting was at the discretion of the Crown, but it was costly because no regular taxation could be imposed without some sort of consenting institution. Doing without estates did not imply that revenues became fixed. Rather, the Crown had to find alternative paths to raise revenues.

The Crown had some leeway in securing revenue because it was not only the executive but also the apex of the judiciary (North and Weingast 1989). Its executive function gave it discretion over currency matters in at least some of its domains, and it also gave it discretion over the organization of tax collection. Its judicial powers allowed the Crown considerable freedom to secure revenues. Indeed, the judiciary's regulatory powers could be used to raise revenue, most famously through the sale of monopolies "for the public good."

European history thus shows that rulers faced different levels of constraint on their expenditure and revenue decisions. If we abstract from these different situations, it makes sense to think that provinces have the capacity to limit rulers' revenues without having the capacity to limit their rulers' use of funds. In contrast, the reverse situation, in which provincial elites cannot set tax rates but do tell the ruler how to spend his revenues, is highly unlikely. We can therefore limit ourselves to the set of regimes where expenditure decisions are less constrained than revenue decisions. For any given province, we can think that elites may have an effective check on taxes, on taxes and expenditures, or on neither. Because kings rule over many provinces, each with its own institutions, the extent of provincial fiscal independence can vary. At one extreme a ruler could have complete fiscal control in all his provinces. At the other extreme he could lack fiscal control over any province—he would, in effect, be a parliamentary monarch. But the king's power could also vary from province to province, leading him to face partial constraints on revenues and possibly partial constraints on expenditures. This form of government has often been called absolutism.

Consider the domains of Philip II of Spain. In Castile the Crown wielded considerably more power over revenues than it did in other parts of the Iberian Peninsula, and its efforts at tax rationalization in the Low Countries were viewed as an affront to provincial liberties. Resistance to new taxes led to the sixteenth-century revolt and ultimately to the loss of the northern Low Countries. Within the Iberian Peninsula taxes were much higher in Castile than elsewhere, and an attempt at tax rationalization there led to the permanent loss of Portugal (Elliott 1986). In France, William Beik (1989) and others have documented that even Louis XIV had to negotiate far more strenuously to extract revenue from provinces with representative assemblies *(pays d'états)* than with those that did not have such institutions. Equally notable, Beik documents that in the case of Languedoc the Crown was forced to leave substantial sums in the province for the provision of public goods.

It is important to note that although representation in Europe has very old roots, its ultimate adoption as the standard mechanism for fiscal decision making was challenged every step of the way. Representation was a key element of rule in many ancient city-states (Athens and Rome, but not Sparta). It was also an important element of the political structure among the populations that invaded the Roman Empire. Nevertheless, it was a structure that most rulers did not like. From the Roman emperors to absolutist kings and to "parliamentary" monarchs like William and Mary, at best, rulers tolerated the institution. Rather than quietly accept representation, both Charles II and Louis XVI lost their heads (Rosenthal 1998). Europe may have had an efficient fiscal mechanism, but it was not easily adopted because it represented a fundamental weakening of the power of sovereigns.

Representation was as unique to Europe as good governance was to China. Until the twentieth century China had no formal institutions outside the imperial bureaucracy that structured negotiations between ruler and subjects over taxes. However, the Chinese were not without voice: an important element behind revolts was the burden of taxation and beliefs about the diversion of revenue into the pockets of corrupt officials. Tax revolts, in fact, were an element of tax negotiation that was common to both Europe and China (Wong 1997: 231–251). Revolts were costly in effort and dangerous for people to mount, but they were also expensive for governments to put down. This latter fact no doubt curbed government appetites for taxation to some degree, even if in the case of Europe a diet of light taxes could never really satisfy the ruler's needs.

We can use these ideas to reconcile our understanding of the political economy of taxation across China and Europe. Rulers in China could keep taxes low because they could field comparatively large armies with low tax rates and a domestic political equilibrium that equated internal fiscal and political stability with a limited amount of diversion of tax revenues into the pockets of officials and the emperors. The emperor could and did buy further goodwill by investing in an array of public goods important to his mostly rural subjects. Meanwhile, in the competitive political economy of Europe, taxes were kept relatively high by the need to defray ever-growing military expenses. Wars made it impossible for rulers to commit to any significant program of domestic public spending—to the extent that when these activities occurred, they were discharged by the private sector or by nongovernmental organizations like guilds or the church. Although European rulers and Chinese emperors lived in luxury unimaginable to their subjects, political mechanisms kept their take of the fiscal system limited. Versailles and the Forbidden City were perhaps politically costly, but they were fiscally cheap. The rise of representative government did not lead to any decline in fiscal pressure, in part because such systems were expensive, but mostly because they too had to face the burden of war.

Reinterpreting History: Equilibria and Unforeseen Consequences

In the universe of economic possibilities available before the Industrial Revolution, the rate of technological change was exogenous. The main sources of economic growth were either market based or related to agricultural productivity. Given these conditions, the Chinese fiscal regime of relatively low taxes and relatively high provision of public goods compares favorably with European fiscal regimes of relatively high taxes and relatively low provision of public goods. It thus seems that the Chinese fiscal regime was the superior one for the economy.

Although the motivations of rulers and their populations might have been similar, the different intensities of warfare led to long-term differences in fiscal structure. Most prominently, Chinese emperors preferred to face the threat of exit than the constraints of voice, and they could do so because they did not face constant warfare. By 1300 European rulers, on the other hand, had exhausted this strategy and had to rely on voice. These differences had important implications for fiscal structures across Eurasia and for how they evolved.

The Chinese achieved their bureaucratic regime of rule without representative institutions and despite dramatic geographic variations and cultural diversity. Chinese historians sometimes express skepticism regarding the efficacy of Confucian ideology, but there can be little doubt that in contrast to European political ideologies, Confucian thought succeeded in providing simple and relatively persuasive rules for the behavior of peasants, elites, and the emperor. Because of these norms, local officials were aided by local elites in raising funds for various projects. Such activities included those initiated by proclamations coming from the emperor to his provincial officials, who in turn passed on instructions to local county officials. In China the eighteenth century witnessed rising levels of public expenditures—if there was a state that sponsored economic development anywhere in the eighteenth century, it was the Qing state, not Britain, France, or any other European state.

The Qing recognized that the geographic diversity of the empire could be as much a source of strength as one of weakness. Officials were members of a larger, vertically integrated bureaucracy. Those serving in more developed provinces were required to coordinate decision making with officials in other provinces and in the capital to create both routine and extraordinary flows of resources to poorer areas. Without these resource transfers it is difficult to imagine how the Qing state could have succeeded in consolidating its frontiers. As a result, officials at least implicitly divided the agrarian empire into three zones. One kind of zone included the economic cores and nearby peripheries of the interior. The most economically prosperous provinces produced fiscal surpluses to be used in poorer peripheries, and especially along the landlocked frontiers that formed a second kind of zone along the northern and southwestern borders of the empire. A third kind of zone was composed of the maritime region along the southeastern and southern borders of the empire which included port areas with thriving trade to other parts of Asia (Wong 2004). In Europe it was the development of voice rather than exit that produced growth in the provision of public goods (and of military resources). In the previous section we argued that constitutional constraints forced rulers to accept voice, however reluctantly. Given that negotiations over budgetary matters were a repeated process, one might assume that rulers could have developed a reputation for producing low-corruption regimes and avoided either the sanctions of exit or the unpleasant oversight of voice. Although this approach is theoretically attractive, it holds little promise to explain the development of taxation in Europe. To be sure, reputation enlarges the set of equilibrium taxes and expenditure shares that can be supported and thus apparently weakens the differences across political regimes. This is particularly true if subjects use trigger strategies to punish misbehavior and rulers never deviate from the equilibrium path. Then rulers and subjects who are patient enough can find equilibria that support efficient (low-corruption, high-tax, high-public-goods) outcomes regardless of the institutional structure. If societies reach reputational equilibria in their taxation, rulers tax lightly or produce lots of public goods for their subjects, otherwise they would suffer tax strikes or revolts.

It is our contention, however, that history is not consistent with the prevalence of reputational equilibria. Institutions mattered in European public finance because rulers could not adhere to behavior consistent with a good reputation. Although some may have behaved well (as Henry IV appeared to do in France), inevitably either warfare or corruption reared its ugly head, and society returned to a more naked political economy in which institutional constraints were binding. The history of Qing China before 1800 conforms with the expectation of a low tax, high public good reputational equilibrium. The subsequent history does not. As we shall see below, faced with increased strife, the Empire sought and found massive new sources of revenue

Hence the European equilibrium may well have been less a consequence of initial constitutional conditions than a consequence of political fragmentation. At the European scale, warfare could not have occurred without fragmented sovereignty. Within each polity fragmented sovereignty was also important in coordinating resistance to tax increases and paving the way for voice. It also had the consequence that taxing commerce at internal and international borders was a much more important source of revenue for European states than for China. In both absolute and proportional terms, more revenue was generated from commerce by European states than in China. Tariffs were both domestic and international. Indeed, the European polities that existed in 1700 were the product of conquest, marriage, and inheritance, and, as noted earlier, each province tended to maintain institutional autonomy long after it had come under the sway of a particular king. Although this autonomy was important for creating voice, it also made possible internal tariffs, a fiscal benefit for the Crown. During the eighteenth century the elimination of such internal tariffs became an important policy goal in France and Spain. Such reform was part of a package of reforms that were intended to increase economic output but were resisted by local elites because they threatened the fiscal equilibrium. In France these internal barriers were swiftly removed during the Revolution as representative institutions arrived. In sharp contrast, the unification of Britain with Ireland in 1801 came long after the rise of representative government. There was thus no simple causal linkage between institutions of political representation and a state's fiscal centralization and integration. More generally and key to our argument, the competitive state system that created warfare also caused serious distortions of trade within Europe.

China's fiscal regime was well suited to promote the material welfare of the general population under a preindustrial set of economic possibilities. The direct consequences of low taxes and high public goods expenditures were economically positive. China's fiscal regime was well able to absorb a variety of natural and social shocks that could have challenged the material security and economic well-being of the people. The equilibrium between principles of taxation and expenditure broadly stayed in balance. In Europe any attempt to exit the high-taxation/low-public-goods equilibrium was inevitably undermined by needs to raise taxes to fund warfare.

Over several centuries before 1850, Chinese rulers were usually able to address a variety of economic opportunities and challenges. Moderate taxation was a key component of a larger kind of balance that the state aimed to maintain across the empire's diverse regions and along the social hierarchy. Maintaining the fiscal equilibrium and social and economic balances more generally became increasingly difficult during the eighteenth century as populations grew and the territory under imperial rule expanded. Indeed, insofar as state policies enhanced people's abilities to reach the economy's production frontier, the state may have made some people more vulnerable to short-term economic shocks from natural or human-made disasters.

In Europe the fiscal equilibrium of high taxes and high military expenditures produced fewer direct economic benefits for ordinary people, but despite the persistent underinvestment in public goods, the European fiscal regime produced some unintended consequences that were positive, while China's did not. Governments as a source of demand for military armaments, for instance, could stimulate technological changes that could be beneficial beyond warfare. Government spending stimulated investment and technological changes that otherwise might not have taken place. These consequences for the economy were indirect because governments were not seeking to improve conditions in the economy generally. For instance, investments in warships were designed to make them faster and more reliable. The knowledge gained from these investments diffused and made all ships faster. As a result, goods and people, rather than just cannons and marines, moved more quickly over time. These suggestions, of course, have been made long ago (Nef 1950). For our purposes it is important to contrast these kinds of unexpected long-term consequences with the more immediate goals pursued by government officials, which in early modern Europe meant warfare and in late imperial China meant social welfare. This point complements the one made in Chapter 3 about the unintended consequences of locating manufacturing in cities. For both observations, we distinguish causal consequences from the intentions or purposes of the people making the political decisions that affected long-run economic growth possibilities.

The two cases of early modern Europe and late imperial China by themselves might suggest that persistent political instability is more advantageous than peace for promoting long-run economic growth. It is helpful, therefore, to recall that much of the world, including Africa, southern and central Europe, and Southeast Asia, all had competing political regimes and often warfare without benefiting from the kinds of windfalls that took place in Europe in the period before the Industrial Revolution. Further research is needed to understand just why those competitive areas did not embark on the path of capital-using technological change. Clearly, however, political competition and conflict are not enough to guarantee technological change and economic growth.

China and Europe after 1850

In some ways the contrasting relationships among state finances, warfare, and economic growth in China and in Europe after 1850 reversed the basic patterns clearly visible a century before. China moved from a low-tax and high-public-goods equilibrium to a high-tax regime in order to finance military expenses—first to put down massive midcentury rebellions and then to begin building armaments to strengthen the empire's defenses against foreign predators. As a consequence, the Chinese state's abilities and willingness to invest in public goods fell well below the levels it had maintained a century earlier. Just as European states had earlier turned to commercial sources of revenue, after 1850 the Chinese empire also expanded its revenue base through new domestic and foreign trade taxes and by increasing the price at which the government's monopoly sold salt.

Europe, however, ceased to engage in the scale of costly warfare that had previously been the driving force behind fiscal expansion. Instead, European states were beginning to supply more public goods. This included financing railroads, beginning in the 1840s and 1850s on the Continent, and improving urban amenities later in the century with sewage systems, plumbing, paved streets, streetlights, and the like. Alongside the growth of public goods provision, Europeans completed their moves toward freer trade that had begun in the eighteenth century. These moves took place both within individual European countries and between them. The British unilaterally abolished the Corn Laws in 1847, and the British and the French signed a major trade treaty in 1860.

These changes in the fiscal regimes of both China and Europe took place after the Industrial Revolution. Neither played a positive causal role in creating the Industrial Revolution. However, we might have expected the Chinese state in the second half of the nineteenth century to play a positive role in mobilizing resources and directing them into projects promoting economic growth. The state certainly was able to raise much more revenue than it had been able to raise in the eighteenth century. But the extremely large increases in taxes that occurred after 1895 were forced on the Chinese by foreign powers wanting indemnities for military actions. Early modern European state expenditures on war could not be expected to yield direct and positive impacts on those economies. Similarly, China's payments of indemnities in the late nineteenth and early twentieth centuries could do little, if anything, to stimulate economic growth.

In 1849 the government raised some 42.5 million taels of revenue, 77% of which came from agriculture and the balance from commerce. Thirty-six years later revenues had climbed to more than 77 million taels; the increase was largely due to a quadrupling of commercial revenues. Expenditure levels had remained in the range of 30 to 40 million taels annually between the 1720s and the early 1840s. They then doubled to 70 to 80 million taels annually between the 1860s and the early 1890s (Hamashita 1989: 66). The capacity to increase revenues and expenditures in this manner is hardly the sign of a weak state—the conventional portrait of China in this period— but it is an indicator of a significant transformation. The state was able to mobilize far more revenues than it had previously found desirable to amass. Although the state took in less than it needed, its revenue was sufficient to begin responding to foreign challenges.

Much of the increased revenue was raised through maritime customs. In addition to serving as security for foreign loans (which were used to help pay for the suppression of the 1867 Muslim rebellion in northwestern China), customs revenues were used in the 1880s to build railroads (Hamashita 1989: 68, 72). The development of imperial control over customs revenues is a clear indication of the state's ability to create new infrastructural capacities. When China's late nineteenth-century central government is not judged by its failure to survive beyond 1911 but is instead compared with its eighteenth-century predecessor, we can see just how much its fiscal capacities had grown. But these Chinese increases were nothing compared with the nearly 302 million taels of revenue gathered in 1911, the final year of the dynasty. By this date agricultural taxes had grown from roughly 30 to roughly 50 million taels, commercial taxes brought in more than 207 million, and another 45 million came from miscellaneous sources. Whatever the late Qing state's weaknesses, raising money was not among them (Wei 1986: 227). Unfortunately, the 1895 Japanese indemnity equaled a full year's receipts, and the 1900 Boxer indemnity was one and one-half times as large. It was the weight of international reparations that made China's fiscal situation so precarious and ultimately untenable.

What if China had been free of its international debts and thus able to put newly raised funds to more productive uses? Are there any indications that the government would have used the funds effectively? Typically the Chinese failure to industrialize in the late nineteenth century is contrasted with Japanese successes, but these contrasts between China and Japan may rest too much on reading backward from mid-twentieth-century differences in economic growth to nineteenth-century differences. An assessment of either what the Chinese state did or what it might have done if it had had more revenues with which to pursue an economic agenda would clearly provide a more positive conclusion. Benjamin Elman's assessment of Chinese science and technology includes analyses of some late nineteenth-century changes. He argues that the Chinese tradition of natural studies and Western science developed together beginning in the 1860s and that both highly educated literati, the social stratum from which officials were recruited, and more modestly educated artisans were drawn to modern science and technologies entering the empire from the West. Furthermore, these developments began a decade before similar changes took place in Japan. Japanese officials visited Chinese arsenals and shipyards to learn how to develop imported technologies (Elman 2005: 283–395).

At the turn of the century, a time during which Tessa Morris-Suzuki (1994) has found that the Japanese were spreading technological knowledge through various local study circles, we also find governmental efforts in China spearheaded by provincial governments to promote the formation of similar groups at the county level (Morris-Suzuki 1994; Jin 1919). When we look directly at nineteenth-century evidence, it is less obvious than we once assumed that Japanese efforts to promote economic growth were more serious than those taken up in China. Had the Chinese had more fiscal and organizational resources to put toward these efforts after 1900, they might have helped promote industrialization and economic growth. But the fiscal difficulties of the indemnities for the Sino-Japanese War and the Boxer Uprising crippled the state's capacities to spend money on projects intended to yield economic benefits. Although in the late nineteenth century the Chinese state was unable to devote as much of its attention to economic development as the Japanese did, officials were able to raise substantially more revenues than they had previously done. If we imagine China less threatened by foreigners, we could reasonably expect that a greater portion of Chinese efforts would have gone toward promoting economic change. Had there been even less contact, we can imagine China possibly continuing for a longer period of time with its earlier kind of fiscal equilibrium and thus not likely to have had either the opportunities or the pressures to make dramatic changes.

In Europe the nineteenth century was also a time of rising taxes, fiscal innovation, and, more generally, increasing government involvement in promoting economic growth. Without going back to the catch-up framework of Gerschenkron (1962), states did become more concerned about promoting growth. As a result and in contrast to China, industrialization in Europe led to a decline in the share of government revenue (and of the economy) devoted to the military. Hence the political transformation that began with the French Revolution propelled Europeans in a direction opposite to China's movements. While the Chinese empire had to spend ever-increasing amounts on military activities (or on war indemnities), continental European states were investing in their economies. England is a somewhat anomalous case because the maintenance of its empire was a very important factor in the relatively high rates of taxation that fell on Britons. But because per capita income was relatively high, England could afford both public goods and the largest navy in the world (Davis and Huttenback 1986).

Aside from the consequences of colonial involvement, European states increased their expenditures on public goods in different ways and at different times in different places. The work of Peter Lindert (2004) has focused on the growth of welfare and education spending. It shows that representative institutions (voice) were critical in the expansion of public services from the 1880s to the mid-twentieth century. But the growth of public spending antedates the rise of the welfare state and the expansion of schooling. In the nineteenth century public spending included transport through the direct financing of roads and canals, subsidies to railroad expansion, or concessions for transport improvements (ports, bridges, and, at times, roads). Such spending (admittedly by local rather than central governments) also provided significant investment in local public utilities as urban areas expanded the demand for sanitation, clean water, street lighting, marketplaces, and local transport services.

The pursuit of increased public goods depended on the mechanism of voice. Most obviously, countries with representative government were more likely to devote a share of their central government budget to these activities—that is, after all, how the expansion of railroads, canals, and other major infrastructure projects was funded. Equally important was that the process of creating structures that favored the local provision of infrastructure or education also depended on mechanisms of voice. These included the bills of the British Parliament that authorized turnpike trusts and railroad corporations (Bogart 2005; Bogart and Richardson forthcoming). Mechanism of voice also included the institutions whereby municipalities could concede the business of providing lighting, clean water, and other local public goods to the public sector or decide to provide it themselves. Finally, mechanisms of voice were also present in the myriad of not-for-profit organizations that bloomed in nineteenth-century Europe. Whether these were credit cooperatives, savings banks, or agricultural improvement districts, they all relied on the capacity of individuals to form organizations whose governance gave their members voice.

The end of the Old Regime in Europe marked a transition to a higher level of public goods provision. Nevertheless, not all was new in the nineteenth century. Military concerns continued to loom large. Thus states did not promote trade or railroads solely because of their economic benefits but, even more important, because of their implications for the balance of power in Europe. For similar reasons, central governments were reluctant to let subnational units (in particular, municipalities) run their own fiscal

affairs. The main motivation for strict restriction of cities' fiscal independence was to avoid competition over revenues between central and local
governments. Because they were fiscally constrained, local governments
had little choice but to turn to the private sector for the development of
local utilities. Public goods provision did indeed depend on the mechanism of voice, but as the Chinese case makes clear, the European political
logic is by no means a universal one—the Chinese had more developed
public goods provision at an earlier time because of attention to issues of
exit rather than those of voice (Wong 2007).

This chapter has examined the differences in public finance by using a
simple model of political economy. In comparing this model with history,
we have been required to make it more complicated and more subtle, and
we have also come to a better understanding of the key differences between
the preindustrial public finance regimes that prevailed in China and in
Europe.

Perhaps the most controversial implication of this chapter is that Chinese
political economy, particularly its fiscal regime, had more positive direct
consequences for economic growth than did European fiscal regimes before the Industrial Revolution. This was because the emperor was far from
being a predatory despot. Rather, the Chinese regime focused on a significant production of public goods with moderate taxation, especially under
the Qing. This regime produced a successful expansion of the agrarian
and commercial economy—precisely the kind of Smithian growth that
European economic historians are so fond of. But Smithian growth need
not beget industrialization (Wong 1997: 9–52).

In Europe, by contrast, the political pressure to raise taxes was a central
element of conflict between rulers and elites. In the short-run perspective
of an agrarian commercial economy, these pressures had little good to
offer, but in the long run they may well have been an irritant that increased
the likelihood of both political and economic change. The military, after
all, was an important source of demand for manufactured goods. But one
should bear in mind that competitive state systems, such as those in Africa or Southeast Asia, have more often than not produced warfare rather
than economic growth.

It is also apparent that the direct benefits of political systems with representation came to be realized only after the onset of the Industrial Revolution, and after the consolidation of fiscal power into a unified central

government. In the early modern period all but the smallest states labored under inefficient and fragmented fiscal regimes. In these regimes, although taxes were high relative to China, public goods provision mattered little. China reminds us that although representation played an important role in the nineteenth and twentieth centuries in Europe, one cannot conclude that representation drives public goods provision everywhere and at all times.

By the mid-nineteenth century China was laboring under increased external and internal pressures, and its failure to develop large-scale fiscal capacities was becoming increasingly costly. Adaptation to a world in which warfare was a major problem proved difficult. The history of China since 1949, however, suggests that the path to higher taxation and public goods provision need not go through representative institutions. The Communist Party in both its Maoist and reform guises has been quite successful at providing public goods, such as primary schooling, health systems, and infrastructure. A case in point is the generation of schoolchildren whose education was ruined or at least severely impaired by the Cultural Revolution. For such a generation of students to have their education destroyed, there had to be schools in China in the 1950s that enrolled very large numbers of pupils. Had Mao behaved like the proper despot of economic theory after 1949, there would have been no need for the Cultural Revolution because few, if any, children would have been going to school.

Since 1978 the Chinese government has embarked on reforms that have privatized much of the economy. To be sure, serious problems remain in factor markets, most notably capital markets. But an important part of the gains from growth has been invested in infrastructure and other public goods. Although the public sector has shrunk dramatically, investment in more classic public services has been increasing. This has occurred despite the fact that the Communist Party has not released its grip on the political process. Thus although China may open up the political process over the next decade or two, it is not going to do so because it has previously failed to provide public goods.

In our analysis we emphasize variations among the fiscal institutions of European polities and only hint at the variation in fiscal institutions across the Chinese empire. We have taken the spatial scale of polities as given and have contrasted empire in China with a competitive political system in Europe. In several previous chapters we have noted that very few competitive political systems have led to the peculiar equilibrium favorable to economic change as experienced by Europe. A similar caveat is in order for empires. China's bureaucracy, focused on public goods and agrarian prosperity, was unique. Of the three other empires the Mongols ruled (Russia, Persia, and central Asia), none had administrative structures like China's. The Mongols were either unwilling or unable to export the political structure into which they embedded themselves in China. Hence the Chinese imperial equilibrium is but one possible outcome for a territorially large entity. We do not claim that Europe is typical of competitive state situations or that China is a typical empire. Rather, they represent two especially successful examples of a competitive state system and an empire, respectively. It is now time to show how the divergent political equilibria at each end of Eurasia came to be sustained.

7

Political Economies of Growth, 1500–1950

We have seen in previous chapters that economic growth due to gains from trade was more easily achieved in China than in Europe during the early modern era. Despite differences among the kinds of economic institutions most typical of China and those most typical of Europe, we can find no evidence that these differences made for significantly different likelihoods of economic growth in one rather than the other. Nor do differences in the representative nature of political institutions play the often-anticipated role of serving economic growth. But it is easy to be suspicious that these claims must somehow be specious, for surely the economic and political practices preceding the Industrial Revolution must have influenced the manifest divergence between the economic trajectories of nineteenth-century China and Europe. We do not, however, claim that different practices preceding the Industrial Revolution had no significance for nineteenth-century patterns of economic growth. Rather, we suggest that some of the most important differences between China and Europe that mattered for nineteenth-century economic growth emerged several centuries before that time. In particular the political structures in place in the period 1650 to 1800 had already been long standing. As Map 7.1 shows, China under the Qing was a large integrated political space as it had been under the Han and much like today's People's Republic. Europe in the mid-eighteenth century, as Map 7.2 shows, was severely fragmented, less than it had been in the Middle Ages and more so than today. Nevertheless at all of these times Europe has been less integrated than China. Unlike many previous observers, we do not find that these differences were due either to a particular cultural genius of Europeans or to political and economic circumstances that endowed them with advantages from a very early time. In this chapter we argue that early modern Chinese political economy was more explicitly intended to foster economic growth than European political economies. Moreover, Chinese officials succeeded in part because they had created political peace and social stability for more people across far more territory than their European counterparts could realistically imagine, let alone pursue. At this point the nineteenth-century economic divergence is not merely a European success story and a story of Chinese failure to emulate those successes. It is also a story of the Chinese loss of an earlier era of political economy, in part due to the political challenges created by Western powers and Japan. This history may seem very distant from a twenty-first century that has witnessed an apparently relentless expansion of the Chinese economy, but the abilities of the Chinese state to foster conditions that have made this growth possible are in part explained by economic history.

Late Empire: Foreigners, Natives, and Chinese Strategies of Rule

While European princes, as well as rulers in the Islamic political world, were being advised about how to undo their princely rivals and suppress internal challengers, many Chinese officials were reading a text that was very different in substance and spirit from Machiavelli's *The Prince*. They studied the *Supplement to the Exposition on the Great Learning,* by the fifteenth-century Confucian scholar Qiu Jun, a work that combined descriptions of statecraft policies popular in earlier centuries with the author's own commentaries. Widely distributed after Qiu Jun presented it to the emperor, who ordered the text to be printed and disseminated across the empire, this work became a ready reference for officials considering a variety of statecraft subjects, including water control, grain storage, tax policy, and local administration of minority populations, among many others. The tradition of statecraft continued to evolve under the Qing emperors and their officials who promoted material well-being and social stability through their economic policies. They learned what the practice of benevolent rule across an agrarian empire could concretely mean. From the vantage point of the empire's sedentary population alive in the late seventeenth and eighteenth centuries, people who accounted for well over 90% of the empire's total, the Manchu emperors advocated and implemented an agenda for managing

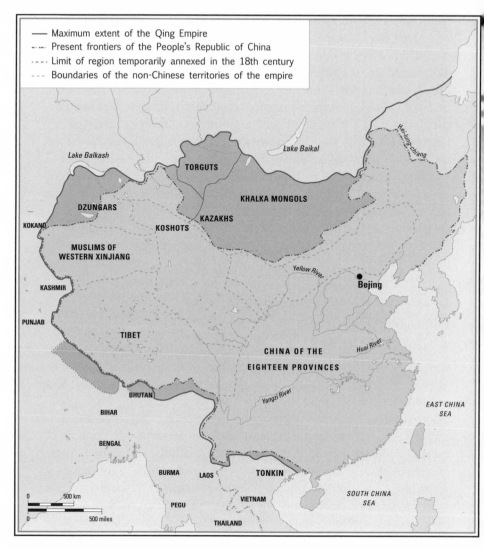

Map 7.1. The Qing Empire

society that was far more energetic and ambitious than that of their Ming predecessors.

The emperor's commitment to neo-Confucian strategies of rule was by itself inadequate to create the conditions for Ming- and Qing-dynasty successes at ruling the agrarian empire. For these strategies to make a differ-

Map 7.2. Europe in 1721, after the treaties of Utrecht and Nystad

ence, elites and commoners alike also had to consider neo-Confucian priorities and policies expressed in works like the *Supplement* sensible and beneficial. At a minimum they had to believe that their interests were better served within this political order than by undertaking the costs of exiting the empire. We do not mean to suggest that people were constantly evaluating the relative benefits and costs of staying within the empire in late imperial times, but simply that if people had been actively dissatisfied, they would have sought to reformulate their relationship to the state through some combination of voice and exit; instead, they remained loyal for the most part. Why? Because most subjects had little incentive to bear the costs of inventing an alternative way of organizing political order outside empire when they enjoyed considerable social space where the state weighed lightly on them and they could enjoy its material benefits.

Given that both elites and commoners accepted imperial forms of rule, how did neo-Confucian strategies of social order deflect and defuse the challenges that strained and often fragmented other empires? First, the core of the social elite was composed of literati educated to seek official positions from which they gained their social status. Second, unlike either the early empire of the Han or the middle empire of the Tang, the late empire of the Ming and Qing dynasties did not have to confront great magnate families. Third, commercial elites were not pressed so hard for resources that they considered mounting major opposition to the center. Landed and commercial elites were instead effectively delegated the tasks of maintaining social order by the bureaucracy, and as long as no serious troubles emerged, they were largely left alone by the state. Elite interests were effectively served by a partnership with officials.

For their part, merchant elites specifically benefited from state policies that facilitated long-distance trade, and their riches (unlike the wealth of Italian and German merchants, which was chronically vulnerable to predations from princes anxious for resources) could usually be protected from extraordinary state exactions. The state could keep its direct costs of governing the empire relatively low because it depended on local elites to shoulder much of the burden of formulating and maintaining institutions of local order, such as granaries and schools, as well as ensuring the upkeep of roads, bridges, and temples. Social order was the joint product of official and elite efforts (Wong 1997: 105–126). When natural disasters or social problems emerged, officials, elites, and common people often expected that joint efforts would solve the crises, and when they did not think that this was likely, they did not imagine that some exit strategy from empire would improve their condition. The late Ming dynasty survived the kinds of domestic threats from regional power holders that undermined the effectiveness of other empires. When it lost control, its ideology and institutions of rule for society were largely adopted by the Manchus who succeeded it.

The Manchu-led Qing dynasty that came to power in 1644 expanded the empire's borders once again into central Asia. Unlike the Mongols, the Manchus largely adopted the bureaucratic institutions of civilian rule to administer the vast peasant population of the empire. They made changes designed to improve communications, bureaucratic effectiveness, and, in particular, responsiveness to imperial orders, but the basic institutional template and ideological justifications of rule followed the principles and policies of earlier rulers of empires.[1] As we look at the role of the Manchus from the vantage point of the role of outsiders either promoting the persistence or hastening the destruction of empire, we can appreciate the degree to which Manchu successes across peasant China depended on their integration into an ongoing bureaucratic structure of rule. The eighteenth-century imperial anxieties about Manchus losing their martial spirit and becoming assimilated into Han Chinese culture reflect the considerable assimilation they underwent (Elliott 2001). The differences between the Manchus and the Han Chinese, important as specialists have shown them to be, remain less stark than those between Mongols and Chinese a few centuries earlier. The political similarities and connections between Manchu and Han are even more apparent, and for us crucial, when we put this Manchu-Han relationship into a common frame of reference with the relationship between imperial Rome and its "barbarians." In contrast to the Western situation where large numbers of distinct groups invaded portions of the Roman Empire, none of whom were able either to ally with or to defeat the others, outsiders in Chinese history were smaller in number relative to those already living under imperial rule. By the time the Manchus appeared on the scene, a demographically small group from beyond the empire had available a repertoire of policies that created benefits for both the rulers of empire and their subjects.

The political economy of the eighteenth-century state generally followed principles articulated in the previous centuries, but it committed officials to a greater degree of intervention and activism for longer periods of time than had been typical under the Ming dynasty. During the eighteenth century domestic commercial taxes were deliberately kept minimal. Merchants largely regulated local markets on their own. For its part, the state depended on markets not only to purchase the commodities consumed by the imperial household and the bureaucracy, but also to purchase the construction materials and hire the labor needed to build and repair government buildings. More significantly for the population, the state also bought grain in times of dearth to transport to places that were suffering the greatest subsistence needs. These features of the state's political economy contributed to the expansion of long-distance trade and the importance of informal institutions addressed in Chapter 3. The state also encouraged the diffusion of handicraft production (which we evaluated in Chapter 4) throughout China. Some officials disseminated information about craft technologies as they moved from post to post across the empire (Wong 1999). As we saw in Chapter 6, the state more generally chose not to tax the craft output of agrarian households, limiting itself to taxing the household's agricultural output. Indeed, it would have been far more costly to tax widely dispersed rural craft production than to tax urban-based production in larger workshops, which makes the state's decision to forgo these taxes more understandable than if the crafts had been concentrated in fewer locations.

The state's role in private and public finance also promoted economic growth. The private credit market we examined in Chapter 5 was largely informal, and the state played only a small role in regulating its activities. Chinese business was able to develop informal mechanisms to finance production and distribution without much recourse to government intervention. The costs of doing business were therefore lower than they would have been had more formal institutions been established. In public finance, as we showed in Chapter 6, the eighteenth-century Qing state invested far more in infrastructure (e.g., water control for production and transport) than was possible in Europe in the same period. The state's social spending overall was higher, and it stimulated and guided local government and elites to fund granaries, schools, road and temple repairs, and social surveillance against crime in their areas.

The contrasting spatial scales of the Chinese empire and European states offers a splendid illustration that the trade-offs offered by the theory of the firm are relevant to understanding the importance of scale in political economy. Firm size (in total capital and employment or in the number of tasks that it takes on) is variable as technology changes, and a manager who wishes to expand his or her firm must develop techniques of administration that make internal management superior to that of the market. The Ming chose a smaller empire, but one in which the population was overwhelmingly sedentary and thus receptive to the value of peace and internal trade. They did so not because they could not muster the might necessary to recover part of the western lands held by precursor dynasties. On the contrary, they limited their spatial ambitions to focus their resources on internal growth. The Qing dynasty, building on that effort, was able simultaneously to expand the set of services it rendered to its peasant population and to bring the empire to its largest scale. Its successful strategy of rule provided the resources for expansion. How different was the experience of state formation in Europe?

State Formation in Europe from Charles V to Napoleon

Machiavelli's *The Prince* was a guide for rulers who faced enemies from all sides. As Machiavelli saw it, the ambitious prince wanted to enhance the size of his realm at the same time as he wanted to avoid being beholden to his subjects. Pursuing his ambitions implied defeating his external enemies while holding the rebellious tendencies of his subjects in check. That *The Prince* was the main secular guide to rulers' behavior reminds us of the long history of European political strife. European states could not be built from a core relationship between subjects and rulers focused on low taxes and public goods. Instead, they had to be built in struggles that included conflicts between dynasties, as well as violent confrontations between subjects and rulers.

Fragmentation in Europe ended haltingly, but by 1300 the trend toward ever-smaller polities that had begun with the collapse of the Roman Empire had reversed, and states were generally growing (Tilly 1990). One reason for this is that by then the external challenges to Europe were limited geographically to the formidable threats represented by the Ottomans. From Spain to Poland, Europe was expanding through use of a military technology that was not only radically different from that of the Roman legions but also unlike what had prevailed at the end of the first millennium (Hoffman forthcoming). On the defensive side the importance of fortifications made it possible for relatively small states (like the Low Countries) to hold off larger ones. But fortifications required resources, and expenses did not stop there. By 1300 feudal levies of troops had long been replaced by soldiers who had to be paid (whether they were foreign mercenaries or domestically levied troops like the Spanish Tercios). By 1400 artillery trains added to the cost of war. Only states with large treasuries could continue to compete in Europe's political contests. Such large treasuries were possessed either by small but very prosperous polities, like Venice or Florence, or by very large ones, like France or Castile. Although many independent polities disappeared, there were serious obstacles to the expansion of states, most notably the general tendency of alliances to form against the major power of the time. Throughout the centuries between Crécy (1346) and Waterloo (1815), international conflict was perhaps only somewhat less pervasive than in the preceding millennium. The persistence of war had several consequences. One of these was the development of a military infrastructure that by the end of the sixteenth century had enabled Europe to extend its political ambitions to many locales across the globe. The other is that the demands of warfare in Europe would make the development of Chinese like-strategies of rule simply impossible before 1815 (Parker 1996).

In 1516 Charles Hapsburg ascended the throne of Spain. This is none other than the Charles V we have already met in Chapter 1. Charles was the focal point of an extraordinary dynastic convergence (Lynch [1964] 1991 Chap 1). Through each of his grandparents he inherited a formerly sovereign entity. Along with the crown of Spain on his head, Charles was also ruler of major parts of the Italian Peninsula, Austria and its dominions, and the Low Countries. Not content with these, he had himself elected emperor of the Holy Roman Empire as well. Soon his domains included most of Latin America after the conquests led by Hernán Cortés and Francisco Pizarro. Consequently, by the time of his abdication in 1556 he was the ruler of an empire of nearly Chinese proportions and one that, even though it did not include France, vastly exceeded the dominions of Charlemagne or Napoleon. But as had been true for Trajan before him, Charles V's capacity to acquire territory exceeded his capacity to rule it. When he abdicated, he split the empire, carving out the imperial crown and the Austrian dominions for his younger brother and leaving the rest to his son Philip II.

Charles V's European empire was definitely un-Chinese and, for that matter, un-Roman.[2] Obviously it was far from compact, and it was not the result of some persistent expansion based on one group's military prowess over another. Furthermore, although Charles's legitimacy as the ruler of these lands was unquestioned, the extent of his authority in any one of his domains was a complicated matter. Charles was hemmed in by the liberties his forebears had granted to the different regions they had acquired, and some of these were quite extensive. More important still, the administration of each region was sui generis, and changing any of the key institutions in a locality required the assent of a local representative body, the presence of the monarch, or both. Because many of his territories were quite small, Charles had much greater difficulty ruling his domains than his Chinese counterparts did. Subjects in Castile fell under a relatively uniform set of institutions, but they inhabited only about two-thirds of the polity we now call Spain. In the Netherlands there were nearly a dozen separate provinces or territories where Charles's authority varied. Moreover, although Castilians and Catalonians may have recognized more connections among themselves than they did with the king's subjects in Naples or Vienna, they were far more likely to emphasize their differences and to take political action to maintain these differences. Hence Charles V's efforts at creating coherence in his European domains failed; his son Philip II continued the effort, only to spark the Dutch revolt.

At the cost of a digression, it is worth noting that European rulers' inability to gain more riches and territory at one another's expense propelled some of them to go overseas. In the Americas large expanses of land were claimed for European crowns and for a time provided massive wealth for the Spanish Crown. Trade with Asia was organized around monopolies that were supposed to make regular contributions to the state's coffers as merchants maneuvered to gain positions at new and old ports from which they could purchase precious spices and luxury goods. In both instances European states built what historians have labeled *empire*. These territorial and commercial expansions do not meet our criteria for empire in terms of population and territory. Indeed, these empires were either purely commercial or heavily extractive—in no case was there any effort to fold newly gained territory into a larger, homogeneous whole. This fragmented strategy persisted into the colonial rush of the nineteenth century. Thus there is a fundamental institutional contrast between Chinese and European empires.

Nowhere is this more evident than in the deep concern of Charles V's subjects for their local privileges, which meant that in Europe larger polities did not realize many of the gains that one might expect (Lynch ([1964] 1991, Elliott 1986). Indeed, these larger territories were themselves institutionally fragmented and constantly at war. From a Chinese point of view, Charles's European dominions were small and not very well integrated. To promote gains from trade, a peaceful empire was more advantageous than smaller war-making states could be. In this matter, the difference between the Hapsburg empires and Britain was in fact less than that between these empires and China. Neither Charles nor his successor could sustain a program of institutional harmonization because of the demands of war. Europe remained a competitive political system. As we saw in preceding chapters, the economic advantages to be realized from competing states came late and were unintended. The dominant impression of political change from 1300 to 1700 must be one of states fighting. To a lesser extent, polity size was growing, but the rise of more uniform institutions came later—after the onset of the economic transformation of the Industrial Revolution.

Europe's Industrialization and Imperialism: State Transformations and Economic Growth

Social scientists often associate the conditions conducive to economic growth with those that enable democratic political regimes. Individuals who enjoy liberties and freedoms typically also benefit from secure property rights. Those places in Europe that developed economically were also those that formulated democratic political institutions. The rise of representative government constitutes a remarkable break in its political history not only for Europe but for the world. Nevertheless, rather than the Glorious Revolution, it was the French Revolution that was a watershed for European political structures (Bogart et al. 2009). In the eighteenth century no European country followed Britain's lead of parliamentary monarchy, just as in the seventeenth century no country had followed the Netherlands by establishing a federal republic. To a large extent such regimes were anathema to Europe's rulers. In the quarter century following the French Revolution, however, Europe experienced a massive political transformation—the creation of unified parliamentary monarchies in France and the Netherlands, a significant reduction in the number of independent entities in Germany and Italy, the creation of a unified authoritarian monarchy in Prussia, and attempts at constitutional monarchies in Spain and Portugal. Napoleon's attempt to forge a large political entity failed, but many of the changes he initiated endured. Most strikingly, none of the restored ruling houses in France, the Netherlands, or Italy gave up on fiscal centralization. Moreover, these changes spread; for instance, when Belgium became independent in 1830, it immediately adopted a form of representative government.[3]

The transformation brought on by the French Revolution has typically received less attention than the rise of democracy in the later nineteenth century for several reasons. Most important, this transformation was quite likely to create or bolster conservative or authoritarian regimes (as it did in Prussia, the Netherlands, the Austrian Empire, and Russia). As a result, although this transformation seems to have been a complement to the surge in infrastructure investment that spread throughout Europe after the demise of Napoleon, it did not lead to the appealing equation of liberalization and growth. But from the point of view of our comparison this is the period when European states begin to look Chinese. Rulers in Europe demonstrated a new emphasis on efficient governance and providing prosperity. That said, it is remarkable how little effect this major political innovation had on fragmentation in Europe. It is true that the number of independent states continued to fall between 1789 and 1815 because Napoleon and the Congress of Vienna redrew the boundaries of Europe. Overall, however, the most radical attempt at reducing fragmentation—Napoleon's gambit to create a single state out of territories in much of western Europe—simply failed. Although many populations might have welcomed the reforms that French conquest brought in its wake, they did not want to be ruled by Frenchmen. Local elites were sometimes divided about reform, but they were always opposed to the elimination of their power and to foreign overlords.

The French Revolution and the regimes created in its wake typically downplayed regional identities in favor of national ones, but these new identities were no more favorable to the creation of a common political space than the older provincial ones. From a Chinese perspective, the partial replacement of Breton identities with French identities, for example, was not much of a step toward creating a European identity.

European history up to the mid-nineteenth century makes it abundantly clear that the fragmentation of the Roman Empire had tremendous consequences for this end of Eurasia. Long after the Great Invasions had passed, and long after Europe had become an exporter of military violence, political processes remained mired in a local logic. There were economic, political, and military reasons for states to grow, and to some extent they did. Territorial growth, however, was painful and slow. After 1815, when Napoleon's defeat closed the path to a unified Europe, the surviving states could enjoy the benefits of a significant reduction of the power of subnational institutions. They also tried to reduce the economic costs of political fragmentation through trade and monetary negotiations. They articulated a political logic of balance of power meant to acknowledge competition among themselves while reining in any unbounded pursuit of power at one another's expense. These efforts extended and elaborated on the political sensibilities formulated in the mid-seventeenth-century Treaty of West-phalia. Had Europeans been able to do more politically, they could have achieved a larger economic space with lower transaction costs and greater gains from trade. Clearly, they believed that such union was not feasible. Thus the approach to regional economic institutions in Europe that by-passes the problem of political union has its roots in the nineteenth century. Clearly, building a large economic space from the bottom up is different than building it from the top down.

Beyond their own fragmented region, Europeans grasped the desirability of pursuing power and wealth internationally. Consequently, at the same time at which the domestic regimes of European countries developed new political institutions and fashioned new political ideologies, some of them embarked on new overseas adventures. During the second half of the nineteenth century much of the world that had not already been settled by white Europeans became formal colonies of European powers. The military expertise they had gained in a dozen centuries of internal warfare allowed Europeans to exploit the labor and raw materials available in many Asian and African areas. More generally, industrialization fostered an international division of labor within which industrial capital concentrated in western Europe and North America bought raw materials and attracted labor from other parts of the world (Findlay and O'Rourke 2007: Chap 7). The British promoted free trade as a virtuous and efficient way to benefit people and their economies. The degree to which these economic principles dominated international exchange remains a topic of disagreement. To be sure, free trade and an international division of labor based on comparative advantage and natural-resource endowments prove to be powerful engines of growth. The European pursuit of these economic possibilities grew out of an early modern era in which Europeans for the most part competed with one another overseas rather than cooperated with one another within Europe.

Nineteenth-century British domination of the world had more than four centuries of European maritime exploration and conquest as its historical background. The ability of the British and other Europeans to exploit economically their international political position depended on technological and institutional changes more likely to occur in Europe than in China or anywhere else. War making drew entrepreneurs seeking to defend their capital into cities where relative prices ended up favoring capital investments, agglomeration favored growth, and certain technologies improved on advances made in military pursuits. In previous chapters we noted what we consider the key reasons for economic growth in China and Europe in the early modern era. We have argued that China was not obviously or certainly failing to grow as Europe did. But key differences in relative factor prices, which we explain through the impact of political differences on economic decision making, explain the far higher likelihood of an industrial revolution occurring in parts of Europe than anywhere in China. Once this economic transformation was under way, it no longer makes sense for us simply to compare the dynamics of economic growth in China and in Europe. We must also evaluate the significance of European impacts on China. It is possible that after the Middle Kingdom was forced to enter the global economy, politics either prevented it from doing so on its own terms or made it much more difficult for such a transformation to succeed.

After 1850 we no longer can analyze China and Europe as two large and important regions independently. Indeed, it is not obvious that the dynamics of political and economic change in one region can be kept separate from changes occurring in the other region. In the European case the influence of China was probably limited, although relations with the Americas and other parts of the globe were of considerable importance (Findlay and O'Rourke 2007: 402–424). In the Chinese case the major focus of politics and of economics could not simply be domestic. Even though China did not become a formal colony of any foreign power in the nineteenth century, the political and economic influence of foreign entrepreneurs and officials was huge. The growing presence of Europeans in nineteenth-century China was accompanied by increasing signs of a weakening central government unable to meet the twin challenges of maintaining the virtues of eighteenth-century statecraft and fashioning a new kind of state power able to manage new kinds of foreign relations. For a century after 1850 the Chinese government failed to maintain itself, let alone provide order across the country.[4] Nonetheless, China emerged after 1949 as a sovereign nation that comprised almost all the territories previously ruled by the Manchus. The Chinese accomplished this feat by asserting the primacy of a unitary state in which authority was vested in the central government. As a consequence, the Chinese were in a position to benefit from the economic advantages of spatial scale once again and in ways that Europeans began to approach concretely only after World War II.

Chinese Empire: Limitations on Growth in a World of European Dominance

For two millennia starting with the Qin, the Chinese economic growth that we have examined in earlier chapters of this book was possible because of the country's imperial scale. During this time the state's political economy helped support the institutional practices and relative prices that favored an agrarian and rural economy. But such strategies proved increasingly difficult to sustain as foreign political pressures created new demands on the Chinese state. We do not believe that their ultimate failure in 1911 can be attributed to the limitations of the earlier dynamics of growth. Instead, the economic advantages of empire were lost in the nineteenth century when the demands of managing both domestic space and foreign relations became increasingly expensive and difficult.

The Chinese political economy of promoting trade across a peaceful empire and supplying social services and goods with relatively modest taxation was no longer feasible in the nineteenth century. Chinese leaders had to invest in new political institutions and economic efforts designed to strengthen the state. They had to raise more taxes and were able to supply their subjects with fewer public goods. Around midcentury the Chinese state began raising taxes on commerce. By the 1870s and 1880s it appeared that the state was coping adequately with its new political agenda. A crucial turning point came in 1895 when the Qing emperor was defeated by Meiji Japan in a naval war waged around the Korean Peninsula. The victorious Japanese imposed a punishing indemnity. To pay the Japanese, the Chinese government was forced to increase its taxes and face growing domestic dissatisfaction. The Qing state confronted an even more difficult challenge after an eight-nation army marched on the capital in 1900 to demand that the Qing state put down the violence of the Boxer movement against foreign Christians. The ensuing indemnity equaled roughly three times the total annual revenue of the government. The only way even to attempt to meet the foreigners' demands was to reorient all government revenues toward that one goal.

It is little wonder that China's eighteenth-century focus on prosperity based on an agrarian rural economy lost pertinence. After 1911 and the fall of the Qing dynasty, such a political economy became completely irrelevant because the Chinese mainland was politically fragmented for most of the years preceding the founding of the People's Republic in 1949.

Even in the decade between 1927 and 1937 when the Nationalists claimed to rule China, they could collect agricultural taxes from only five provinces. Their rule over many areas depended on understandings with military warlords, and they could claim sovereignty in name only over other parts of the former Qing Empire, such as Tibet. Taiwan, which had been settled by Chinese immigrants centuries earlier and had been incorporated administratively by the eighteenth-century state, was no longer a part of China but a formal colony of the Japanese. More ominously, the Japanese established a puppet state in the northeastern area of Manchuria, taking away from Chinese rule the Manchu homeland to which millions of Han Chinese had migrated in the nineteenth century. Together, these changes meant that China faced a very uncertain future in the 1930s.

Political competition and military conflict were chronic features of Republican-era China. The kinds of conditions fostering economic growth in the empire that we have examined in earlier chapters of this book were largely lacking. Instead, political conditions in China resembled more closely the war-making competition and chronic fiscal shortfalls of early modern Europe. If European history had supplied all the lessons, we could have expected the Chinese mainland to become a set of states in competition with one another. Chinese political development could be presented as a late copy of dynamics that had worked themselves out in Europe centuries before. In this light the Chinese phase of political competition would have been set off by imperialism more than by any other factor. Although foreigners' interventions in nineteenth-century China caused severe political dislocation, there was no attempt to control any significant part of the empire until 1895 when Taiwan came under Japanese rule. In the absence of colonization we might expect competitive political dynamics similar to those in early modern Europe to have played a decisive role in early twentieth-century China. From a European perspective, China might have remained politically fragmented because so many empires broke apart. But if we generalize from European history or put the Chinese empire into a common category with other landed empires, we simply fail to explain what did in fact happen. Fragmentation did not endure.

Historians depict nineteenth-century Chinese history as a narrative of decline qualified by some signs of adaptive abilities to develop new institutions to accommodate the increased presence of Western merchants, missionaries, and diplomats. But although it was obvious to Chinese leaders that they faced multiple challenges, none could anticipate in the 1850s and 1860s or even the 1880s and 1890s that their system of government would fail in 1911. It may well be that leaders in other large nineteenth-century polities also lacked the foresight to recognize growing signs of failure, but in the Chinese case leaders confronted the end of their imperial system by developing new strategies and institutions to create a government that replaced empire. Although their success was certainly in doubt for several decades of war in the first half of the twentieth century, defeat of the Japanese and the conclusion of a civil war did not lead to a divided country. It culminated in the establishment of a regime claiming in large measure to rule all the territories and peoples once ruled by the Qing dynasty. When political stability was reestablished, the Chinese could once again enjoy many advantages of a large political unit. Obviously, the leaders of the People's Republic of China did not take effective advantage of these possibilities until three decades of rule had passed. In many ways China's experience since Mao's death reminds us that the region had a real economy before the Qing Empire's demise and that foreign political demands clearly constrained how that economy could evolve.

The failure of the Qing dynasty to manage the transition to a modern economy turns out to be distinct from the possibility of a large-scale polity reemerging after a period of disunion. In one sense such an event lends credence to those who suggest that the Communist Party is simply the most recent dynasty in a long line of rulers who have controlled the Chinese mainland. But in another sense the Chinese state that emerged after 1949 was one that could take advantage of practices begun by earlier generations who had managed to adopt and adapt a variety of foreign economic, social, and political ideas and institutions. The fact that little advantage was taken of this legacy until thirty years after the founding of the People's Republic does not make those earlier experiences any less relevant to understanding how and why China has grown so rapidly since the early 1980s. Understanding how the spatial scale of a polity matters to economic growth today, however, is a question quite different from the one that has occupied our attention in this book: how differences in spatial scale affected China and Europe before the nineteenth-century divergence. We have offered an abbreviated sketch of some features of Chinese political change in the nineteenth and twentieth centuries to remind the reader of the durability of a spatially large polity on the Chinese mainland. Empire, as we have used the term, has survived in China at the same time at which Europe has (since the 1950s) been moving more explicitly toward political and economic unification. We have allowed the narratives of European national state making to supply the norms for political development for too long. If it is disorienting to realize that Europe has been moving toward a Chinese norm of political scale rather than China moving toward becoming like any particular European state, that is only a measure of the bias of long-standing approaches in Western scholarship. The historical perspective we have gained here at least begins to correct that bias.

Political Competition and Economic Growth

Although the two ends of Eurasia achieved radically different political equilibria, the dominant underlying political economy analysis used to explain both is remarkably similar. For Europe, scholars have emphasized the importance of institutions of parliamentary representation and interstate competition for growth. Conversely, for China, and for despotic governments more generally, scholars have found only economic stagnation. In Europe the advent of good institutions was thought to be responsible for the onset of sustained growth, while in China the stifling oppression of the omnipotent emperor led to a population living near the Malthusian minimum. As the reader has discovered, our thesis is rather different. At the aggregate level, interstate competition was quite costly and certainly had a negative impact on the size of the market, while we see emperors surviving in part because they cared about their subjects' welfare. Nevertheless, the superiority of a particular form of governance should not be overstated because well into the nineteenth century massive variation in political structure remained within Europe, and massive variation in levels of well-being characterized life both within China and within Europe.

In China, scholars have recently been uncovering mounting evidence of regional differences in income before the twentieth century that is not consistent with an empire whose subjects were eking out little more than subsistence. Moreover, imperial policies do not seem to have been so extortionate that they led to low levels of investment or to massive poverty. On the contrary, it seems that these policies aimed at expanding the regions of prosperity across the realm. The evidence for Europe is even more at odds with the old assumptions, given that representative governance was not consolidated until the last quarter of the twentieth century, even in the parts of Europe that were not behind the iron curtain. To be sure, one could argue (and we have done so elsewhere) that rulers were unwilling to adopt the more efficient structures of governance because that would have reduced their power (Rosenthal 1998). In the light of China's history, that amendment is insufficient. The level of economic growth in Wilhelmine Germany was remarkably robust even though by English or French standards it was an incomplete democracy. Equally problematic, the levels of economic achievement of England had few echoes in Ireland (although it was formally part of the same polity) during the 120 years in which the union between the two countries prevailed. And these examples are small matters relative to examining either Austria-Hungary or the Iberian Peninsula. In short, the logic whereby the competitive state system provides great rewards simply does not hold throughout Europe. Economically more efficient states, like the Netherlands in the seventeenth century or England in the eighteenth, did not gain territory in Europe. States that transformed themselves may have garnered a higher rate of economic growth, but their territorial expansion in Europe was nil—to the extent that there was a reward, it came in the form of colonial empires.

We do not mean to suggest that efficient forms of governance neither exist nor prevail in the long run, but rather that the pressure to adopt representative institutions was weak. Moreover, the impact of reform was dramatically different across space. Political structures affected economic growth historically and continue to do so today, but the putative virtues of European state formation for economic growth have been misspecified, and contemporary political changes in Europe suggest that China is at least as much a political norm for effective state policies on the economy as any individual European state or the European Union can claim to be. We emphasize that in historical terms political regimes were adopted largely for fiscal reasons, not because of a love of liberty or an unwillingness to put up with a corrupt monarch. Furthermore, the conflict over representation was, more than anything else, a struggle over the control of expenditures and the level of taxes. Hence one cannot argue that representation was somehow promoted by individuals who wanted to reduce the distortions inherent in despotic taxation. Rather, these individuals wanted to strip the power of choosing the level of taxes and the distribution of expenditures from the sovereign. The European dynamics of political transformation did matter for economic growth because, as we argued in Chapter 3, the competitive state system was directly (though unforeseeably) responsible for Europe's adoption of capital-intensive methods of production, while China's peaceful empire privileged recourse to labor-intensive methods. In this chapter we have seen how the political structures that were in place at the time of Charles V in Europe and the Ming dynasty in China have continued to influence the process of institutional change. To be sure, Europeans are no longer quite as enamored of their parochial privileges, but national and, to a surprising extent, provincial identities already in place in 1500 continue to hamper European unification. China's growth, by contrast, is occurring under the guidance of a very strong center that must sometimes reckon with provincial priorities. How the spatial scale of polities continues to matter to economic growth today is a topic to which we now turn as part of a more general conclusion about the ways in which China and Europe have been changing in recent times. In particular, the end of political-military competition, coupled with a general openness of international markets, makes it easier to sustain fragmentation in Europe. If Catalonians, Scots, and Flemish were forced to endure the risk of invasion from neighbors and were shut out of international trade, they would be much less likely to seek independence than they are now.

Findings, Methods, and Implications

This book has considered a classic question in economic history: why did sustained economic growth arise in Europe rather than in China? The preceding seven chapters argue that political processes drove the economic divergence between the two world regions. This divergence became increasingly visible in the nineteenth century, but its causes are located in far earlier times. For centuries, China's peaceable empire was more prosperous and more stable than Europe's warring polities. But war, which offered to those who lived through it little more than misery (and even less to those who perished), also produced a series of distortions that pushed Europe toward urbanization and capital-using technologies several centuries before 1700. Stressing the political contexts of these two world regions does not mean that we wish to overturn the economic arguments. On the contrary, for preindustrial economies, the theories of the school of economists epitomized by Adam Smith and David Ricardo are extraordinarily insightful.

The problem with earlier attempts to assess the significance of political differences for economic development rests on the inference that the competition so useful for economic development is also salutary among polities. That view has relevance for modern times because if political actors are themselves subject to the rule of law, their political campaigns may well impose a far lesser economic burden than the follies of rapacious dictators. By implication, scholars have concluded that a competitive and innovative Europe outperformed an imperial and traditionalist China. This volume has argued against such easy inferences from the contemporary world to the past. We suggest that the historical costs of political competition were very high. Although political competition has been overwhelmingly prevalent throughout human history and throughout the world, it has rarely created prosperity. In the past, rather than gentlemanly electoral jousting, political competition involved real internal and international violence. The need to secure the resources for political action drives a political actor to intrude into his own economy and destroy those of his rivals. In historical environments in which rulers faced few constraints, the economic consequences of such competition were dire—as Hobbes famously put it, life was nasty, brutish, and short.

The roots of the economic divergence between China and Europe did indeed lie in their political differences, but we view European political competition less as the source of economic virtue and more as a vice that reduced the possibility of economic growth. Europe's persistent poverty before the late eighteenth century resulted from the limited domestic realms of rulers and the resulting restrictions on markets. The rise of capital-intensive methods of production that characterize the modern economy was an unintended consequence of Europe's political anarchy, not a carefully crafted result of government efforts. Conversely, China's vast and stable empire was the source of its millennium-long prosperity, a linkage presented in Chinese historical texts in terms of the state promoting prosperity in order to sustain a vast and stable empire. Together these two observations make it impossible to presume that China failed either because its economic system was incapable of development or because it was hobbled by overarching cultural, environmental, or political factors.

It turns out that European institutions were not obviously superior to Chinese ones in the ways that are conventionally believed. Therefore, we cannot accept the still-common narratives of a European march forward toward technological breakthrough contrasted with Chinese stagnation. Because we have evened the playing field, it becomes worthwhile to study these economies jointly. We believe that the intellectual payoffs from such a focus are demonstrated in the previous chapters. On one level we argued that other economic or cultural factors that are often invoked (e.g., demography, informality, capital markets) either have their roots in the political processes we highlight or else fail to stand up to evidence. On a second level we have traced the implications of differences in international relations for technological change, credit markets, and government spending.

This has allowed us to show that the chronic threat of war in Europe produced unanticipated positive conditions for economic change, and its absence allowed the Qing dynasty to implement policies favorable to Smithian growth but unlikely to produce industrialization.

Our analysis has been less concerned with explaining precisely when and why Europe overtook China's economic leadership than in tracing the consequences of two political structures (empire and fragmentation) on economic change. We have built our argument in terms of an increasing likelihood that new forms of economic production would emerge in parts of Europe rather than in any part of China and have demonstrated that what drives these different probabilities can be brought back to differences in political structures. The more typical comparative analyses that seek to explain when and why Europe overtook China in the early modern era face two dangers we can more easily avoid. First, given the state of quantitative information, a precise dating is likely to be inaccurate. In fact, any statement more precise than "sometime between 1450 and 1800 per capita income came to be higher in Europe than China" is unlikely to be very meaningful. This may be a measure of the dismal precision of social sciences, but we should not presume more. Second, analyses that seek to pinpoint a moment of major shifts tend also to search for all the factors present in that historical moment. Such accounts of change are usually quite thick with description. They thus invoke many causal factors whose relative importance or significance is difficult to discern. By arguing for the growing probability that Europe rather than China would be the world region where modern economic development would begin, we offer a kind of explanation similar to those more common in the social sciences: a thesis about expected likelihoods of certain events or effects taking place given the presence of certain other conditions or factors.

Our approach to comparative economic history differs significantly from those currently on offer. Rather than one big theory, our explanation relies on a number of small sharp theories. Each theory or model has clear implications for differences in the structure of economic activity both between Europe and China and within each region. For instance, in Chapter 2 we considered the effect of household structure on the labor market by positing a model of how household structure affects the size of the labor market, and then we formulated a series of propositions about the average skill of wage earners in economies with different household structures.

We seek to be explicit in creating specific causal chains because such chains can be fruitful, in particular when large amounts of data are unavailable. In Chapter 4, to briefly offer a second example, we first used a Leontief production function and then a Cobb-Douglas production function to work through the effects of war on relative factor prices, thus revealing differences in urban and rural locations of production as a function of the fear of military disturbances. We moved from a static model to a dynamic argument that considers war's influences on relative factor prices and the direction of technological change. At all stages the links in our reasoning are explicitly identified and evaluated.

Our comparative economic history is economic because it consciously applies economic theories to the questions we face. It is explicitly comparative and historical because we attend to various elements of context, in particular, seeking to explain how specific sets of institutions operate in different settings, whether these are household structures and kinship systems, financial markets and credit practices, or commercial dispute resolution by government officials and merchants themselves. Our scales of comparison take China and Europe as large and different world regions within each of which there is all manner of variation. We argue that variation in some phenomena, such as intensities of commercial production, should arise both within each region and between China and Europe for simple economic reasons. Among the differences that emerged between China and Europe, we distinguish those for which political factors were most crucial.

Our strategy of analysis applies a number of general principles to specific regions over long periods of time. We are by no means modest in our ambition, but our claims are certainly bounded—they exist within certain contexts. We do not offer any universal explanation of economic change or any general theory about the impact of politics on economic change. Indeed, we are somewhat skeptical that much universal explanation is plausible in the social sciences, historical or otherwise. More specifically, we have offered an explanation of why modern economic growth began in Europe rather than in China. Many of our explanations are specific to major aspects of this large problem. A few are more general, such as the argument in Chapter 6 about the composition of public goods and levels of taxation in China and Europe; we explain both why China had lower taxation and higher public goods provision than Europe did before the nineteenth century and how China's levels of taxation subsequently rose and public goods provision fell for reasons similar to those at work in an earlier period of European history. Although circumstances have changed—in particular, military budgets have shrunk relative to other government spending—tensions over fiscal policy remain at the core of politics. Furthermore, and as we discuss later, the institutions that distribute power between the center (Beijing or Brussels) and the provinces or countries (e.g., Sichuan or Guangdong, Spain or Sweden) have tremendous persistence.

Overall, however, our explanation of why modern economic growth began in Europe rather than China has stopped around 1800. In this book we seek to understand the factors that caused the great divergence in technological change, and that process was completed by 1800. Thus we have not discussed much nineteenth- or twentieth-century material nor evaluated other world regions outside China and Europe. Certainly, the process of economic growth changed during the nineteenth and twentieth centuries and thus includes new problems and possibilities we have not had reason to consider. Nevertheless, our historical perspective on institutional change has implications for how we view twentieth-century transformations in China and Europe, as well as what we might anticipate in the future. We argue that institutional change is always, at least in part, an extension and elaboration of previous practices, whether consciously conceived as such or not. Moreover, contrasts between China and Europe help highlight the challenges these regions face and the opportunities they can seize.

The global twentieth-century economic environment is, of course, fundamentally different from the settings in China and Europe with which we have been principally concerned in this book. Technological progress and political change have altered both the kinds of institutions people can construct and the choices they are likely to make. For instance, the importance of relative factor costs for production choices that is basic to our account in Chapter 4 of manufacturing locations in early modern China and Europe matters far less in the twentieth century. Nowadays, war is not as important, and entrepreneurs and policy makers throughout the world pursue capital deepening. Local variations in relative factor prices may affect the process, but even the most labor-intensive outsourcing involves capital deepening in poor economies. Similarly, changes in labor markets and demography render the arguments we analyzed in Chapter 2 quite irrelevant after 1900 or so: firm size is now so large that household structure is much less important for labor markets than in the past. We are neither surprised nor dismayed to confirm that some of our substantive analyses work for particular times and places and do not readily extend to other cases. On the contrary, these limitations are what we expect of many explanations in the social sciences.

Many scholars accept a periodization of history in which the end of World War II marks a significant rupture with the preceding decades and centuries and thus will naturally be skeptical that much of what we have considered in this book could matter to the past half century. As a result, readers may not be especially disturbed by the reminder that some of our empirical analyses are not directly relevant to the study of the present-day world. If this temporal divide created a consistent division of labor between those working on earlier periods and those working on the recent past, scholars might comfortably continue along their separate ways to develop their distinct literatures. But this is hardly possible because so much of the social sciences and humanities makes claims to levels of generality that depend on propositions persuasive for the present being plausible for earlier eras. Many of us are quite ready to look on the past with our eyes fixed largely on the present. Similarly, many scholars are comfortable making the ideas and institutions of Europe and neo-Europes the norms with which we generalize about the world, an ease demonstrated by *Violence and Social Orders* by North, Wallis, and Weingast (2009), already discussed in our introduction. Much of our book has aimed to counter this convention. We have put China and Europe on the same analytical platform, and, guided by some basic principles of economic theory and knowledge of Chinese and European history, we have evaluated factors of possible significance for economic performance in the past. Now we turn to the post–World War II era to suggest that much about the recent pasts and possible futures of the Chinese and European economies can be better understood by including an understanding of history.

Because institutional changes take place in particular contexts with important historical dimensions, politics can always influence economic practices. We have made much of the recurring capacity of states to create ideas and institutions of empire across the Chinese mainland and the absence of a comparable capacity in Europe. For both China and Europe, the years from 1914 to 1947 were a succession of catastrophes, most of which had political origins and international scope. Although economic growth might have been rapid in some places during the 1920s, the longer period bracketed by the two world wars was a very dark period at both ends of Eurasia, which were beginning to converge toward polities of more similar size. In particular, war-torn China fragmented and began to resemble a more familiar fragmented Europe. Thus if we were to focus on the first half of the twentieth century, it would be easy to conclude that our contrast is no longer relevant: the empire was vanishing.

If we fast-forward to the late twentieth century, we witness a reunified China and a Europe moving in fits and starts toward reduced competition, more coordination, and even integration. Europeans have begun to achieve a spatial level of political coordination and economic integration that China repeatedly achieved in earlier periods of history and continued to pursue after the founding of the People's Republic in 1949. Europeans were encouraged to achieve greater political cooperation because the globe had been divided by the Cold War. The fault lines created by the Cold War made intra-European political competition less plausible. Although economic recovery from World War II was pursued at the national level, it was framed within a new international competition between the capitalist West and the socialist East. The Communist threat made the battle lines of the world wars obsolete and enabled the seeds of European economic integration to be sown. But economic coordination remained limited and integration slowed because regional policy making continued to be hostage to nationalist visions of economic growth. We can look back from the present and see the precursors of the European Union (EU) in such institutions as the European Coal and Steel Community and later the Common Market, but these were hardly key components of political policies that framed economic activities. The more visible flowers of unification bloomed decades later.

In China a different rupture with earlier practices took place in the 1950s and 1960s. By the mid-1950s central planning replaced markets that had spanned urban and rural areas and that had induced many people to adopt technologies and institutions first formulated in the West. Although many of the economic practices and their institutional settings we have analyzed in previous chapters were demolished by the Communist regime, certain key political and economic elements remained or resurfaced at various points after 1949. The People's Republic formed a unitary centralized state governing virtually all the territory amassed by the Qing Empire at its height. The advantages of centralized bureaucratic rule, as well as the institutional limitations of such rule, were rediscovered by the

Communists even as they forged a political ideology and institutions that consciously owed more to Soviet influences than to earlier Chinese ones. The ideological and institutional ruptures between the late imperial past and the socialist present of the 1950s and 1960s obscures just how much these two unitary and centralized states shared.

To appreciate the significance of China's late imperial past for its present and future practices, we must consider some persistent differences in Chinese and European political economies. If we turn to contemporary public finance and recall the argument presented in Chapter 6—that the eighteenth-century Chinese state made all taxation decisions at the central level—and contrast this with the absence of an EU level of government in this same era, we can uncover some of the bases on which we hold very different expectations of public finance in Beijing and Brussels. For EU administrators to acquire a budget equal to 10% of EU gross domestic product would require a far greater transfer of sovereignty than most Europhiles contemplate. At the same time, it is difficult to imagine the central government in China managing such a small percentage of Chinese gross domestic product in the future. Similarly, Beijing produced a fiscal stimulus response to the 2008 financial crisis that far exceeded what Brussels could even imagine. The Chinese approach combined funds from the center with directions for provincial-level stimulus targets. It also left many details for provincial authorities to decide. In its structure it is highly reminiscent of the ways in which mid-eighteenth-century Chinese officials mounted famine-relief campaigns that involved central government authorities making plans and the coordination of the efforts of multiple provincial-level administrations. The EU-level response to the 2008 financial crisis was simply pallid. Bailouts and fiscal stimulus packages were left to the national governments. Beijing, in contrast, put up half the funds for its stimulus package and dictated the kinds of infrastructure projects that would be supported. Even more recently, Brussels has allocated no funds to respond to the Greek financial crisis; at best, it can coordinate the different national governments. In the end, each member state decides whether to help out. The EU simply does not have the money to do much, and, of course, Europe had no early modern parallel to China's famine-relief campaigns.

Over the past three decades, China has embarked on processes of economic transformation that promise a great deal of improvement for extraordinarily large numbers of people. The number of potential consumers in these countries has made the heads of global firms giddy with anticipation.

But exactly what are the bases of this stellar performance? Among contemporary China specialists it is generally well understood that growth in the 1980s largely occurred without the benefit of the formal institutions deemed so important both for Europe's economic history and in the prescriptions made for development in the contemporary world. Much of China's industrial growth in the 1980s and early 1990s was produced by township and village enterprises (TVEs), firms outside the state plan that lacked clear property rights structures and engaged in exchanges without the benefits of a court system to enforce contracts. One hears some China scholars and observers remark that this was a natural way to begin growth. It did not pay for Chinese officials to develop formal institutions to manage production and exchange early on. Instead, informal institutions could shoulder the burden until China became rich enough that it could afford to improve its legal infrastructure. That scholarship leaves in the dark why such "natural" growth experiences do not occur more generally throughout the world and, conversely, why post-Communist China was able to rely on informal institutions during the explosive TVE growth period. Our account in Chapter 3 suggests that informal institutions had long been important historically in China not to palliate failed formal institutions but as complements that enabled market exchange. Chinese policies after 1949 took away many informal institutions and put in their place formal institutions quite different from those of a market economy. Mao's radical rule was brief enough that the earlier history was not forgotten. When in the mid-1970s leaders decided to allow and accept growth outside the formal state sectors and plans, people depended greatly on earlier informal institutions as the basis on which they began to pursue development. Chinese economic growth in the 1980s was thus built on the past.

Since the early 1990s policies and economic conditions have changed, and so have Chinese enterprises. Industrial production increasingly takes place in sophisticated factories whose owners and managers require more clearly stipulated property rights than those of the TVE era. But contract enforcement remains uneven at best, and not all property rights deemed necessary and appropriate in Euro-American contexts have been specified clearly in Chinese situations. We believe that such differences can often be explained, at least in part, by preferences and practices of earlier eras. The extension of our argument in Chapter 3 to more recent conditions counsels us to avoid simple projections about institutional convergence that accompanied the once-popular "end of history" kinds of arguments.

Similarly, our analysis does not support the view that China's development can serve as a refutation of American economic practices specifically and Western ones more generally. It also does not support any arguments about a "clash of civilizations." It has become popular to see different economic practices as evidence of persistent differences that make foes of people in different world regions. As we have repeatedly indicated, economic principles at work in one world region apply equally well in another. The differences we have found depend on history's influence over institutions that are, to some degree, always embedded in broader social contexts that have features distinguishing them from others.

This perspective figures prominently in our account of credit institutions and financial markets in Chapter 5. In spatial terms we developed and applied an argument to explain variation among early modern European situations, as well as between them and the far less well-documented range of situations in late imperial China. Different types of debt were developed in Europe, and financial markets in many countries responded to new demands for credit. European governments did not collect large amounts of data on private financial markets, but their policies greatly influenced the institutional particularities of financial markets. The diversity of financial practices, however, did not produce clear and important economic differences among different parts of Europe. Europe was able to tolerate financial diversity and variation with no sharp impact on economic efficiency. Scholarship on Chinese economic history has yet to discover and analyze data that would allow us to assess the nature of variation across the empire. However, we have been able to show both that the absence of European-style financial institutions does not mean that the Chinese were bereft of credit mechanisms, and that it is unlikely that the limitations of capital availability were a crucial constraint on economic growth in the era preceding the Industrial Revolution. Moreover, when we turn to the recent past, we can see that politicians from different European countries have continued to be willing to pay a high price for financial diversity—most notably in the regulatory failures that led to the Icelandic financial collapse.

In contrast, a strong centralized government in Beijing after 1949 was able to redefine the institutional bases of Chinese credit institutions and financial markets, thereby asserting its capacities to define formal institutions. Its ability to coordinate banking policy has avoided the tensions and inconsistencies that have plagued the EU. This contrast is plausible despite the repeated rounds of banking and financial reforms that have changed the formal system and permitted some local and less formal forms of financing to thrive. Irrespective of the relative virtues of the Chinese and European financial systems, it is at best premature to anticipate that Chinese practices should converge toward any European or American practices that can confidently be assessed as superior. Some of the formal reforms undertaken by China have made some of its banking practices conform more closely to international standards defined by some mix of European and American practices, but the Chinese financial system remains very distinct from those present in Europe and the United States (Z. Fan 2007). Both are subject to reforms, some of which make them more similar. Other features, less commonly noted, reflect their persistent differences.

The politics of contemporary economic differences have historical dimensions that almost all observers of the contemporary world ignore. We suspect that this ignorance handicaps our abilities to anticipate the likely range of future changes in any of these situations. This book is certainly not intended primarily to proclaim the virtues of historical social sciences for confronting present problems and imagining future possibilities. It has taken on a more modest challenge of exploring and explaining the relative performance of China and Europe over many centuries. We chose to do so by combining our different expertises; that in turn forced us to reconsider and reject some approaches to comparative economic history.

In understanding persistent differences in economic institutions, social scientists have become fond of frameworks that emphasize the long shadow of history. A variety of cognitive, cultural, or political factors conspire to make that shadow so powerful that societies become locked into specific institutions. Whether these are informal institutions, religious constraints, or family practices, these modes of behavior lie outside the standard policy domain and largely doom these societies to poverty. Even when they do not suggest that institutional change is virtually impossible because of path-dependent constraints, social scientists have come to recognize the tremendous difficulty some societies experience in making institutional innovations (La Porta et al. 1997, 1998; Acemoglu et al. 2001; Engerman and Sokoloff 1997). Even though a set of technologies and institutions that massively raised individual welfare has been developed, only a fraction of the world has yet to take full advantage of these innovations. Explaining the persistent differences between societies that have embarked on modern economic growth and those that have not done so attracts scholarly attention to institutional differences. With respect to arguments about different kinds of path-dependent institutional lock-in, we suggest that such ideas should be pursued with extreme caution: appearances can be very deceiving. What seem to be path-dependent institutions can change rapidly if the economic or political contexts change. To the extent that we seek a revolution, ours is more narrowly political. Rather than consign some societies to poverty in the absence of radical cultural change, one should seek to alter the political structures that shackle growth. Our research indicates that this would require more than the simple transcription of Western models (e.g., democracy). Rather, the history of China and Europe favors a gradual evolution in which either indigenous elements are transformed to serve new purposes or external institutions are inserted into a local structure.

This economic history also argues that if social science is to contribute to the process of change, it must ally local historical expertise with the abstract concerns of economic and political theory. This is not as easy as it seems because of disciplinary conflicts. Too often economists consign the knowledge of historians to the bin of irrelevant details, while historians and area-studies scholars treat economic theory as a construct with little relevance to the real world. It is also difficult because scholars working on Europe or North America have too often evaluated specific institutions with a home-country bias. From their point of view, because Europe experienced economic growth earlier than elsewhere, it must have had better institutions. This has led them to a line of inquiry that rationalizes the inferiority of alternative structures. Economists are particularly tempted by such analyses because they fit neatly in the discipline's focus on optimal decision making. Unfortunately, as the preceding chapters show, this approach can lead one seriously astray.

This set of observations on our method of comparative economic history and its virtues for analysis, both historical and contemporary, concludes our book. We have sought in the preceding seven chapters to provide a combination of Chinese and European historical narratives and economic analysis adequate to persuade the reader that understanding the politics of economic change in China and Europe before the Industrial

Revolution is both possible and useful. In particular, we suggest that these efforts enable us to identify key factors that explain the economic evolution of these two world regions better than those previously proffered. If we have achieved any success at reaching our objective, we hope that the reader will also consider the book's approach for subjects far beyond our particular historical subject that lie in the recent past and will confront us all in the future.

Notes

2. Population, Resources, and Economic Growth

1. These assumptions make about as much sense as one that would assume that marginal productivities are equal for all households at all times.
2. The analogy comes from flipping coins an even number of times and examining the share of heads. As the number of flips increases, the proportion of heads gets concentrated around 1/2, while at the same time the likelihood of a sequence that has exactly half heads goes to zero. The first effect drives the shrinking labor market, while the second drives the increasing share of households in the labor market.

4. Warfare, Location of Manufacturing, and Economic Growth in China and Europe

1. A factor share is the ratio of expenditure on one factor to total expenditure. If w is the wage rate and r is the interest rate, the factor share for labor is $wL/(wL + rK)$, while the factor proportion is simply L/K.

5. Credit Markets and Economic Change

1. Mathematically, if the individual discounts the future at rate d, then the interest rate, r, must be such that $d = 1/(1 + r)$.
2. The one mysterious period is the long hiatus in the empire under the Sung. For some three centuries the Chinese mainland was divided into competing regimes. A European, at least, would have surmised that either the Sung or its rivals would have developed credit institutions in a gambit to reunify the empire.

6. Autocrats, War, Taxes, and Public Goods

1. After that time some states launched road-building efforts to move their troops; the same roads were also useful in speeding up transport (see Arbellot 1973).

2. There are exceptions, of course, such as the French state investment in royal roads in the eighteenth century. It is worthwhile to note, however, that these roads had important strategic value and that this investment came late in the preindustrial period.
3. Richard Bonney (2007) puts the cost of Versailles at 92 million livres. That amount was less than 2% of tax revenues during Louis's half-century reign.

7. Political Economies of Growth, 1500–1950

1. Crucial Manchu innovations took place in the dynasty's relations to other groups along the empire's northern frontiers, especially with different Mongol, Uighur, and Tibetan groups, but these important changes, the subject of much recent and current research in Qing history, concern areas that are not the sites of economic practices with which we have been concerned in this book.
2. We concentrate on the European empire because it is the most relevant to the issues in this book. We return briefly to the colonial empires in the last part of this chapter.
3. As in all things in Europe, there are exceptions. Notably, the Austro-Hungarian Empire was immune to the reform epidemic. Its various nineteenth-century guises emphasized the institutional distinctiveness of its different components (down to the emperor of Austria separately ruling as the king of Hungary).
4. For a narrative of this period of Chinese history the reader may consult Spence (1990: 137–513).

References

Acemoglu, D., S. Johnson, and J. Robinson. 2001. "The Colonial Origins of Comparative Development: An Empirical Investigation." *American Economic Review* 91, 5: 1369–1401.

———. 2005. "The Rise of Europe: Atlantic Trade, Institutional Change, and Economic Growth." *American Economic Review* 95, 3: 546–579.

Adshead, S. A. M. 2004. *T'ang China: The Rise of the East in World History.* London.

Alesina, A., and E. Spolaore. 2003. *The Size of Nations.* Cambridge.

Allen, R. C. 1992. *Enclosure and the Yeoman; The Agricultural Development of the South Midlands. 1450–1850.* Oxford.

———. 2001. "The Great Divergence in European Wages and Prices from the Middle Ages to the First World War." *Explorations in Economic History* 38, 4: 411–447.

———. 2004. "Mr. Lockyer Meets the Index Number Problem: The Standard of Living in Canton and London in 1704." Mimeo, Oxford University.

———. 2009a. *The British Industrial Revolution in Global Perspective.* Cambridge.

———. 2009b. "The Industrial Revolution in Miniature: The Spinning Jenny in Britain, France, and India." *Journal of Economic History* 69, 4: 641–672.

Allen, R. C., J.-P. Bassino, D. Ma, C. Moll-Murata, and J. L. van Zanden. 2007. "Wages, Prices, and Living Standards in China, 1738–1925: In Comparison with Europe, Japan, and India." Mimeo, Oxford University.

Altorfer, S. 2004. "The Canton of Berne as an Investor on the London Capital Market in the Eighteenth Century." Working paper, London School of Economics.

Andaya, L. 1999. "Interactions with the Outside World and Adaptation in Southeast Asian Society, 1500–1800." In *The Cambridge History of Southeast Asia,* vol. 1, part 2, chap. 1, ed. N. Tarling. Cambridge: 1–57.

Anderson, B. L. 1969a. "The Attorney and the Early Capital Market in Lancashire." In *Liverpool and Merseyside: Essays in the Economic and Social History of the Port and Its Hinterland,* ed. R. Harris. London: 50–77. (1972. Reprinted in *Capital Formation in the Industrial Revolution,* ed. F. Crouzet. London: 223–267.)

————. 1969b. "Provincial Aspects of the Financial Revolution of the Eighteenth Century." *Business History* 11, 1: 11–22.

Arbellot, G. 1973. "La grande mutation des routes en France au milieu de XVIIIe siècle." *Annales, Histoires, Sciences Sociales* 28, 3: 745–772.

Arrighi, G. 2007. *Adam Smith in Beijing: Lineages of the Twenty-first Century.* New York.

Baehrel, R. 1961. *Une Croissance, la basse-Provence rurale fin 16ᵉ–1789.* Paris.

Bairoch, P., J. Batou, and P. Chèvre. 1988. *The Population of European Cities from 800 to 1850.* Geneva.

Bates, R., A. Greif, M. Levi, J.-L. Rosenthal, and B. Weingast. 1998. *Analytic Narratives.* Princeton.

Béaur, G. 2000. *Histoire agraire de la France au XVIIIe siècle: Inerties et changements dans les campagnes françaises entre 1715 et 1815.* Paris.

Becker, G. 1981. *A Treatise on the Family.* Cambridge.

Beik, W. 1989. *Absolutism and Society in Seventeenth-Century France: State Power and Provincial Aristocracy in Languedoc.* Cambridge.

Berg, M. 1986. *The Age of Manufactures: Industry, Innovation, and Work in Britain, 1700–1820.* Oxford.

————. 1994. "Factories, Workshops, and Industrial Organization." In *The Economic History of Britain since 1700,* vol. 1, *1700–1860,* 2nd ed., ed. R. Floud and D. N. McCloskey. Cambridge: 123–150.

Bernhardt, K. 1992. *Rent, Taxes, and Peasant Resistance: The Lower Yangzi Region, 1840–1950.* Stanford, Calif.

Beveridge, W. 1965. *Prices and Wages in England from the Twelfth to the Nineteenth Century.* London.

Bielenstein, H. 1986. "Wang Mang: The Restoration of the Han Dynasty and Later Han." In *The Cambridge History of China,* vol. 1, ed. D. Twitchett and M. Loewe. Cambridge: 223–290.

Bisson, T. N. 2009. *The Crisis of the Twelfth Century: Power, Lordship, and the Origins of European Government.* Princeton.

Bodde, D. 1986. "The State and Empire of the Ch'in." In *The Cambridge History of China,* vol. 1, ed. D. Twitchett and M. Loewe. Cambridge: 20–103.

Bogart, D. 2005. "Turnpike Trusts and the Transportation Revolution in Eighteenth-Century England." *Explorations in Economic History* 42: 479–508.

Bogart, D., M. Drelichman, O. Gelderblom, and J-L Rosenthal. 2009. "State and Private Institutions." In *Unifying the European Experience: An Economic History of Modern Europe,* ed. S. Broadberry and K. O'Rourke. Cambridge.

Bogart, D., and G. Richardson. Forthcoming. "Property Rights and Parliament in Industrializing Britain." *Journal of Law and Economics.*

Bonney, R., ed. 1995. *Economic Systems and State Finance.* New York.

————, ed. 1999. *The Rise of the Fiscal State in Europe, c. 1200–1815.* New York.

———. 2007. "Vindication of the Fronde? The Cost of Louis XIV's Versailles Building Program." *French History* 21, 2: 205–225.

Botticini, M. 2000. "A Tale of 'Benevolent' Governments: Private Credit Markets, Public Finance, and the Role of Jewish Lenders in Medieval and Renaissance Italy." *Journal of Economic History* 60, 1: 164–189.

Bourgon, J. 2004. "Rights, Freedoms, and Customs in the Making of Chinese Civil Law, 1900–1936." In *Realms of Freedom in Modern China,* ed. W. Kirby. Stanford, Calif.: 84–112.

Boyer-Xambeu, M. T., G. Deleplace, and L. Gillard. 1995. *Bimétalisme, taux de change et prix de l'or et de l'argent; 1717–1873.* Cahier de L'I.S.M.E.A., Serie A. F. 19–20. Paris.

Brandt, L. 1989. *Commercialization and Agricultural Development: Central and Eastern China, 1870–1937.* Cambridge.

Brandt, L., and T. Rawski. 2008. *China's Great Economic Transformation.* Cambridge.

Brandt, L., S. Rozelle, and M. Turner. 2004. "Local Government Behavior and Property Right Formation in Rural China." *Journal of Institutional and Theoretical Economics (JITE)* 160, 4: 627–662.

Braudel, F. 1966. *The Mediterranean and the Mediterranean World in the Age of Philip II.* 2nd rev. ed. Glasgow.

———. 1967. *Civilisation matérielle et capitalisme, XVe–XVIIIe siècle.* Paris. English translation. 1973. *Capitalism and material life, 1400–1800.* Translated from the French by Miriam Kochan. New York.

Brennan, T. 1997. *Burgundy to Champagne: The Wine Trade in Early Modern France.* Baltimore.

———. 2006. "Peasants and Debt in Eighteenth Century Champagne." *Journal of Interdisciplinary History* 37, 2: 175–200.

Brenner, R. 1976. "Agrarian Class Structure and Economic Development in Pre-industrial Europe." *Past and Present* 70: 30–75.

Brewer, J. 1989. *The Sinews of Power: War, Money, and the English State, 1688–1783.* New York.

Brown, H. Phelps, and S. V. Hopkins. 1981. *A Perspective of Wages and Prices.* London and New York.

Bury, J. B. 1928. *The Invasion of Europe by the Barbarians: A Series of Lectures.* London.

Caferro, W. 1998. *Mercenary Companies and the Decline of Siena.* Baltimore.

Calomiris, C. W. 1995. "The Costs of Rejecting Universal Banking: American Finance in the German Mirror, 1870–1914." In *Coordination and Information: Historical Perspectives on the Organization of Enterprise,* ed. N. R. Lamoreaux and D. M. G. Raff. Chicago: 257–315.

Campbell, B. 2006. "The Land." In *A Social History of England, 1200–1500,* ed. R. Horrox and M. Ormrod. Cambridge: 179–237.

Campbell, J. B. 2002. *War and Society in Imperial Rome, 31 BC–AD 284.* London.

Carosso, V. 1967. *Investment Banking in America, a History.* Cambridge.

Chaianov, A. Vasilevich. 1966. *The Theory of Peasant Economy.* Homewood, Ill.

Ch'iu, P. 2008. *Dangfalu oushang jingji: Ming Qing Zhongguo de shangye falu* (When law meets economics: Commercial law in Ming Qing China). Taipei.

Clark, G. 2001. "Debt, Deficits, and Crowding Out: England 1727–1840." *European Review of Economic History.* 5, 3: 403–436.

———. 2007. *A Farewell to Alms: A Brief Economic History of the World.* Princeton.

Coase, R. 1937. "The Nature of the Firm." *Economica*, n.s., 4, 16: 386–405.

Collins, M. 1991. *Banks and Industrial Finance in Britain, 1800–1939.* Cambridge.

Courdurié, M. 1974. *La dette des collectivités publiques de Marseille au XVIIIe siècle: Du debat sur le prêt à intérêt au financement par l'emprunt.* Marseille.

Daudin, G. 2005. *Commerce et prospérité: la France au XVIIIe siècle.* Paris.

Davis, L. E., and R. A. Huttenback. 1986. *Mamon and the Pursuit of Empire: The Political Economy of British Imperialism, 1860–1912.* Cambridge.

Delille, G. 2003. *Le maire et le prieur: Pouvoir central et pouvoir local en Méditerranée occidentale (XVe–XVIIIe siècle).* Civilisations et sociétés, vol. 112. Bibliothèque des écoles françaises d'Athènes et de Rome, vol. 259/2. Paris.

De Long, B., and A. Shleifer. 1993. "Princes and Merchants: European City Growth before the Industrial Revolution." *Journal of Law and Economics* 36: 671–702.

de Moor, T., and J. L. van Zanden. 2008. "Girl Power: The European Marriage Pattern and Labour Markets in the North Sea Region in the Late Medieval and Early Modern Period." *Economic History Review* 63, 1: 1–33.

Deng, G. 1993. *Development versus Stagnation: Technological Continuity and Agricultural Progress in Pre-modern China.* London.

de Roover, R. 1948. *The Medici Bank: Its Organization, Management, Operations and Decline.* New York.

———. 1953. *L'évolution de la lettre de change, xivE–xviiiE siècles.* Paris.

de Vries, J. 1984. *European Urbanization, 1500–1800.* Cambridge.

———. 2008. *The Industrious Revolution: Consumer Behavior and the Household Economy, 1650 to the Present.* Cambridge.

de Vries, J., and Ad van der Woude. 1997. *The First Modern Economy.* Cambridge.

Deyon, P. 1996. "Proto-industrialization in France." In *European Proto-industrialization*, ed. S. Ogilvie and M. Cerman. Cambridge: 38–48.

Diamond, J. 1997. *Guns, Germs, and Steel: The Fates of Human Societies.* New York.

Dickson, P. G. M. 1967. *The Financial Revolution in England.* London.

Di Cosmo, N. 2004. *Ancient China and Its Enemies: The Rise of Nomadic Power in East Asian History.* Cambridge.

Diderot, D., and J. D'Alembert, eds. 1751–1772. *Encyclopédie ou Dictionnaire raisoné des sciences, des arts et des métiers.* 35 vols. Paris.

Dincecco, M. 2009. "Fiscal Centralization, Limited Government, and Public Revenues in Europe, 1650–1913." *Journal of Economic History* 69, 1: 48–103.

———. 2010. "Fragmented Authority from Ancien Régime to Modernity: A Quantitative Analysis," *Journal of Institutional Economics* 6: 305–328.

Ding, C. 1987. "Zhongguo jindai jiqi mianfang gongye shebei, ziben, chanliang, chanzhi de tongji he guliang" (Statistics and estimates of industrial equipment, capital, production and value of Chinese modern cotton industry). In *Zhongguo jindai jingji shi yanjiu ziliao* (Materials on the Study of the Economic History of Modern China), vol. 6. Shanghai.

Ditmar, J. 2009. "Cities, Institutions, and Growth: The Emergence of Zipf's Law." Manuscript, University of California, Berkeley.

Domar, E. 1970. "The Causes of Slavery or Serfdom: A Hypothesis." *Journal of Economic History* 30, 1: 18–32.

Drelichman, M. 2005. "The Curse of Montezuma: American Silver and the Dutch Disease." *Explorations in Economic History* 42, 3: 349–380.

Drelichman, M., and H.-J. Voth. 2009. "Lending to the Borrower from Hell: Debt and Default in the Age of Philip II, 1556–1598." Mimeo, University of British Columbia.

Drèze, J., and A. Sen. 1989. *Hunger and Public Action.* New York.

Duby, G. 1974. *The Early Growth of the European Economy: Warriors and Peasants from the Seventh to the Twelfth Century.* Ithaca, N.Y.

———. 1979. *L'économie rurale et la vie des campagnes dans l'Occident médiéval: France, Angleterre, Empire, IX–XVe siècles; Essai de synthèse et perspectives de recherches.* Paris.

Dykstra, M. n.d. "Commercial Dispute Mediation in Chongqing: 1875–1949." Mimeo, University of California, Los Angeles.

Dyson, H. 2003. *French Property and Inheritance Law: Principles and Practice.* Oxford.

Ehrenberg, R. 1922. *Das Zeitalter der Fugger: Geldkapital und Creditverkehr im 16. Jahrhundert.* 3rd ed. Jena.

Elliott, J. H. 1986. *The Count-Duke of Olivares: The Statesman in an Age of Decline.* New Haven.

Elliot, M. 2001. *The Manchu Way: The Eight Banners and Ethnic Identity in Late Imperial China.* Stanford, Calif.

Elman, B. 2005. *On Their Own Terms: Science in China, 1550–1900.* Cambridge.

Elvin, M. 1972. "The High-Level Equilibrium Trap: The Causes of the Decline of Invention in the Traditional Textile Industries." In *Economic Organization in Chinese Society,* ed. E. Willmott. Stanford, Calif.: 137–172.

———. 1973. *The Pattern of the Chinese Past.* Stanford, Calif.

Emigh, R. 2003. "Property Devolution in Tuscany." *Journal of Interdisciplinary History* 33, 3: 385–420.

Engerman, S., and K. Sokoloff. 1997. "Factor Endowments, Institutions, and Differential Growth Paths among New World Economies: A View from Economic Historians of the United States." In *How Latin America Fell Behind: Essays on the*

Economic Histories of Brazil and Mexico, 1800–1914, ed. Stephen Haber. Stanford, Calif.: 260–304.

Epstein, S. R. 1998. "Craft Guilds, Apprenticeship, and Technical Change in Pre-industrial Europe." *The Journal of Economic History* 58, 3: 684–713.

———. 2000. *Freedom and Growth: The Rise of States and Markets in Europe, 1300–1750.* London.

Fan, J. 1998. *Ming Qing Jiangnan shangye de fazhan* (The development of commerce in Ming Qing Jiangnan). Nanjing.

———. 2007. *Ming Qing shangshi jiufen yu shangye susong.* (Ming Qing commercial dispute resolution and commercial disputes). Nanjing.

Fan, Z. 2007. *Quyu jinrong tiaokong lun* (A study of regional financial regulation). Beijing.

Faure, D. 2006. *China and Capitalism: A History of Business Enterprise in Modern China.* Hong Kong.

———. 2007. *Emperor and Ancestor: State and Lineage in South China.* Stanford, Calif.

Fei, S. 2009. *Negotiating Urban Space: Urbanization and Late Ming Nanjing.* Cambridge.

Ferguson, N. 1998. *The World's Banker: The History of the House of Rothschild.* Vol. 1. London.

Ferrie, J. P. 1999. *"Yankeys Now": European Immigrants in the Antebellum United States, 1840–1860.* New York.

Findlay, R., and K. O'Rourke. 2007. *Power and Plenty, Trade, War, and the World Economy in the Second Millennium.* Princeton.

Fogel, R. W. 2004. *The Escape from Hunger and Premature Death 1700–2100, Europe, America, and the Third World.* Cambridge.

Frank, A. G. 1998. *ReOrient: Global Economy in the Asian Age.* Berkeley, Calif.

Fu, Y. 1956. *Ming Qing shidai shangren ji shangye ziben* (Merchants and merchant capital in the Ming Qing period). Beijing.

Fuji, H. 1953–1954. "Shin'an shōnin no kenkyū" (A study of the Xin'an merchants). *Tōyō Gakuhō* 36, 1: 1–44; 2: 32–60; 3: 65–118; 4: 115–145.

Fujita, M., P. R. Krugman, and A. Venables. 2001. *The Spatial Economy: Cities, Regions, and International Trade.* Cambridge.

Galenson, D. W., and C. L. Pope. 1989. "Economic and Geographic Mobility on the Farming Frontier: Evidence from Appanoose Country, Iowa, 1850–1870." *Journal of Economic History* 49, 3: 635–655.

Geary, P. J. 2002. *The Myth of Nations: The Medieval Origins of Europe.* Princeton.

Gelderblom, O. 2000. *Zuid-Nederlandse kooplieden en de opkomst van de Amsterdamse stapelmarkt (1578–1630).* Hilversum.

———.Forthcoming. *Confronting Violence and Opportunism: The Organization of Long-Distance Trade in Bruges, Antwerp, and Amsterdam, c. 1250–c. 1650.* Princeton.

Gelderblom, O., and J. Jonker. 2004. "Completing a Financial Revolution: The Finance of the Dutch East India Trade and the Rise of the Amsterdam Capital Market, 1595–1612." *Journal of Economic History* 64, 3: 641–672.

———. 2006. "Exploring the Market for Government Bonds in the Dutch Republic (1600–1800)." Mimeo, Utrecht University.

———. 2008. "Collective Spirit or Aggregate Wealth? Understanding the Structure and Growth of Holland's Public Debt, 1514–1713." Mimeo, Utrecht University.

Gernet, J. 1962. *Daily Life in China on the Eve of the Mongol Invasion, 1250–1276.* Stanford.

Gerschenkron, A. 1962. *Economic Backwardness in Historical Perspective: A Book of Essays.* Cambridge.

Goetzmann, W., and E. Koll. 2006. "The History of Corporate Ownership in China: State Patronage, Company Legislation, and the Issue of Control." In *A History of Corporate Governance around the World: Family Business Groups to Professional Managers,* ed. R. K. Morck. Chicago: 149–184.

Goodman, M. 1997. *The Roman World: 44 BC–AD 180.* London.

Graff, D. 2002. *Medieval Chinese Warfare, 300–900.* London.

Grant, M. 1978. *History of Rome.* New York.

Grantham, G. 1993. "Divisions of Labour: Agricultural Productivity and Occupational Specialization in Pre-industrial France." *Economic History Review,* n.s., 46, 3: 478–502.

Great Britain. 1870. *Report from the Select Committee on Pawnbrokers.* House of Commons Sessional Papers. Vol. VIII.

Greif, A. 1989. "Reputation and Coalitions in Medieval Trade: Evidence on the Maghribi Traders." *Journal of Economic History* 49, 4: 857–882.

———. 2006. *Institutions and the Path to the Modern Economy: Lessons from Medieval Trade.* Cambridge.

Grove, L. 2006. *A Chinese Economic Revolution: Rural Entrepreneurship in the Twentieth Century.* Lanham, Md.

Guinnane, T. W. 2002. "Delegated Monitors, Large and Small: Germany's Banking System, 1800–1914." *Journal of Economic Literature* 40, 1: 73–124.

Guinnane, T. W., R. Harris, N. R. Lamoreaux, and J.-L. Rosenthal. 2007. "Putting the Corporation in Its Place." *Enterprise and Society* 8, 3: 687–729.

Gutmann, M. 1980. *War and Rural Life in the Early Modern Low Countries.* Princeton.

Habbakuk, H. J. 1962. *American and British Technology in the Nineteenth Century: The Search for Labour-Saving Inventions.* Cambridge.

Haber, S. 1991. "Industrial Concentration and the Capital Markets: A Comparative Study of Brazil, Mexico, and the United States, 1830–1930." *Journal of Economic History* 51, 3: 559–580.

Haber, S., N. Maurer, and A. Razo, 2003. *The Politics of Property Rights; Political Instability, Credible Commitments, and Economic Growth in Mexico, 1876–1929.* Cambridge.

Hajnal, J. 1965. "The European Marriage Patterns in Perspective." In *Population in History,* ed. D. Glass and D. Eversely. London: 101–138.

Hale, J. R. 1985. *War and Society in Renaissance Europe, 1450–1620.* Baltimore.

Hall, J. A. 1985. *Powers and Liberties: The Causes and Consequences of the Rise of the West.* Oxford.

Hamashita, T. 1989. *Chūgoku kindai keizaishi kenkyū* (Studies on modern Chinese economic history). Tokyo.

Hamilton, G. 2006. *Commerce and Capitalism in Chinese Societies.* New York.

Hanley, A. G. 2005. *Native Capital: Financial Institutions and Economic Development in São Paulo, Brazil, 1850–1920.* Stanford, Calif.

Harris, R. 2005. "The English East India Company and the History of Company Law." In *VOC 1602–2002: 400 Years of Company Law,* Series Law of Business and Finance, vol. 6, ed. E. Gepken-Jager, G. van Solinge, and L. Timmerman. New York: 219–247.

———. 2008. "The Institutional Dynamics of Early Modern Eurasian Trade: The Commenda and the Corporation." Working paper.

Harrison, L., and S. Huntington, eds., 2000. *Culture Matters: How Values Shape Human Progress.* New York.

Hayhoe, J. 2008. *Enlightened Feudalism: Seigneurial Justice and Village Society in Eighteenth-Century Northern Burgundy.* Rochester, N.Y.

Heather, P. 2006. *The Fall of the Roman Empire: A New History of Rome and the Barbarians.* Oxford.

Herlihy, D., and C. Klapisch-Zuber. 1985. *Tuscans and Their Families: A Study of the Florentine Catasto of 1427.* New Haven.

Hirschman, A. O. 1970. *Exit, Voice, and Loyalty: Responses to Decline in Firms, Organizations, and States.* Cambridge.

Hoff, K., and J. E. Stiglitz. 2004. "After the Big Bang? Obstacles to the Emergence of the Rule of Law in Post-Communist Societies." *American Economic Review* 94, 3: 753–763.

Hoffman, P. T. 1996. *Growth in a Traditional Society: The French Countryside, 1450–1815.* Princeton.

———. Forthcoming. "Prices, the Military Revolution, and Europe's Comparative Advantage in Violence." *Economic History Review.*

Hoffman, P. T., and K. Norberg, eds. 1994. *Fiscal Crises, Liberty, and Representative Government, 1450–1789.* Stanford, Calif.

Hoffman, P. T., G. Postel-Vinay, and J.-L. Rosenthal. 2000. *Priceless Markets: The Political Economy of Credit in Paris, 1660–1870.* Chicago.

———. 2008. "The Old Economics of Information and the Remarkable Persistence of Traditional Credit Markets in France, 1740–1899." Unpublished manuscript, California Institute of Technology.

———. 2011. "History, Geography, and the Markets for Mortgage Loans in Nineteenth-Century France." In *Understanding Long-Run Economic Growth: Essays in Honor of Kenneth L. Sokoloff,* ed. D. L. Costa and N. R. Lamoreaux. Chicago.

Hoffman, P. T., and J.-L. Rosenthal. 1997. "The Political Economy of Warfare and Taxation in Early Modern Europe: Historical Lessons for Economic Development." In The *Frontiers of the New Institutional Economics,* ed. J. Drobak and J. Nye. San Diego, Calif.: 31–55.

Homer. S., and R. Sylla. 1991. *A History of Interest Rates.* 3rd ed. New Brunswick.

Huang, J. 1994. *Zhongguo yinhang ye shi* (A history of the Chinese banking industry). Taiyuan.

———. 2002. *Shanxi piaohao shi* (A history of the Shanxi native banks). Taiyuan.

Huang, P. 1985. *The Peasant Economy and Social Change in North China.* Stanford, Calif.

———. 1990. *The Peasant Family and Rural Development in the Yangzi Delta, 1350–1988.* Stanford, Calif.

———. 1996. *Civil Justice in China: Representation and Practice in the Qing.* Stanford, Calif.

Hunt, E. S. 1994. *The Medieval Super-Companies: A Study of the Peruzzi Company of Florence.* Cambridge, UK.

Ihara, H., and H. Umemura. eds. 1997. *Sō to Chūo ūrashia* (The Song and Central Eurasia). Vol. 7 of *sekai no rekishi* (World History). Tokyo.

Jin, Q., ed. 1919. *Jiangsu sheng shiye shicha baogao* (The complete Jiangsu Province industrial survey report). Hong Kong.

Jones, E. L. 1981. *The European Miracle: Environments, Economies, and Geopolitics in the History of Europe and Asia.* Cambridge.

———. 1988. *Growth Recurring: Economic Change in World History.* Oxford.

Jones, J. R. 1972. *The Revolution of 1688 in England.* New York.

Keller, W., and C Shiue. 2007. "Markets in China and Europe on the Eve of the Industrial Revolution." *The American Economic Review* 97: 1189–1216.

Kertzer, D., and M. Barbagli. 2001–2002. *The History of the European Family.* 2 vols. New Haven.

Kim, S. 1995. "Expansion of Markets and the Geographic Distribution of Activities: The Trends in U.S. Regional Manufacturing Structure, 1860–1987." *Quarterly Journal of Economics* 110, 4: 883–908.

Kindleberger, C. 1984. *A Financial History of Western Europe.* London.

Kirby, W. 1995. "China Unincorporated: Company Law and Business Enterprise in Twentieth-Century China." *Journal of Asian Studies* 54, 1: 43–63.

Kishimoto, M. 2007. "Land Markets and Land Conflicts in Late Imperial China." Paper delivered at the Utrecht Conference on Law and Economic Development in Historical Perspective.

Kohl, B. 1998. *Padua under the Carrara, 1318–1405.* Baltimore.

Kuran, T. 2003. "The Islamic Commercial Crisis: Institutional Roots of Economic Underdevelopment in the Middle East." *Journal of Economic History* 63, 2: 414–446.

———. 2004. "Why the Middle East Is Economically Underdeveloped: Historical Mechanisms of Institutional Stagnation." *Journal of Economic Perspectives* 18, 3: 71–90.

Lamoreaux, N. R., and J.-L. Rosenthal. 2005. "Legal Regime and Business's Organizational Choice: A Comparison of France and the United States during the Mid-Nineteenth Century." *American Law and Economic Review* 7, 1: 28–61.

Landa, J. 1994. *Trust, Ethnicity, and Identity: Beyond the New Institutional Economics of Ethnic Trading Networks, Contract Law, and Gift-Exchange.* Ann Arbor.

Landes, D. S. 1979. "Watchmaking: A Case Study in Enterprise and Change." *Business History Review* 53, 1: 1–39.

———. 1983. *Revolution in Time: Clocks and the Making of the Modern World.* Cambridge.

———. 1998. *The Wealth and Poverty of Nations: Why Some Are So Rich and Some So Poor.* New York.

La Porta, R., F. Lopez-de-Silanes, A. Shleifer, and R. W. Vishny. 1997. "Legal Determinants of External Finance." *Journal of Finance* 52, 3: 1131–1150.

———. 1998. "Law and Finance." *Journal of Political Economy* 106, 6: 1113–1155.

Lavely, W., and R. Bin Wong. 1992. "Family Division and Mobility in North China." *Comparative Studies in Society and History* 34, 3: 439–463.

———. 1998. "Revising the Malthusian Narrative: The Comparative Study of Population Dynamics in Late Imperial China." *Journal of Asian Studies* 57, 3: 714–748.

Lee, J., and C. Campbell. 1997. *Fate and Fortune in Rural China: Social Organization and Population Behavior in Liaoning, 1774–1873.* Cambridge.

Lee, J., C. Campbell, and T. Guofu. 1992. "Infanticide and Family Planning in Rural Liaoning, 1774–1873." In *Chinese History in Economic Perspective*, ed. T. Rawski and L. Li. Berkeley, Calif.: 149–176.

Lee, J., and Wang Feng. 2001. *One Quarter of Humanity: Malthusian Mythology and Chinese Realities, 1700–2000.* Cambridge.

Lee, J., and R. Bin Wong. 1991. "Population Movements in Qing China and Their Linguistic Legacy." In *Languages and Dialects of China*, ed. W. Wong, Journal of Chinese Linguistics Monograph Series no. 3. Berkeley, Calif.: 52–77.

Le Roy Ladurie, E. 1966. *Les Paysans de Languedoc.* 2 vols. Paris.

Levi, M. 1989. *Of Rule and Revenue.* Berkeley, Calif.

Li, B. 1998. *Agricultural Development in Jiangnan, 1600–1850.* New York.

———. 2003. *Duo shijiao kan Jiangnan jingji sh.i* (A multiperspective exploration of the economic history of Jiangnan, 1250–1850). Beijing.

Li, J. 1990. *Mingdai haiwai maoyi shi* (The history of maritime foreign commerce during the Ming dynasty). Beijing.

Li, M. 2003. Essays on public finance and economic development in a historical institutional perspective: China 1840–1911. Ph.D. diss., Stanford University.

Liang, Z. 1996. *Qingdai xiguanfa: Shehui yu guojia* (Customary law in the Qing dynasty: Society and the state). Beijing.

Lindert, P. H. 2004. *Growing Public: Social Spending and Economic Growth since the Eighteenth Century.* Cambridge.

Luckett, T. 1992. "Credit and Commercial Society in France, 1740–1789." Ph.D. diss., Princeton University.

Lufrano, R. 1997. *Honorable Merchants: Commerce and Self-Cultivation in Late Imperial China.* Honolulu.

Lüthy, H. 1959–1961. *La banque protestante en France de la révocation de l'Edit de Nantes à la Révolution.* 2 vols. Paris.

Lynch, J. [1964] 1991. *Spain, 1516–1598: From Nation State to World Empire.* London.

Ma, D. 2006. "Law and Commerce in Traditional China: An Institutional Perspective on the 'Great Divergence.'" *Keizai-Shirin* 73, 4: 1–28.

Macauley, M. A. 1998. *Social Power and Legal Culture: Litigation Masters in Late Imperial China.* Stanford, Calif.

Magnac, T., and G. Postel-Vinay. 1997. "Wage Competition between Agriculture and Industry in Mid-Nineteenth-Century France." *Explorations in Economic History* 34, 1: 1–26.

Malthus, T. R. [1806] 1992. *An Essay on the Principle of Population; or, A View of Its Past and Present Effects on Human Happiness.* Cambridge.

Mamoru, T., and T. Yukio, eds. 1997. *Zuitō teikoku to kodai chōsen* (Sui Tang empires and ancient Korea). Vol. 6 of *sekai no rekishi* (world history). Tokyo.

Mann, S. 1987. *Local Merchants and the Chinese Bureaucracy, 1750–1950.* Stanford, Calif.

———. 1992. "Household Handicrafts and State Policy in Qing Times." In *To Achieve Security and Wealth,* ed. J. Leonard and J. Watt. Ithaca, N.Y.: 75–96.

Mathias, P., and P. O'Brien. 1976. "Taxation in Britain and France, 1715–1810: A Comparison of the Social and Economic Incidence of Taxes Collected for the Central Governments." *Journal of European Economic History* 5, 3: 601–650.

McCloskey, D. 1975. "The Persistence of English Common Fields." In *European Peasants and Their Markets,* ed. W. Parker and E. Jones. Princeton: 73–114.

———. 1976. "English Open Fields as Behavior towards Risk." *Research in Economic History* 1: 124–170.

McGuire, M., and M. Olson. 1996. "The Economics of Autocracy and Majority Rule: The Invisible Hand and the Use of Force." *Journal of Economic Literature* 34, 1: 72–96.

McNeill, W. H. 1976. *Plagues and Peoples.* Garden City, N.Y.

———. 1982. *The Pursuit of Power: Technology, Armed Force, and Society since A.D. 1000.* Chicago.

Meskill, J. 1979. *A Chinese Pioneer Family: The Lins of Wu-Feng Taiwan, 1729–1895.* Princeton.

Michaud, C. 1991. *L'Eglise et l'argent sous l'Ancien Régime: Les receveurs généraux du clergé de France aux XVIe et XVIIe siècles.* Paris.

Michie, R. C. 1999. *The London Stock Exchange: A History.* Oxford.

Mokyr, J., ed. [1985] 1989. *The Economics of the Industrial Revolution.* Totowa, N.J.

———. 1990. *The Lever of Riches: Technological Creativity and Economic Progress.* New York.

———. 2002. *The Gifts of Athena: Historical Origins of the Knowledge Economy.* Princeton.

———. 2009. *The Enlightened Economy; An Economic History of Britain 1700–1850.* New Haven.

Montesquieu, C. de. [1748] 1951. *De L'esprit des lois.* Paris.

Mori, M. 1969. "Jūroku-jūhachi seiki ni okeru kōsei to jinushi denko kankei" (Famine relief and landlord-tenant relations from the sixteenth to the eighteenth century). *Tōyōshi kenkyū* 27, 4: 69–111.

Morris-Suzuki, T. 1994. *The Technological Transformation of Japan.* Cambridge.

Moulinas, René. 1981. *Les Juifs du Pape en France.* Toulouse.

Muller, R. C. 1997. *The Venetian Money Market: Banks, Panics, and the Public Debt, 1200–1500.* Baltimore.

Munro, J. 2005. "Spanish Merino Wools and the Nouvelles Draperies: An Industrial Transformation in the Late Medieval Low Countries." *Economic History Review* 58, 3: 431–484.

Neal, L. 1993. *The Rise of Financial Capitalism: International Capital Markets in the Age of Reason.* Cambridge.

———. 1994. "The Finance of Business during the Industrial Revolution." In *The Economic History of Great Britain since 1700,* vol. 1, *1700–1860,* 2nd ed., ed. R. Floud and D. N. McCloskey. Cambridge: 151–181.

Neal, L., and S. Quinn. 2003. "Markets and Institutions in the Rise of London as a Financial Center in the Seventeenth Century." In *Finance, Intermediaries, and Economic Development,* ed. S. Engerman et al. Cambridge: 11–33.

Needham, J., ed. 1954–2008. *Science and Civilization in China.* Cambridge.

Nef, J. 1950. *War and Human Progress: An Essay on the Rise of Industrial Civilization.* Cambridge.

Ng, C. 1983. *Trade and Society: The Amoy Network on the China Coast, 1683–1735.* Singapore.

Nishijima, S. 1984. "The Formation of the Early Chinese Cotton Industry." In *State and Society in China: Japanese Perspectives on Ming-Qing Social and Economic History,* ed. L. Grove and C. Daniels. Tokyo: 17–77.

———. 1986. "The Economic and Social History of the Former Han." In *The Cambridge History of China,* vol. 1, ed. Michael Loewe. Cambridge: 551–552.

Niu, G. 2008. *17–19 shiji Zhongguo de shichang yu jingji fazhan* (Seventeenth- to nineteenth-century Chinese markets and economic development). Hefei.

North, D. C. 1981. *Structure and Change in Economic History.* New York.

———. 1990. *Institutions, Institutional Change, and Economic Performance.* Cambridge.

North, D. C., and R. P. Thomas. 1971. "The Rise and Fall of the Manorial System: A Theoretical Model." *Journal of Economic History* 31, 4: 777–803.

North, D. C., J. J. Wallis, and B. R. Weingast. 2009. *Violence and Social Orders: A Conceptual Framework for Interpreting Recorded Human History.* New York.

North, D. C., and B. R. Weingast. 1989. "Constitutions and Commitment: Evolution of the Institutions Governing Public Choice in Seventeenth-Century England." *Journal of Economic History* 49, 4: 803–832.

Nunn, N. 2008. "The Long-term Effects of Africa's Slave Trades." *Quarterly Journal of Economics* 123, 1: 139–176.

Ogilvie, S. 2003. *A Bitter Living: Women, Markets and Social Capital in Early Modern Germany.* Oxford.

Ogilvie, S., and M. Cerman. 1996. *European Proto-industrialization.* Cambridge.

Ostrogorsky, G. 2002. *History of the Byzantine State.* Piscataway, N.J.

Pan, M. 1996. "Rural Credit and the Concept of 'Peasant Petty Commodity Production' in Ming-Qing Jiangnan." *Journal of Asian Studies* 55, 1: 94–117.

Parker, G. 1996. *The Military Revolution: Military Innovation and the Rise of the West, 1500–1800.* Cambridge.

Patlagean, E. 2007. *Un Moyen Age grec: Byzance, 9e–15e siècle.* L'evolution de l'humanité. Paris.

Pezzolo, L. 2005. "Bond and Government Debt in Italian City States, 1250–1650." In *The Origins of Value: The Financial Innovations that Created Modern Capital Markets.* ed. W. N. Goetzmann and K. Geert Rouwenhorst. Oxford: 145–163.

Pfister, U. 1994. "Le petit crédit rural en Suisse au XVIe–XVIIIe siècles." *Annales, Histoire Sciences Sociales* 6: 1339–1358.

Pomeranz, K. 1997. "Traditional Chinese Business Forms Revisited: Family, Firm, and Financing in the History of the Yutang Company of Jining, 1756–1956." *Late Imperial China* 18, 1: 1–38.

———. 2000. *The Great Divergence: Europe, China, and the Making of the Modern World Economy.* Princeton.

Postel-Vinay, G. 1994. "The Disintegration of Labour Markets in Nineteenth-Century France." In *Labour Market Evolution,* ed. G. Grantham and M. MacKinnon. London and New York: 64–84.

Potter, D. 2004. *The Roman Empire at Bay AD 180–395.* London.

Potter, M., and J.-L. Rosenthal. 1997. "Politics and Public Finance in France: The Estates of Burgundy, 1660–1790." *Journal of Interdisciplinary History* 27, 4: 577–612.

Quinn, S. 2004. "Money, Finance, and Capital Markets." In *Industrialization, 1700–1860.* Vol.1 of *The Cambridge Economic History of Modern Britain,* ed. R. Floud and P.Johnson. Cambridge: 147–174.

———. 2008. "Securitization of Sovereign Debt: Corporations as a Sovereign Debt Restructuring Mechanism in Britain 1694–1750." Working paper.

Rankin, M. 1986. *Elite Activism and Political Transformation in China.* Stanford, Calif.

Rawski, T. 1989. *Economic Growth in Prewar China.* Berkeley, Calif.

Reddy, W. M. 1984. *The Rise of Market Culture: The Textile Trade and French Society, 1750–1900.* New York.

Ricardo, D. [1817] 1973. *The Principles of Political Economy and Taxation.* London.

Rosenthal, J.-L. 1992. *The Fruits of Revolution: Property Rights, Litigation and French Agriculture (1700–1860).* Cambridge.

———. 1993. "Credit Markets and Economic Change in Southeastern France 1630–1788." *Explorations in Economic History* 30, 1: 129–157.

———. 1998. "The Political Economy of Absolutism Reconsidered." In *Analytic Narratives,* ed. R. Bates et al. Princeton: 63–108.

Rossabi, M. 1983. *China among Equals: The Middle Kingdom and Its Neighbors, 10th–14th Centuries.* Berkeley, Calif.

———, ed. 1988. *Khubilai Khan, His Life and Time.* Berkeley, Calif.

Ruskola, T. 2000. "Conceptualizing Corporations and Kinship: Comparative Law and Development Theory in a Chinese Perspective." *Stanford Law Review* 52: 1599–1729.

Sabean, D. 1998. *Kinship in Neckarhausen, 1700–1780.* Cambridge.

Scheidel, W., ed. 2009. *Rome and China: Comparative Perspectives on Ancient World Empires.* Oxford.

Schnapper, B. 1957. *Les rentes au XVIe siècle: Histoire d'un instrument de crédit.* Paris.

Scoville, W. 1960. *The Persecution of Huguenots and French Economic Development, 1680–1720.* Berkeley, Calif.

Sen, A. 1981. *Poverty and Famines: An Essay on Entitlement and Deprivation.* Oxford.

Servais, P. 1982. *La rente constituée dans le ban de Herve au XVIIIe siècle.* Brussels.

Shiba, Y. 1970. *Commerce and Society in Sung China.* Ann Arbor.

———. 1977. "Ningpo and Its Hinterland." In *The City in Late Imperial China,* ed. G. W. Skinner. Stanford, Calif.: 422.

Shiga, S. 2002. *Shindai Chūgoku ho to saiban* (Law and adjudication in Qing China). 2nd ed. Tokyo.

Shiue, C. 2002. "Transport Costs and the Geography of Arbitrage in Eighteenth Century China." *The American Economic Review* 92, 5: 1406–1419.

Skinner, G. W. 1977a. "Cities and the Hierarchy of Local Systems." In *The City in Late Imperial China*, ed. G. W. Skinner. Stanford, Calif.: 275–351.

———. 1977b. "Regional Urbanization in Nineteenth-Century China." In *The City in Late Imperial China*, ed. G. W. Skinner. Stanford, Calif.: 211–252.

Smith, A. [1776] 1976. *An Inquiry into the Nature and Causes of the Wealth of Nations.* Chicago.

Smith, P. J. 1991. *Taxing Heaven's Storehouse: Horses, Bureaucrats, and the Destruction of the Sichuan Tea Industry, 1074–1224.* Harvard-Yenching Institute Monograph Series. Cambridge.

Sokoloff, K., and D. Dollar. 1997. "Agricultural Seasonality and the Organization of Manufacturing in Early Industrial Economies: The Contrast between England and the United States." *Journal of Economic History* 57, 2: 288–321.

Sokoloff, K., and V. Tchakerian. 1997. "Manufacturing Where Agriculture Predominates: Evidence from the South and Midwest in 1860." *Explorations in Economic History* 34, 3: 243–264.

Soltow, L., and J. L. van Zanden. 1998. *Income and Wealth Inequality in the Netherlands, 16th–20th Century.* Amsterdam.

Spence, J. 1990. *The Search for Modern China.* New York.

Stasavage, D. 2003. *Public Debt and the Birth of the Democratic State: France and Great Britain 1688–1789.* Cambridge.

Tabellini, G. 2008. "The Scope of Cooperation: Values and Incentives." *Quarterly Journal of Economics* 123, 3: 905–950.

Tanaka, M. 1984. "Rural Handicraft in Jiangnan in the Sixteenth and Seventeenth Centuries." In *State and Society in China: Japanese Perspectives on Ming-Qing Social and Economic History*, ed. L. Grove and C. Daniels. Tokyo: 79–100.

Tang, X. 1987. *Zhongguo jindai caizheng jingjishi lunwen xuan* (Selected essays on modern Chinese fiscal and economic history). Chengdu.

Tawney, R. H. 1966. *Land and Labor in China.* Boston.

Taylor, K. 1999. "The Early Kingdoms." In *The Cambridge History of Southeast Asia*, vol. 1, part 1, chap. 2, ed. N. Tarling. Cambridge: 137–182.

Terada, T. 1972. *Sansei shōnin no kenkyū* (An analysis of Shanxi merchants). Kyoto.

Tilly, C. 1984. *Big Structures, Large Processes, Huge Comparisons.* New York.

———. 1990. *Coercion, Capital, and European States, AD 990–1990.* Cambridge.

Tonami, M., and Y. Takeda, eds. 1997. *Zuitō teikoku to kodai chōsen* (The Sui-Tang Empire and Ancient Korea). Vol. 6 of *sekai no rekishi* (world history). Tokyo.

Tracy, J. D. 1985. *A Financial Revolution in the Habsburg Netherlands.* Berkeley, Calif.

Trivellato, F. 2009. *The Familiarity of Strangers: The Sephardic Diaspora, Livorno, and Cross Cultural Trade in the Early Modern Period.* New Haven.

Tsuya, N., F. Wang, G. Alter, and J. Lee. 2010. *Prudence and Pressure: Reproduction and Human Agency in Europe and Asia, 1700–1900.* Cambridge.

Twitchett, D., ed. 1979. *The Cambridge History of China*. Vol. 3, *Sui and T'ang China, 589–906 AD, Part One*. Cambridge.

Twitchett, D., and H. Franke, eds. 1994. *The Cambridge History of China*. Vol. 6. *Alien Regimes and Border States, 710–1368*. Cambridge.

Twitchett, D., and M. Loewe, eds. 1987. *The Cambridge History of China*. Vol. 1, *The Ch'in and Han Empires*. Cambridge.

Van Dyke, P. 2005. *The Canton Trade: Life and Enterprise on the China Coast, 1700–1845*. Hong Kong.

Vardi, L. 1993. *The Land and the Loom: Peasants and Profit in Northern France, 1680–1800*. Durham.

Varian, H. [1978] 1984. *Microeconomic Analysis*, second ed. New York.

Velde, F., and D. Weir. 1992. "The Financial Market and Government Debt Policy in France, 1746–1793." *Journal of Economic History* 52, 1: 1–40.

Veyne, P. 1976. *Le pain et le cirque: Sociologie historique d'un pluralisme politique*. Paris.

Vogel, E. 1979. *Japan as Number One*. Cambridge.

Vogt, J. 1965. *The Decline of Rome*. New York.

Von Glahn, R. 1996. *Fountain of Fortune: Money and Monetary Policy in China 100–1700*. Berkeley.

Wallerstein, I. 1974–1989. *The Modern World-System*. 3 vols. New York.

Wallis, J. J. 2000. "American Government Finance in the Long Run: 1790 to 1990." *Journal of Economic Perspectives* 14, 1: 61–82.

Wang, Y. 1973. *Land Taxation in Imperial China, 1750–1911*. Cambridge.

Weber, M. 1930. *The Protestant Ethic and the Spirit of Capitalism*. Translated by Talcott Parsons. London.

Wee, H. van der. 1988. "Industry Dynamics and the Process of Urbanization and De-urbanization in the Low Countries from the Late Middle Ages to Eighteenth Century, A Century." In *The Rise and Decline of Cities in Italy and the Low Countries*, ed. H. van der Wee. Leuven: 307–381.

Wee, H. van der, and M. Verbreyt. 1997. *The Generale Bank, 1822–1997: A Continuing Challenge*. Tielt.

Wei, G. 1986. "Qingdai houqi zhongyang jiquan caizheng tizhi de wajie" (The collapse of the fiscal system of central authority in the late Qing). *Jindaishi yanjiu* 1: 207–230.

Weir, D. R. 1984. "Life under Pressure: France and England, 1670–1870." *Journal of Economic History* 44, 1: 27–47.

Will, P.-E., and R. Bin Wong. 1991. *Nourish the People: The State Civilian Granary System in China, 1650–1850*. Ann Arbor.

Wittfogel, K. 1957. *Oriental Despotism: A Comparative Study of Total Power*. New Haven.

Wong, R. Bin. 1994. "Dimensions of State Expansion and Contraction in Imperial China." *Journal of Economic and Social History of the Orient* 37, 1: 54–66.

————. 1997. *China Transformed: Historical Change and the Limits of European Experience.* Ithaca, N.Y.

————. 1999. "The Political Economy of Agrarian Empire and Its Modern Legacy." In *China and Imperial Capitalism: Genealogies of Sinological Knowledge,* ed. T. Brook and G. Blue. Cambridge: 210–245.

————. 2001. "Formal and Informal Mechanisms of Rule and Economic Development: The Qing Empire in Comparative Perspective." *Journal of Early Modern History* 5, 4: 387–408.

————. 2004. "Relationships between the Political Economies of Maritime and Agrarian China, 1750–1850." In *Maritime China and the Overseas Chinese Communities,* ed. Wang Gungwu and Ng Chin-Keong. Wiesbaden.

————. 2007. "Les politiques de dépenses sociales avant ou sans démocratie." *Annales, Histoire Sciences Sociales* 62, 6: 1405–1416.

————. Forthcoming. "Taxation and Good Governance in China." In *Fiscal States in Europe and Asia,* ed. B. Yun Casalilla et al. Cambridge.

Wrigley, E. A. 1967. "A Simple Model of London's Importance in Changing English Society and Economy, 1650–1750." *Past and Present* 37: 44–70.

————. 1985. "Urban Growth and Agricultural Change: England and the Continent in the Early Modern Period." *Journal of Interdisciplinary History* 15, 4: 683–728.

————. 1988. *Continuity, Chance and Change: The Character of the Industrial Revolution in England.* Cambridge.

Wrigley, E. A., and R. Schofield. 1981. *The Population History of England.* Cambridge.

Xu, D., and C. Wu, eds. 2000. *Chinese Capitalism, 1522–1840.* New York.

Yan, S. 2008. "Essays on Real Wages and Wage Inequality in China, 1858 to 1936." Ph.D. diss., University of California, Los Angeles.

Yang, D. T. 2008. "China's Agricultural Crisis and Famine of 1959–1961: A Survey and Comparison to Soviet Famines." *Comparative Economic Studies* 50, 1: 1–29.

Yang, G. 1988. *Ming Qing tu di qi yue wen shu yanjiu* (Studies of Ming-Qing-era land contracts). Beijing.

Yang, L. M. 2002. "Essays on Public Finance and Economic Development in a Historical Institutional Perspective." Ph.D. diss., Stanford University.

Ye, S., and L. Pan. 2004. *Zhongguo gujindai jinrong shi* (A history of ancient and modern Chinese banking). Beijing.

Zanden, J. L. van. 2007. "The Skill Premium and the 'Great Divergence.'" Unpublished manuscript, Utrecht University.

Zanden, J. L. van, and A. van Riel. 2004. *The Strictures of Inheritance: The Dutch Economy in the Nineteenth Century.* Princeton.

Zelin, M. 1990. "The Rise and Fall of the Furong Well-Salt Elite." In *Chinese Local Elites and Patterns of Dominance,* ed. J. Esherick and M. Rankin. Berkeley, Calif.: 82–109.

———. 2004. "Economic Freedom in Late Imperial China." In *Realms of Freedom in Modern China,* ed. W. Kirby. Stanford, Calif.: 57–83.

———. 2005. *The Merchants of Zigong: Industrial Entrepreneurship in Early Modern China.* New York.

Zelin, M., J. K. Ocko, and R. Gardella, eds. 2004. *Contract and Property in Early Modern China.* Stanford, Calif.

Zheng, C. 1989. *Ming Qing nongcun shangpin jingji* (Ming-Qing agrarian commercial economy). Beijing.

Zhou, Y. 2000. *Wan Qing caizheng yu shehui bianqian* (Late Qing fiscal administration and social change). Shanghai.

Zhou, Z. 2002. *Wan Qing caizheng jingji yanjiu* (Research on late Qing fiscal administration). Jinan.

Acknowledgments

This book is the result of a conversation begun more than two decades ago in a class organized by James Z. Lee. It was sustained by the community of scholars in California and, in particular, those of the All-UC group in Economic History, who heard and commented on draft versions of many chapters. Actual writing was spurred by classes we taught together at UC Irvine and UCLA. The Paris School of Economics hosted a one-day conference on China and Europe, where we presented the last two chapters for the first time. The final version was much improved by a conference organized by the UCLA Center for Economic History in May 2009. Robert Allen, Steve Haber, James Robinson, and Ross Thomson deserve particular thanks for their comments that day. Dan Bogart, Oscar Gelderblom, Philip Hoffman, Naomi Lamoreaux, Gilles Postel-Vinay, and Howard Rosenthal took the time to read and comment on the entire manuscript. Timothy Guinnane and Kenneth Pomeranz, who read the manuscript for Harvard University Press, were exacting and extremely helpful readers. Michael Aronson and Heather Hughes at Harvard University Press, Melody Negron at Westchester Book Services, and Charles Eberline improved the book through a simple, speedy, and smooth production process. Sabrina Boschetti stepped into the breach at the last minute to help compile the references. Paula Scott kindly read and edited the manuscript. If our voices have blended into one, she is to be thanked.

Index

Acemoglu, D., 116
Africa, 5, 14; North Africa in Roman Empire, 26, 30; North Africa in Charlemagne's dominion, 31–32; bias in histories of colonial, 97, 126; competitive state systems of, 200, 205; European exploitation of labor and raw materials, 220
Agriculture, 121–123, 163, 175–176, 189–190. *See also* Waterworks
Alexandria, 15*f*
Allen, Robert, 7, 47, 49, 103, 121, 124, 130, 165
Americas: natural resource bonanza for Europe, 5– 8, 100; bias in histories of, 97, 239; deployment of machinery in manufacturing, 121; conquest and confiscation, 179; Charles V's dominion over, 191
Amsterdam, 80, 92, 116, 125, 211*f*
Ancestor worship, 62–63
Anhui Province, 70–72
An Lushan, 21, 22
Antwerp, 72, 92, 97, 116, 125
Aquitania, 15*f*
Arab Caliphs, 30–31
Arabia, 15*f*
Aragon, 32
Armenia, 15*f*; representation as key element of rule, 195
Athens, 15*f*; representation as key element of rule, 195
Attila, 115
Augustus, 27
Aurelian, 28
Austria, 32, 211*f*, 216, 244n3; taxation, 173; elites, 179
Austrian Netherlands, 211*f*
Austro-Hungarian Empire, 171, 185, 211*f*, 226, 244n3

Autocracy, 3, 51, 162, 184, 243n1, 244n2; enlightened despot, 6–7, 56; inaccurate characterization of, 167–170; Wittfogel's study of, 169–170; North on, 170; McGuire and Olson's model, 170–173; taxes and public goods vs. war expenditures, 180; Communist Party's public goods provision, 206; Germany's robust economy and autocratic government, 226. *See also* Representative government

Balkans, 31
Baltics, 92
Bank of England, 92
Banks: commercial family, 62, 71–72; Chinese, 86, 129; European exchange, 92; borrowing vs. lending prices, 133–134; from one market to many, 137; "native banks," 139, 153; European interest rates and credit markets, 140–151; France's industrialization and banking network, 149, 218; Germany's universal banks and credit system, 149. *See also* Credit market
Barcelona, 32
Beijing, 13, 155, 232, 235, 237
Beik, W., 195
Belgica, 15*f*
Berg, M., 118
Bias, in scholarship, 97, 126, 229, 239. *See also* Despotic government
Bithynia, 15*f*
Black Death, 46, 47, 103, 131–132
Bonaparte, Napoleon, 216, 218–219
Bonney, Richard, 176
Brazil, ix, 160
Britannia, 15*f*. *See also specific nations*
Brussels, 235

Harvard University Press is a member of Green Press Initiative (greenpressinitiative.org), a nonprofit organization working to help publishers and printers increase their use of recycled paper and decrease their use of fiber derived from endangered forests. This book was printed on recycled paper containing 30% post-consumer waste and processed chlorine free.